The Moby Dick Project

The Moby Dick Project

RECONNAISSANCE BALLOONS OVER RUSSIA

Curtis Peebles

SMITHSONIAN INSTITUTION PRESS
Washington and London

Editor: Nancy P. Dutro

Library of Congress Cataloging-in-Publication Data

Peebles, Curtis.
The Moby Dick Project:
reconnaissance balloons over Russia/by
Curtis Peebles.
p. cm.
Includes bibliographical references.
ISBN 1-56098-025-7
1. Aerial reconnaissance, American—
Soviet Union. 2. Balloons.
I. Title.
UG763.P44 1991
358.4'5'0973—dc20 90-21131
British Library Cataloging-in-Publication Data
available
Manufactured in the United States of America
97 96 95 94 93 92 91 5 4 3 2 1

∞The paper used in this publication meets the minimum requirements of the American National Standard for Permanence of Paper for Printed Library Materials Z39.48-1984.

What a gleamy and dazzling thing,
this splendid, great white whale!

—Herman Melville, 1851

Contents

Introduction

Today the world exists in an "Age of Surveillance." United States, Soviet, and Chinese photo reconnaissance satellites keep watch on the earth, their cameras covering thousands of targets. The satellites are technological marvels. The U.S. Big Bird satellite is able to return photos sharp enough for a man to be visible. The Soviet effort is massive—over thirty launches per year and as many as six satellites operational at any given time. Other satellites listen for radio and radar transmissions. Some use huge dish antennas to pick up the slightest electronic whispers from thousands of miles out in space. The advent of intelligence-gathering satellites has had a profound effect on international relations, military planning, and arms control. They allow both sides to know with an acceptable degree of uncertainty the activities and status of the other side. Because this is how it is now, one tends to imagine that is how it has always been. Yet this is not true. In the early years of the Cold War, the Soviet Union was a blank threatening void. The most basic information was not only unknown but seemingly unknowable. This uncertainty had a damaging effect. Like a dark specter, the threat of a surprise Soviet nuclear attack loomed over U.S./Soviet relations. The United States could never feel secure until it knew the capabilities and intentions of the Soviet Union.

This book is a history of the first attempt to light that darkness: reconnaissance balloons. This has been a largely unknown chapter in the history of both aerial reconnaissance and U.S./Soviet relations. The U-2 is common knowledge, but when most people are told that before the U-2 the U.S. used balloons for reconnaissance of Russia, the response is one of disbelief. This is not surprising as very little has been written on this subject—a brief mention here, a few pages somewhere else. Additionally, with a few exceptions, much of this scant information is wrong. A number of myths have built up over the balloons. One is that development of the reconnaissance balloons was started in the late 1940s when the Cold War first began. Another is that the Skyhook balloon that Capt. Thomas Mantell was killed chasing (because he believed it was a flying saucer) was a reconnaissance balloon prototype. A further myth was that the Skyhook balloon was a highly classified project until the early 1950s. Still another was that the reconnaissance balloon program continued to make overflights for several years; as will be seen, the operational period was far shorter. The final myth is that the 1958 balloon flights were not authorized by President Eisenhower. As will be shown, none of these is true.

The use of reconnaissance balloons over Russia was not an isolated event but, rather, the culmination of a long history. Chapters 1 and 2 cover these early efforts in balloon reconnaissance during the French Revolution, U.S. Civil War, and World Wars I and II. Use of reconnaissance balloons over Russia was practical only because of postwar technical advances, specifically, the use of thin plastic film in the Skyhook balloons. Chapter 3 covers this part of the story. Chapters 4 through 7 cover first the reconnaissance balloons' development, crew training, and finally, their use over Russia, China, and Eastern Europe. Chapter 8 is an assessment of their accomplishments, shortcomings, and final triumph.

Many people helped with the writing of this book. First I would like to thank Paul M. Lovrencic, George R. Mathews III, Robert L. Burch, and James A. Winker for their assistance in making the story of balloon reconnaissance come alive. Also helping were Phil and Sue Henderson, Peter Campbell, Dave Cherwink, Jim Taylor, Phil C. Hurley, Lloyd H. Cornett, Jr., Martin M. Teasley, James E. Oberg, Harry N. Miller, R. W. Koch, Leroy C. Stables, Jeffrey Richelson, Vincent Lally, Svein Tonning, Nils Petter Gleditsch, Mary Fuller, Col. Robert J. Dzur, Donald B. Vest, Sandy Weisenburger, Anne W. Turner, Barba L. Little, Doris M. Lama, Lynn O. Gamma, David H. Herschler, Barbara Carmichael, Lt. Cmdr. W. H. Stieglitz, Vincent P. Murone, Kenneth Hartung, John R. Burke, P. L. Gruendl, G. R. Aitken, Arthur O. Korn, Steven A. Thompson, John C. Reilly, Jr., George Cully, Dr. Ruth Liebowitz, and Wesley B. Henry. I would also like to thank the Air Force Historical Research Center at Maxwell AFB, the Air Force Systems Command, the U.S. Navy Naval Historical Center (Ships History Branch) at the Washington Navy Yard, the Strategic Air Command, the Dwight D. Eisenhower Library, the U.S. Department of State, General Mills, Raven Industries, *Air Force Magazine, Naval Aviation News,* Mil-Air Books, the Air Force Museum, the Air Force Tactical Air Command, the Air Force Inspection and Safety Center at Norton AFB, the Air Force Geophysical Laboratory, the International Peace Research Institute (Oslo, Norway), the San Diego State University Library, the San Diego Aerospace Museum, and Document Control at Cipher Data.

1

The Roots of Balloon Reconnaissance

The principle by which a balloon flies was first discovered by the ancient Greek mathematician Archimedes. In a treatise entitled "On Floating Bodies," he noted that an object submerged in water is buoyed upward by a force equal to the water it displaces. It followed that if a balloon was filled with a gas lighter than air, it would rise until its weight matched that of an equal volume of the surrounding air.

It would be nearly 2,000 years before man would use this principle to take flight. The men who would do so were Joseph Montgolfier and his brother, Etienne. They were manufacturers of paper and suppliers to the kings of France. In 1782, Joseph began his first experiments with paper globes filled with hydrogen. They floated only briefly as the hydrogen leaked out of the unsealed paper. What happened next is lost in myth and legend. According to one version, his wife's chemise, which was hanging by the front of the fire to dry, was carried upward with the smoke. Another has it that the inspiration came from a paper cone, thrown into a fire, rising up the chimney. However the idea came, Joseph and Etienne Montgolfier realized rising smoke could be used to lift a balloon. They began building successively larger hot air balloons. On September 19, 1783, before an audience that included King Louis XVI, the Montgolfiers flew a balloon carrying a sheep, a chicken and a duck. Two months later, on November 21, 1783, the first humans took flight. François Pilâtre de Rozier and the marquis d'Arlandes went aloft in a brightly painted hot air balloon. They flew for twenty-five minutes and traveled five miles. The road to the sky, and all that lay beyond, was open.

At the same time, a manned hydrogen balloon was also being built. A

French physicist, Jacques Charles, working with Jean and Noel Robert, had covered a silk balloon with a rubber coating that prevented the hydrogen from escaping. It had the features of all gas balloons to follow. The pilot would ride in a gondola suspended from the balloon by ropes. To go up, ballast, in the form of sandbags, was dropped. To come down, gas was vented from the balloon.

On December 1, 1783, Charles and Noel Robert went aloft. Their flight lasted two hours and covered twenty-seven miles. After landing, Robert climbed out and the balloon, now lightened, rose again. Charles thus made the world's first solo flight.[1,2]

Reconnaissance

The France in which the balloon made its appearance was a troubled land. The country was nearly bankrupt. The new middle class was frustrated by a political and social system in which privilege depended on noble birth and not on talent. Peasants were burdened by feudal laws and taxes to the king, nobles, and church. The new ideas of Voltaire, Rousseau, and the American Revolution were sweeping the land. The States-General that convened on May 5, 1789, demanded a constitution. The French Revolution had begun. Before it ended, the fires of revolution would consume both the old order and the revolutionaries.

In April 1792, the French Republic declared war on the monarchies of Austria, Prussia and Holland. In 1793, several prominent citizens suggested the use of tethered balloons to spot enemy positions. On April 2, 1794, the Compagnie d'Aérostiers, the world's first air force, was established under the command of Capt. Jean Marie-Joseph Coutelle. Total personnel were thirty-four officers and men, plus one balloon: *L'Entreprenant (The Enterprise)*. The "Aérostiers" wore a distinctive blue uniform with black collars and red piping.

The Aérostiers made their first reconnaissance flight on June 2, 1794, at Maubeuge near the Belgian border. On such flights, two people would go aloft. One observed the enemy positions and troop movements while the other relayed the information to the ground with signal flags or by putting a message in a sandbag and sliding it on metal rings down the tether lines. The initial flights were so successful that the Aérostiers were ordered to make twice-daily ascents.

The Austrians tried to counter the balloon by firing at it with cannons; their tailpieces were placed in ditches in order to raise their maximum elevation. These first antiaircraft guns sent one shot sailing over the balloon while another cannonball grazed the gondola. Captain Coutelle shouted "Vive la République" and ordered the ground crew to let out more line to get the balloon out of range. Even at this early stage, it was clear that safety was found in height.

At the end of June, the Aérostiers moved from Maubeuge to Charleroi in Belgium. The reconnaissance of the beseiged Dutch garrison by Coutelle and the French general Antoine Morlot indicated its positions were weak. Soon after, the Dutch surrendered.

A few days later, at the battle of Fleurus in Belgium, came the Compagnie d'Aérostiers' greatest victory. Coutelle and Morlot were aloft before the battle had started. Commanders on the ground attached questions to a line that Coutelle pulled up. General Morlot observed the action and issued orders that were slid down the tether line. They were in the air some ten hours, directing the battle. When it was over, the French had won.

Ironically, the battle of Fleurus also marked the decline of the Aérostiers. Although they performed well at the battle of Mayence in 1795, high-level indifference and hostility, particularly that of a rising young general named Napoleon Bonaparte, took its toll. Napoleon took a balloon company to Egypt in 1798, but left its equipment aboard ship. After Napoleon returned to France in July 1799, he closed down the balloon school and factory. Soon after, in November 1799, Napoleon helped overthrow the French Republic and was named first consul. He was now the true ruler of France. In his subsequent battles in Austria, Prussia, Spain and Russia, Napoleon never used balloons.[3]

Despite the end of the Compagnie d'Aérostiers, balloons were used sporadically for military purposes during the first half of the nineteenth century. During the Algerian campaign of 1830, the French aeronaut Jean Margat made at least one flight. In 1859, two French balloonists, Louis and Eugène Godard, made a series of ascents during the Italian campaign. It was not only the French who were making flights. The Russian Army used balloons during the siege of Sebastopol in the Crimean War (1854–1856). The Danes and the Milanese launched propaganda-carrying balloons. The U.S. Army considered using balloons during the Second Seminole War (1835–1842) to spot small bands of Indians hiding in the swamps and forests of the Florida Everglades. The field commanders, however, were halfhearted and the war ended soon afterward.[4]

One application of balloons foreshadowed events of nearly a century later. In the years 1848–1849, a series of revolutions raged across Europe. One of these was the Italian War of Independence. The Austrian Army besieging Venice could not find positions for heavy guns. As a substitute, two Austrian Lieutenants, Franz and Josef Uchatius, developed a bomb-carrying unmanned hot air balloon. It was made of thin paper, could remain aloft for a half hour and carry a 48-lb bomb. The bomb was dropped by a time fuse. One hundred balloons were launched against Venice. One of the bombs exploded in St. Mark's Square. Others, caught by a shifting wind, drifted back over Austrian lines. Losses on either side were minimal.[5] The focus of military ballooning now shifted to the U.S.

Civil War

In the 1840s and 1850s, relations between North and South were getting worse. Many in the northern states became convinced that slavery and the power of the slaveholders must not expand. The South saw slavery both as an economic necessity for its agricultural society and as a means of social control. The more slavery was attacked, the tighter the South clung to it and the more insecure it became. The South demanded that slavery be allowed to expand into the Southwest and Midwest—the very thing the North would never allow. A series of compromises papered over the split but it could not be contained forever. The final trigger was the election of Abraham Lincoln in November 1860. In the months that followed, eleven Southern states seceded from the Union. On April 12, 1861, the Confederates fired on Fort Sumter and the Civil War began.

Among those who rushed to the Union cause were a number of balloonists: T. S. C. Lowe, John Wise, John La Mountain, and James Allen. They had all learned their craft following the summer circuit of small towns, traveling shows, county fairs, and Fourth of July celebrations.

For the balloonists, the first weeks and months after the Civil War began was a time of confusion as they sought a friendly ear in the government or the army and competed to be named head of the Union aeronautical program.

James Allen was the first to volunteer, on April 19. He subsequently joined the Rhode Island Providence Marine Corps of Artillery, commanded by Col. Ambrose E. Burnside. Two weeks later, John La Mountain submitted a long study of military ballooning and a character reference from thirty-three local citizens to Secretary of War Simon Cameron and the New York State military commissioners. A second letter followed a week later. In late May, after a month with no response, La Mountain received a letter from Maj. Gen. Benjamin F. Butler, commander of the Department of Virginia, offering to hire him as a civilian balloonist. La Mountain accepted, saying he would start for General Butler's headquarters at Fort Monroe by mid-June.

Also in late May, Allen was ordered to join the Rhode Island troops in Washington. He loaded two balloons, a gas generator, tether line, and a winch aboard a train. While in Washington, Allen talked with War Department officials. On June 9, 1861, Allen made the first official army balloon ascent from a spot near the capitol building. The next day, Allen was ordered to accompany the Rhode Island troops on their march toward Harpers Ferry. Although Allen traveled with Burnside's regiment, he made no flights owing to the failure of the hydrogen generating equipment.

The same day Allen was setting out, Maj. Hartman Bache wired John Wise, another aeronaut, about the price of a balloon. Ironically, the 53-year-old Wise had offered his services as a militia unit commander. Wise wired his interest and on June 26, Bache ordered a 20,000-cubic-foot balloon. Wise indicated it would cost $850 and be ready in two weeks.

It was soon clear the leading contender for head of the program was Thaddeus Sobieski Constantine Lowe. The start of the Civil War found Lowe in an uncomfortable position. On April 20 (a week and a day after Fort Sumter was fired on), he made a 900-mile flight from Cincinnati in preparation for a transatlantic attempt. He landed near Unionville, South Carolina. As he made his way back to Cincinnati, he was arrested several times as a suspected Union spy. He was freed each time when he was recognized by local citizens. When he finally arrived in Washington, Lowe had an important advantage over his rivals. In planning the transatlantic flight, he had worked with Joseph Henry, the Secretary of the Smithsonian Institution. Henry could open the doors of official Washington, arranging meetings with Secretary of War Cameron and President Lincoln.

On June 18, 1861, Lowe made a tethered demonstration flight with his balloon *Enterprise* (the same name as the Aérostier's first balloon). The flight was made from the Columbian Armory (now the site of the

National Air and Space Museum). With Lowe were George McDowell of the American Telegraph Company and Herbert C. Robinson, a telegraph operator. Rising 500 feet above the Mall, they could see for twenty miles. Messages from the balloon were telegraphed to the president, the War Department, Gen. Winfield Scott, Alexandria, and Philadelphia. It was a demonstration of both real-time intelligence and Lowe's public relations skills. The balloon, with the three still on board, was taken to the White House and staked out on the South Lawn. Lowe had a long talk with President Lincoln late into the night. Lincoln was particularly interested in Lowe's plan to direct artillery fire at targets out of sight of the gunners.

Lowe was given the chance to try his balloon on the battlefield. He was to make a reconnaissance of the area between Fairfax Court House and Manassas, where 20,000 Confederate troops were reported. Lowe's first combat mission was made on the early evening of June 22 at Arlington House, Virginia, outside Washington. It was followed early the next morning by a brief ascent at Baileys Crossroads to check for Confederate troops that might block the way. With the road clear, Lowe moved the inflated *Enterprise* to Fall Church, Virginia. On June 24 and 25, Lowe made several ascents with army officers as observers. One flight produced a sketch map of Confederate campfires.

The flights convinced the army, and a balloon corps was established in the Topographical Engineers. It would not be a formal organization like the Aérostiers, but a competition between Lowe, Allen, La Mountain, and Wise.[6]

That same summer, both sides were preparing for their first major battle. The site reflected a peculiarity of geography and the attitudes it created. The two capitals, Washington D.C. and Richmond, were only 100 miles apart. The belief grew that the loss of either capital would end the war. The newspaper battle cry, "On to Richmond," grew loud. To meet the need for quick action, a plan was drawn up for a Union attack on Confederate Gen. Pierre G. T. Beauregard's 25,000 troops at Manassas Junction, behind a stream called Bull Run. It was not "on to Richmond"—the inexperience of both officers and men prevented this—but it could eliminate a major Confederate force only thirty miles from Washington.[7]

As preparations for the attack began, the Union balloonists underwent a time of trial. On July 9, Allen tried to make a reconnaissance of Confederate positions near Washington, but was foiled by an inexperienced ground crew and a gas generator that left the balloon half filled. The next day was no more successful. Allen was ordered to prepare his balloons for the Manassas attack. On July 14, disaster struck. First, Allen's smaller balloon burst as it was being filled at a city gas main. Then, the same day, his larger balloon, while being moved to Falls Church, Virginia, was caught by a wind gust, hit a telegraph pole, and burst. Lowe was asked by Major Bache on July 17 to prepare his balloon and join Gen. Irvin McDowell's troops, moving toward Manassas. Lowe began to fill the *Enterprise* at a gas main. The next day, Wise and the army's specially designed balloon arrived (its cane-and-willow basket had an iron floor for protection against ground fire). Lowe was ordered to halt preparations so Wise could inflate his balloon.

In the early morning hours of July 21, the day of the battle, Wise and his twenty-man ground crew left Washington. Heavy trees slowed their progress. By noon they could hear the sounds of battle. As they rushed toward it, the balloon became wedged in tree branches and ripped when the crew tried to free it.[8]

Nearby, the Battle of Bull Run was reaching its climax. The Union army had wheeled around the Confederate left flank and made early advances. It then came under repeated blows from Confederate reinforcements. The Union army faltered, then broke and ran. As they fled, they collided with picnickers from Washington who had come out to see the show. The road back to Washington was a jam of disorganized troops, panicking civilians, carriages, and abandoned weapons. It was not to be a short, easy war.[9]

In the wake of the Bull Run fiasco, there was a general fear the Confederates were about to march on Washington. Wise's army balloon was repaired by July 23. He was ordered by Capt. A. W. Whipple of the Topographical Engineers to move the balloon toward Arlington House. During the transfer on July 26, a strong breeze brushed the tether lines against telegraph lines, cutting them and setting the balloon free. The balloon was too damaged to be used. Captain Whipple went into an obscene tirade directed at Wise and his son Charles. It was John Wise who had the last word on the early days of Civil War ballooning: "With regard to the Bull Run campaign, the balloon part of the disastrous affair was just about as good as the fighting part." Wise soon left military service and resumed making exhibition balloon flights.

Lowe, during this time, was at Fort Corcoran at Arlington, making tethered flights. Finally, in desperation, he decided to make a free flight. Lowe took off shortly after dawn on July 24; a west wind swept him over Confederate lines. He then dropped ballast, the balloon rose, caught an easterly wind and recrossed Union lines. It was the first overflight. Lowe was not yet safe: Union troops fired on his balloon and he landed in no-man's-land. Lowe's wife, Leontine Gachon Lowe, hurried to the area and rounded up a group of Union troops to rescue him. They could see Lowe, but were unable to reach him owing to Confederate troops nearby. That evening, Mrs. Lowe, dressed as a farm woman, drove a wagon to where the balloon was hidden. Lowe loaded the balloon, then hid in the wagon. The Lowes reached safety in Alexandria.

The Union balloon effort was teetering on the edge of failure. Lowe rushed back to Washington to see President Lincoln. He described the problems caused by having three aeronauts competing under loose army control. Lincoln told him to see Lt. Gen. Winfield Scott, the 75-year-old senior Union military commander.[10] General Scott did not have the slightest interest in balloons, Lowe, or his ideas and refused to see him. Lowe stormed back to the White House to ask Lincoln's help. On July 27, the president accompanied Lowe to Scott's headquarters. Lincoln explained that Lowe, a "personal friend," was "organizing an Aeronautic Corps for the army and is to be its chief" and ordered Scott to help in any way possible.[11] On August 2, 1861, Lowe was given a contract to build a balloon and was hired as a civilian aeronaut at $10 per day (roughly that of a colonel).

Lowe began an intensive series of flights against the Confederate troops besieging Mason's, Clark's, Munson's and Upton's hills outside Washington. He flew on twenty-three of thirty-four consecutive days in August and September and made a number of night ascents to count Confederate campfires. In late September, he directed artillery fire by telegraph from his balloon. The reconnaissance also forced the Confederates to spend time camouflaging their positions and building decoy targets (tree trunks painted black were called Quaker guns). He also strengthened his position by taking aloft several Union generals, including George McClellan.

It was at this same time that Lowe's last rival made his belated operational debut. John La Mountain, it will be remembered, was separate from the Topographical Engineers or Lowe's emerging organization. He was a civilian employee of Gen. Benjamin F. Butler. La Mountain did not arrive at Fort Monroe until late June—he had problems raising the money to reach Virginia. Once there, his troubles continued. La Mountain had early stressed the usefulness of his gas generator, which decomposed water into hydrogen. Once at Fort Monroe, he had to admit it was unworkable. Instead, $480 of iron and acid were needed to produce hydrogen. General Butler agreed but La Mountain would have to forego his salary temporarily.[12]

La Mountain did not make his first flight until July 31. His balloon, *Atlantic,* floated on its tether 1,400 feet above Fort Monroe. From his vantage point, La Mountain spotted a hidden Confederate camp. During his flights, La Mountain made detailed reports and diagrams. One read, "on the left bank of the James River, about eight or nine miles from Newport News, is a large encampment of the enemy, from 150 to 200 tents."[13] The results of La Mountain's reconnaissance were mixed. He failed to spot Confederate troop movements toward Hampton Roads, but did spot Rebel positions and enemy shipping on the James River. La Mountain's operations at Fort Monroe ended with a night ascent on August 10, when his iron and acid supply was exhausted. He had to return to Troy, New York, for his larger balloon, *Saratoga,* and a hydrogen generator. When La Mountain returned to Fort Monroe on September 12, he discovered General Butler had been replaced. La Mountain was sent to Washington for orders. The struggle with Lowe had begun.[14]

At a meeting with army officers and Lowe, La Mountain said he was planning to make free flights. Lowe was dubious, but the army saw an advantage in using both tethered and overflights.

La Mountain made his first overflight of Confederate lines on October 15, near Camp Williams. A long overflight was made on October 18 from Cloud's Mill. He crossed Confederate lines at 1,400 feet and observed "every Confederate position between the [Potomac] river and the Blue Ridge." This included troop concentrations at Fairfax Station, Manassas, and Centreville; gun batteries at Aquia Creek; and the movement of several trains. Recrossing Union lines, his balloon was fired on by Union troops but escaped with only minor damage.

Normally, La Mountain flew alone; in mid-November, however, he took a newspaper reporter along. The subsequent account was the first to describe an overflight of enemy territory:

> Being at [La Mountain's] quarter, he kindly invited me to accompany him on a reconnaissance. Having faith with him in that ever-present upper current towards the east, I did not hesitate, though I knew that the lower current towards the west would in a very few minutes carry us far over inside the enemy's lines. Stepping into the car with him, he cut loose, and in a moment, as it were, our great army lay beneath us, a sight well worth a soul to see—brown earth fortifications, white tented encampments, and black lines and squares of

solid soldiers in every direction. So enchanted was I with the scene that I well nigh forgot that we were drifting enemyward, until Fairfax Court House lay beneath us, and I had my first sight of the enemy, in the roaming squads of rebel cavalry visible in that vicinity. Soon Centreville and Manassas came in full sight, and there in their bough huts lay the great army of the South. All along they stretched out southeasterly toward the Potomac, on whose banks their batteries were distinctly visible. So plain were they below, their numbers could be noted so carefully that not a regiment could escape the count. . . .

The Professor, satisfied with the reconnaissance, as well he might be, after noting down the strength of the forces and their position, discharged ballast and started for that higher current to bring us back. Now I acknowledge I looked anxiously and (I am sure I was excusable) nervously for a backward moment, conscious that to come down where we were was death, or at least the horrors of a Richmond tobacco prison. Up, up we went, but still bearing west and south. I looked at the Professor's face. It was calm and confident, so I felt assured that all was right. That assurance became a settled thing, when in a few moments we commenced passing gently back to the east. *We had struck the Professor's current.* Back, back we went, as though a magnet drew us, until our own glorious stars and stripes floated beneath us, and we came down gradually and smoothly into the encampments of General Franklin's division, where we were surrounded by enthusiastic soldiers who had been excitedly watching the trip.

La Mountain's free-flight operations ended soon after this. On November 16, the *Saratoga* was lost when its ground crew let it escape in high winds.[15]

Mr. Lowe's Air Force

At this same time, Lowe was in the process of putting together the Union Balloon Corps. On September 16, 1861, at the urging of Gen. Fitz-John Porter, Lowe submitted a plan for construction of four balloons—two of 20,000 cubic feet and two of 30,000 cubic feet—and portable gas generators for field operations. General McClellan approved the plan. Lowe would be paid up to $1,500 for each large balloon and $1,200 for each smaller one. Soon after, two more small balloons were ordered. The Union Air Force, by the spring of 1862, consisted of eight balloons—*Enterprise, Union, Intrepid, Constitution, United States, Washington, Eagle,* and *Excelsior* (three other balloons would later be added—*Pioneer, North America,* and *General Scott*; these were not part of the regular inventory).

Ground equipment was critical. Twelve portable gas generators were also built (six were ready by the spring of 1862). These were 11-foot tanks with internal shelves to hold iron filings. Sulphuric acid was poured through a funnel on the top. The hydrogen gas was fed through a limewater washer and cooler to remove the acid and cool the gas. A hand pump was used to fill the balloon.

A four-balloon company required wagons to carry the generator, washer and cooler, plus the iron filings and glass carboys of acid. If a telegraph was used, several more wagons were needed for the five miles of insulated wire, tools, and other equipment. Personnel consisted of an aeronaut, a captain, and fifty men. An experienced crew could have a balloon in the air three hours after halting.

Throughout the fall, winter, and spring, Lowe also recruited a staff of aeronauts. Nine individuals would fly for the Union Balloon Corps at one time or another: William Paullin, John B. Starkweather, Ebenezer Locke Mason, Ebenezer Seaver, James Allen, Ezra Allen, John Steiner, Jacob C. Freno, and John R. Dickinson. Several—Paullin, Steiner, and the Allen brothers—had extensive ballooning experience. (James Allen, it will be noted, was one of Lowe's competitors for command of the Balloon Corps.) Lowe soon had balloon detachments at Port Royal, South Carolina, and on the Mississippi River. Their effectiveness was limited, however, by the disinterest of local commanders.

This was only one of the problems still besetting the Union Balloon Corps. There was a high turnover in personnel. Dickinson's only known flight was in October 1861 and he apparently served only a brief time. Paullin was dismissed in January 1862; Mason and Seaver, fed up with late paychecks, refused to fly and were fired in the spring of 1862. Starkweather resigned in the summer of 1862. Freno, who had earlier been kicked out of the 66th Pennsylvania Infantry for cowardice and other offenses, was fired by Lowe in December 1862 for being AWOL, gambling, disloyal statements, and undermining morale.

Considerable effort was also wasted in feuding between Lowe and La Mountain. La Mountain's free flights had generated considerable newspaper publicity which Lowe saw as both a threat to his own control and as raising unrealistic hopes. After the *Saratoga* was lost, La Mountain cast envious eyes on Lowe's new balloons. In his request, he accused Lowe of hoarding materials. In turn, Lowe referred to La Mountain as "a man who is known to be unscrupulous, and prompted by jealousy or some other motive, has assailed me without cause." This feuding, which was a continuation of their prewar rivalry, was finally resolved on February 19, 1862, when General McClellan ordered La Mountain dismissed.

Lowe had finally emerged as undisputed leader of the Union balloon effort, but at a cost. The aeronauts had spent as much time fighting each other as they had observing Confederate troops. This had done nothing to build confidence among Union commanders.[16]

While Lowe was building an air force, Gen. George B. McClellan was preparing the Army of the Potomac. He had given up the idea of a direct assault on Richmond; rather, an end run would be made. Richmond was at the northern end of the Virginia peninsula—a long spit of land bordered by the James and York rivers. At its southern end, the Union held Fort Monroe. Here McClellan would land his army, drive up the lightly held peninsula, take Richmond, and end the war. The buildup of troops at Fort Monroe began in mid-March 1862, with the attack beginning on April 4. McClellan had planned to take Yorktown in only a few hours. Reaching Yorktown the next day, he found a flooded area and defensive works. The indecisiveness, bewilderment, and inability to carry out plans that were McClellan's fatal flaw now became apparent. He decided to halt the advance and reduce Yorktown's defenses by a time-wasting siege. To reinforce this belief in Yorktown's strong defenses, the Confederate commander, Maj. Gen. John B. Magruder, maneuvered his 15,000 troops so as to appear far greater in number. While McClellan hesitated, Confederate troops in northern Virginia were moved to the peninsula as reinforcements.[17,18]

Lowe, attached to Gen. Fitz-John Porter's division, arrived at the front lines on April 5 and made his first flight at 5:20 P.M. that evening with one of Porter's staff officers. Over the next several days, Lowe made several flights with Porter and draftsmen who prepared sketch maps.

With the observations underway, Lowe returned to Fort Monroe for a second balloon, leaving James Allen in charge. When he returned to Yorktown on the night of April 10, Lowe was nearly captured by Confederate pickets. The next morning, General Porter had his own hair-raising adventure. Arriving at the balloon camp at 5:00 A.M., he ordered James Allen to prepare the balloon. Only one tether line was attached, rather than the three normally used to steady the balloon. The line had been damaged in an acid spill and broke when Porter was fifty feet in the air. Unable to reach the tangled valve cord, he found himself drifting over Confederate lines. Showing admirable cool, Porter made observations of the enemy emplacements. After finishing the brief observations, he dropped sandbags and rode a western air current back over Union lines, then climbed into the netting and released the valve. Porter had valved so much gas that the balloon descended at a high rate of speed until the envelope had gathered into the upper hemisphere and acted as a parachute. Porter landed unharmed. Among the crowd that collected at the landing site was Lowe who had seen the rapid descent.

It would be claimed that the balloon escaped a second near-disaster moments later. In 1886, the Detroit Free Press carried an interview with an anonymous ex-Confederate spy. He said he was one of five individuals who, traveling separately, had tried to sabotage the balloon. The man claimed he had disguised himself as a lame tobacco peddler. Reaching the balloon camp a week after crossing the lines, he discovered two of the group had been caught and the balloon was heavily guarded. General Porter's free flight gave him a chance. He was in the crowd that gathered around the balloon. With a pipe in his mouth he was about to strike a match when "a big sergeant" grabbed him by the neck and yelled, "You infernal idiot! Do you want to fire the balloon?" The Confederate spy left while he still had the chance. Only two made it back; the other three were shot.

Throughout April, Lowe and the other aeronauts made regular flights in the *Constitution* and *Intrepid.* These were used to spot targets for an upcoming artillery barrage set for May 4. It had taken nearly a month for the 10-inch and 13-inch siege mortars to be readied. The balloon flights were made in the face of increasing Confederate artillery fire. Although none hit the balloon, some shells came uncomfortably close and posed considerable dangers to ground crews.

A number of observers made flights. One of them was a flamboyant cavalryman known both for his horsemanship and his long hair—Jr. Lt. George Armstrong Custer. Less than confident in the balloon, Custer went up with James Allen. During the ascent, Custer sat on the floor of the basket and asked Allen if it was safe. Seeking to reassure the novice Lieutenant, Allen jumped up and down. At this point, Custer expected the floor to collapse. Soon Custer relaxed and began observation. He would write later:

> I endeavoured to locate and recognize the different points of interest, as they lay spread out over the surface upon which the eye could rest. The point over which the balloon was held was probably one mile from the nearest point of the enemy's line. In an open country balloons would be invaluable in discovering the location of the enemy's camp and works. Unfortunately, however, the enemy's camps, like our own, were generally pitched in the woods to avoid the intense heat of a summer sun; his earthworks along the Warwick were also concealed by growing timber, so that it would have been necessary for the aeronaut to attain the highest possible altitude and then secure a position directly above

> the country to be examined. With all the assistance of a good field glass, and watching opportunities when the balloon was not rendered unsteady by the different currents of air, I was enabled to catch glimpses of canvas through openings in the forest, while camps located in the open space were as plainly visible as those of the Army of the Potomac. Here and there the dim outline of an earthwork could be seen more than half concealed by the trees which had been purposely left standing on their front. Guns could be seen mounted and peering sullenly through the embrasures, while men in considerable numbers were standing in and around the entrenchments, often collected in groups, intently observing the balloon, curious, no doubt, to know the character or value of the information its occupants could derive from their elevated post of observation.

He was apparently considered a good observer as Custer was soon making flights on a nearly daily basis.[19]

The Confederate Air Force

It was during the siege of Yorktown that the first Confederate balloon made its appearance. Southern aeronauts faced many of the same problems as their Northern counterparts, along with particular ones of their own. It was also a symbol of the difficulties facing the Confederate war effort. The earliest Southern balloon was a small unmanned signal balloon sent aloft outside Washington in July 1861. The first manned balloon's origins are not clear. Confederate Gens. Pierre G. T. Beauregard and Joseph E. Johnston seem to have had a balloon in late August 1861. General Beauregard, after attempting to get a balloon through government channels and failing, bought one through a private source. The balloon apparently was poorly constructed, as Beauregard's inspector general subsequently said it was not successful. It may have made one flight—on September 4, 1861, a manned balloon was seen rising from Confederate positions on Munson's Hill. (There were several reports of Southern balloons in June and July which were probably sightings of Lowe.)

It appears Generals Beauregard and Johnston brought the balloon with them when their troops moved from northern Virginia to the peninsula. The balloon was not an impressive sight—"nothing but a big cotton bag, coated over so as to make it airtight, and intended to be inflated with hot air." Lowe agreed, noting it had "neither shape nor buoyancy."[20]

Its pilot was 21-year-old Capt. John Randolph Bryan, an aide at Gen. John B. Magruder's headquarters. He had learned of the need for a pilot and volunteered. Reporting to General Johnston's headquarters, he was questioned about his knowledge of the area and how to identify the different branches of the Union army. Passing the test (he had known the area since childhood), he reported to the balloon site. It was located behind a large thicket of pine trees about half a mile behind the lines. The trees would shield it from Union artillery fire. The balloon was attached to a half-mile-long rope which was passed through a windlass to raise and lower the balloon. Captain Bryan was briefed on the current disposition of Union forces and asked to note the location of each infantry, artillery, or cavalry unit. He was also given a signal flag and told how to indicate to the ground crew whether he wanted the balloon raised or lowered and how fast.

On April 13, 1862, the day after he was assigned to the balloon, Captain Bryan was ordered to make an ascent. The balloon was inflated by burning pine knots and turpentine, the hot air being transferred into the balloon by a flue. As the balloon slowly rose above the trees, Bryan saw a battery of Union guns being prepared to fire on him. He signaled the ground crew to let the balloon climb rapidly. (Because of the low elevation of the guns, a balloon could only be hit when it was close to the ground.) Once above the danger zone, he saw "a wonderful panorama spread out beneath me. Chesapeake Bay, the York and James Rivers, Old Point Comfort and Hampton, and the fleets lying in both the York and the James, and the two opposing armies lying facing each other."

Bryan had little time for observation; the hot air in the balloon cooled rapidly. Nor was the balloon a very stable reconnaissance platform. Because of its low payload, only one tether line was used rather than the three on Lowe's balloons. This meant the balloon would sway in the breeze.

Coming down posed its own risks. The tether line indicated the descent path and several more Union artillery batteries were now ready. Bryan frantically signaled for a fast descent and he was able to make it through a severe barrage. Once on the ground, he rode to Johnston's headquarters where the general personally noted the observations on the battle map.

The second Confederate ascent was made one or two days later at a point nearer to Yorktown. To make the descent safer, a team of six horses was hitched to the windlass. They would gallop down an adjacent road, pulling the balloon down rapidly.

The third flight was on the night of May 3/4. Bryan and the ground crew were awakened by a courier who told them Confederate forces were about to abandon Yorktown and move up the peninsula. General Johnston had received word of a Union attack that was to take place the next morning and Bryan was ordered to spot their line of march. The fire was lit and the balloon inflated. The process always attracted a large crowd of Confederate soldiers who had never seen a balloon. The bright firelight drew a larger crowd than normal which interfered with preparations. Bryan pushed his way through and entered the gondola. Bryan was not concerned about a night ascent; the dark sky would conceal the balloon while bright moonlight would enable him to spot Union positions. The danger proved to be closer to home, however. As the balloon reached 200 feet, he felt a sudden jerk and it began to climb. One of the crowd had stepped into a loop of rope. As it was paid out, the rope tightened around the soldier's leg and dragged him toward the windlass. One of his friends grabbed an axe and cut the rope, releasing both him and the balloon.

The balloon began drifting across the lines and seemed destined to land either behind Union lines or in the York River. Then the wind carried him back over Confederate territory at a point held by the 2d Florida Regiment. The troops saw the balloon and, thinking it was a Union spy, opened fire and began chasing it on foot. Bryan yelled he was a good Confederate to no avail. The night's adventures were not yet over. The wind picked up and changed direction again, back toward the York River. The hot air had nearly cooled and the balloon was close to the ground. Bryan heard the tether splash in the water and prepared to swim. Before it landed, the wind carried the balloon to shore where Bryan was able to slide down the rope and tie it to an apple tree. He then, none the worse for the night's hardships, borrowed a horse from a farmer and rode to General Johnston's headquarters. Bryan indicated what roads the Union troops would use. On this note, the first major use of balloons by the Confederates ended.[21]

The Battle of Fair Oaks

At the same time Bryan was making his wild flight, the siege of Yorktown reached an anticlimax. On the evening of May 3, the night before the bombardment of Yorktown was to begin, Lowe made an ascent but spotted nothing out of the ordinary. At midnight he was awakened by an officer from Gen. Samuel P. Heintzelman's staff. A large fire was noted behind Confederate lines and it was suspected they were burning supplies and pulling out. Lowe's first ascent in the predawn hours of May 4 showed an absence of the usual number of campfires. Lowe made another flight with General Heintzelman at dawn. In the early morning light, the situation was clear. Yorktown was abandoned. McClellan had gained an empty prize at the cost of a month lost.[22]

The Army of the Potomac began moving toward Richmond. The march was slowed by a number of factors. The roads were poor and maps worse. It also rained heavily that first full spring of the war. A more important reason was McClellan was beset by shadows. The intelligence reports provided by the private detective Allan Pinkerton indicated McClellan was outnumbered two to one. In fact, the reverse was true—Pinkerton's estimates were two to four times the actual Confederate strength. Moreover, the accuracy of the reports got worse as the army neared Richmond. Additionally, McClellan (a Democrat) felt abolitionist Republicans were undermining him, wanting him to fail. Thus any setbacks were the administration's fault, not his.[23]

Lowe and Allen followed the slowly moving Union forces. Lowe operated with Gen. George Stoneman's cavalry which was leading the Union advance on Richmond. Stoneman had at first been sceptical about the usefulness of balloons but soon changed his mind. Between May 21 and 25, Lowe and Stoneman made several ascents from near Seven Pines on the Chickahominy River to observe Confederate strong points and direct artillery fire covering the attack on Mechanicsville. After one flight, General Stoneman said "that he had seen enough to be worth a million dollars to the government."

By late May, the balloons *Constitution* and *Intrepid* were based at Seven Pines while the *Washington* operated from Stoneman's headquarters at Mechanicsville. In addition to reconnaissance, Lowe also used the balloons for psychological warfare. The Seven Pines camp was only seven miles from Richmond and was easily visible. Lowe made sure the name *Constitution*, painted on the balloon, always faced the city. It was a reminder the enemy was at the gates.

Confederate Gen. Joseph E. Johnston needed no reminder. At the end of May, he saw a chance. McClellan and three of his corps (Porter, Franklin, and Sumner) were on the north bank of the Chickahominy. Two others (Keyes and Heintzelman) were on the south bank. On the night of May 30, a violent rainstorm deluged the lines. The flooding Chickahominy, Johnston realized, would put some or all of the bridges over the river out of service. This would leave the two corps south of the river temporarily isolated. Johnston could crush them. On the morning of May 31, the attack was launched. Lowe, in the balloon *Washington,* saw the Confederate troops moving toward Fair Oaks. With the telegraph lines down, he sent a messenger to warn McClellan. Lowe then rode six miles from Mechanicsville to the other balloon camp near Seven Pines and Fair Oaks. The *Intrepid,* which could carry both an aeronaut and telegraph operator, was only half inflated. Lowe, therefore, made a quick ascent in the one-man *Constitution.* He confirmed his earlier observation, descended, and sent another warning.

Lowe now faced the problem of inflating the *Intrepid.* The large balloon could reach 1,000 feet and, with a telegraph operator, relay constant progress reports. The portable gas generator would take an hour to fully inflate the balloon. By then, the Union forces could be overwhelmed. As the two armies drew closer, Lowe realized he might be able to transfer the hydrogen from the *Constitution* into the *Intrepid,* but they lacked a pipe. Then Lowe spotted a ten-inch cooking pot. He had the bottom cut out and the transfer was quickly made. From the *Intrepid,* Lowe and his telegraph operator watched the Battle of Fair Oaks unfold nearly at their feet. At one point, Lowe was making reports every fifteen minutes which were relayed to a worried President Lincoln. Years later, Lowe wrote, "of all the battles I have witnessed, that of Fair Oaks was the most closely contested and most severe." It was fought in a wooded swamp with knee-deep water. The wounded drowned where they fell. The Confederates made major advances the first day. With Lowe's warning, McClellan ordered Gen. Edwin V. Sumner to support the beleaguered corps. Sumner was able to get his corps across a bridge that was in the process of floating away. The Union lines held and the battle ended in a stalemate.

Lowe's work won the praise of the Union commanders. Maj. Adolphus W. Greely, chief signal officer of the army, wrote in 1900, "It may be safely claimed that the Union Army was saved from destruction at the Battle of Fair Oaks . . . by the frequent and accurate reports of Professor Lowe."[24,25]

There were two major effects from the battle of Fair Oaks. McClellan halted his advance for over three weeks while he prepared for a defensive stalemate. The other was that during the evening of May 31,

General Johnston was severely wounded. The next day, Confederate President Jefferson Davis named Gen. Robert E. Lee the new commander. The Union's greatest nemesis was now on center stage.

The Seven Days Battles

General Lee's first step was to begin construction of defensive trenches opposite the Union lines. Unlike McClellan, Lee was not satisfied with a static defensive battle. On June 12, he sent Gen. James Ewell Brown Stuart and a cavalry brigade completely around the Union lines. Stuart crossed the Chickahominy at its northern end and swung around the Union right flank. He then crossed the railroad near the supply base at White House, moved around the southern end of the Union position and returned to Richmond on June 15. The raid showed the Union right flank was vulnerable, and with it, the supply lines the army depended on. The Army of Northern Virginia was ready to strike.[26]

Confederate aeronautical activity did not end with the loss of their first hot air balloon. In May, a Richmond newspaper reported Prof. James C. Patton of Petersburg, Virginia had offered his services as an aeronaut but, unable to reach General Johnston's headquarters, had to return home. Lowe, La Mountain, Allen, Wise, and the other Union aeronauts would have understood.

That same spring, the Confederate's second and most famous balloon was being completed. It was the creation of Capt. Langdon Cheeves, a retired lawyer and one of the signers of the South Carolina Ordinance of Secession. When the war started, he had joined the Confederate Army as an engineer. Cheeves had served at Port Royal, South Carolina, where he may have seen one of Lowe's balloons flown by John Starkweather. The balloon was built at Cheeves's own expense at the Chatham Armory at Savannah, Georgia. According to the story, which became part of Southern folklore, the envelope was made from silk dresses collected from throughout the Confederacy. The result was a patchwork of patterns and colors—thus its name: the "Silk Dress Balloon." Truth was not so romantic. Captain Cheeves bought 40-foot lengths of silk in Charleston and Savannah. The material was cut into segments called gores, sewed together, and then coated with a varnish made from rubber train springs dissolved in naphtha. This made it gas-tight. The volume of the finished balloon was about 7,500 cubic feet. Cheeves packed up the balloon and went to Richmond.[27]

Preparations for Lee's attack were now complete. It was a bold, risky plan. McClellan had 105,000 troops (30,000 north of the Chickahominy, the rest south of the river facing Lee's new fieldworks). Lee had 80,000 to 85,000. Lee proposed to leave 25,000 as a screening force to defend Richmond. The rest would wheel around and smash into the Union's weak right flank. With two to one superiority, Lee intended to cut the Union supply lines, trap the Union forces against the Chickahominy and White Oak swamp, and destroy the Army of the Potomac. He could win the war in a single strike. Equally, he could lose the war. McClellan could plow right through the outnumbered screening force and take Richmond. But Lee knew the mind of his enemy—he had to as he was betting the survival of the Confederacy.

The attack began in earnest on June 27 when Lee's forces attacked Porter's troops at Gaines' Mill. McClellan at first thought it was only an artillery duel. Then a staff officer from headquarters went up with Lowe and saw the danger. Once on the ground, he got on his horse and galloped off to report.

Lowe was not alone in the sky. June 27 also marked the debut of the Silk Dress Balloon. The aeronaut on its first mission was the Confederate artillery chief Maj. E. P. Alexander. He was able to provide a warning as Union Gen. Henry Slocum's division crossed the river to reinforce Porter's battered forces. This move, on the afternoon of the 27th, had been ordered by McClellan in response to Lowe's warning. The Seven Days Battles, as they became known, had the distinction of being the first in which both sides had aerial reconnaissance.

The Gaines' Mill battleground was a tangle of thick trees, fields and gullies. The smoke from the guns formed a heavy fog in the ravines. Confederate soldiers later remembered it as disjointed—moments without connection played out against endless noise. By dusk, all the Confederate divisions were in action. Porter's line collapsed and the remnants fled across the river. That night, McClellan, playing the role Lee had written for him, ordered a retreat to the James River.[28]

As the Union army fell back, the Silk Dress Balloon made daily flights. It was filled at the gasworks at Richmond and then taken by train engine down the York River Railroad to a spot near the lines.[29] The Union retreat was a series of running battles—Savage Station (June 29), Frayser's Farm and White Oak Swamp (June 30). Although Lee's troops inflicted heavy losses on the Union forces, he was unable to deliver a crushing blow.

The last battle of the Seven Days was at Malvern Hill on July 1. That night, the Union troops withdrew to Harrison's Landing, as a newspaper correspondent wrote, "more dead than alive."

Lowe's Balloon Corps played a limited role in the Seven Days Battles. Both Lowe and Allen fell ill from the fevers which swept the Union troops after two months in the Virginia swamps. Allen recovered to take temporary command. Lowe was so ill by the time the army reached Harrison's Landing that he returned to Philadelphia. His father, Clovis Lowe, was left to fly the mission.[30]

When McClellan's troops reached Harrison's Landing, the Silk Dress Balloon changed its observation procedures. The closest point on the York River Railroad was seven miles from the Union positions. Observations made from this great a distance were limited in value. To get closer, it was decided to use a ship. The gasworks at Richmond was close to the James River. The balloon was filled, then transferred to the CSS *Teaser*, a mine layer. The ship would then sail down the river until it reached a position near the Union forces. The first shipboard mission was flown on July 1, 1862. This continued until the Fourth of July, when the CSS *Teaser* went aground on a sand bar at Turkey Bend. At the same time, the Union ironclad USS *Monitor* and its escort ship USS *Maratza* sailed up the James River. The *Teaser* opened fire but was soon hit and abandoned. With it was lost the Silk Dress Balloon.[31]

Interlude

Harrison's Landing provided a safe refuge for the battered Army of the Potomac. During early August, Clovis Lowe made reconnaissance flights over the James River while towed behind a steamer. These were the final balloon missions of the Peninsular Campaign. On August 3, 1862, McClellan was ordered to begin his final withdrawal.

The end of the Peninsular Campaign marked the start of several months of relative inactivity. Lowe had recovered from his illness and had returned to Washington on September 5. His major problem was to reestablish his close relations with the army command. On March 31, 1862, before the start of the Peninsular Campaign, control of the Balloon Corps was transferred to Lt. Col. Rufus Ingalls, chief quartermaster of the Army of the Potomac. Lowe was required to submit all requests through the Quartermaster's Office. Direct tactical control was in the hands of Brig. Gen. Andrew A. Humphreys, McClellan's chief topographical engineer. Humphreys understood the problems and needs of the Balloon Corps and helped the often freewheeling Lowe cope with military red tape.

After the retreat from Virginia, all this was gone—Humphreys now commanded a division. Lowe wrote, requesting travel orders to rejoin the army, to the assistant adjutant general, A. V. Colburn, who responded that Lowe should stay in Washington until McClellan made his intentions clear.[32]

At the same time, the price of McClellan's failure was becoming clear. He had taken the bulk of Union forces to the gates of Richmond and the brink of victory. The military strength and morale of the Union had taken a major blow. The Confederates now held the initiative and Lee meant to use it by taking the war to the gates of Washington. The failure of the Peninsular Campaign also meant the last chance for a quick Union victory was gone. The Southern insurrection was becoming total war. The great issues of freedom and slavery, which even at this late date many tried to avoid, could no longer be ignored. The United States that emerged from this grim struggle would be a far different place.

The Confederate's first step toward victory was to clear Northern Virginia of Union forces. This had to be done before McClellan's forces returned from the peninsula and joined the units commanded by Gen. John Pope, giving the Union overwhelming numbers. To prevent this, Lee sent Stonewall Jackson around Pope's flank to strike at the Union supply base at Manassas Junction some twenty miles behind the lines. After destroying the base, Jackson and his 25,000 men took refuge on the old Bull Run battlefield. Pope went after them, finally catching them on August 29, 1862. The next day, as Pope's troops pursued Jackson's battered forces, Lee's army attacked his flank. Hemmed in on two sides, Pope's army was crushed. The Second Battle of Bull Run was a stunning Confederate victory. Pope was relieved and sent to Minnesota to fight Indians.

Now Lee moved north, crossing into Maryland on September 5. The offensive had several goals: to bring Maryland into the Confederacy and to destroy the Army of the Potomac. The political importance was far greater. A British cabinet meeting was set for late September to discuss recognizing the Confederacy. If recognition was granted, Southern independence was virtually assured. The British decision rested on news of Lee's invasion. The Army of Northern Virginia moved behind the South Mountains. This shielded it from Union eyes and gave room to maneuver. If McClellan crossed the mountains without knowing

Lee's location, Lee could slip past and take Washington. Yet, if McClellan waited too long, the Union would be lost. Lee's army was in three parts: one near the Pennsylvania border, another holding the South Mountains, and a third under Stonewall Jackson heading for Harper's Ferry.

A Confederate officer lost a copy of the operational orders. Two Union enlisted men found it. The orders were taken to McClellan's headquarters. An officer recognized the handwriting and assured McClellan it was real.

With Lee's location and future movements known, McClellan broke through the mountains and forced Lee to pull together his scattered units and make a stand at Sharpsburg on Antietam Creek. And there, on September 17, the Battle of Antietam was fought. It was the bloodiest day in American military history—over 12,000 Union soldiers were killed or wounded, and the Confederates lost about 11,000. The next night, Lee took his crippled forces back across the Potomac, the invasion of the North a failure.

On September 22, in the wake of Lee's failure, President Lincoln signed the Emancipation Proclamation. The war was no longer just to restore the Union but to destroy slavery.[33,34]

It was not until after the Union victory at Antietam that Lowe's enforced idleness ended. On September 18, the day after the battle, Lowe was ordered to bring his balloons to Sharpsburg. He arrived a week later. Lowe met with McClellan who expressed his regret that Lowe had not been present "as the balloon would have been invaluable to him during that engagement." They discussed the future of the Balloon Corps. Lowe explained the difficulty in obtaining orders and transport. Lowe also noted that his lack of an officer's commission meant he "was subject to every young and inexperienced lieutenant and captain." McClellan said he would recommend the Balloon Corps be made a distinct branch of the army and Lowe be commissioned as its commander. Lowe wrote later: "At last it seemed that my greatest ambition was about to be fulfilled."

Starting the next morning and continuing for nearly a month, Lowe and James and Ezra Allen made flights from Sharpsburg and Bolivar Heights above Harper's Ferry.

Finally, after six weeks of inactivity, McClellan moved south to begin a new offensive. Lowe was not to participate in the initial phase. The army would be in the vicinity of the Blue Ridge Mountains and the balloons would be of little value. Lowe and the others were to wait in

Washington. McClellan was in a perfect position to destroy, one at a time, the separate parts of Lee's army. However, McClellan then hesitated to move against either. On November 5, Lincoln ordered him removed. His replacement was Maj. Gen. Ambrose E. Burnside.

McClellan's removal meant Lowe had lost his most important supporter.

Burnside proposed a new plan. His army would move southeast to Falmouth on the Rappahannock River, then cross the river on pontoon bridges at Fredericksburg and head for Richmond. This would put the Army of the Potomac closer to Richmond than Lee's forces were. Lee would be compelled to fight against long odds.

The plan was approved on November 14. The next day, the first two army corps began their advance. By November 17, they had reached Falmouth, overlooking Fredericksburg, which was held by only a small Confederate detachment. The march was so quick, Lee was taken by surprise. However, the bridging equipment had not arrived. Rather than finding a shallow ford, Burnside decided to wait. His greatest shortcoming was an inability to improvise to meet unexpected developments. For thousands of his troops, it was a fatal shortcoming.

In the meantime, Lowe was trying to reestablish his links with the army. On November 20, he wrote to Maj. Gen. J. G. Parke, Burnside's chief of staff, to inform him of his capabilities and requirements, and to request orders. On November 24, Parke responded, ordering Lowe, his men and balloons to join Burnside's forces at Fredericksburg. Lowe arrived in late November, with James and Ezra Allen following soon after. Burnside told them he wanted to keep the balloons' presence a secret until the crossing of the Rappahannock actually began. This, however, meant Lowe could not make any preattack reconnaissance.

Fredericksburg

During the weeks following Burnside's arrival at Fredericksburg, Lee had been pouring reinforcements into the area. Only a relatively small number of skirmishers held the town. The bulk of the forces—35,000 troops under Gen. James Longstreet—were in defensive positions on a line of low hills a mile or two behind the town. Burnside had almost no information about Confederate troop positions. Yet he remained determined to press forward with the attack despite the opposition of his corps commanders. Lowe was still on the ground, forbidden to fly. In retrospect, this was a poor decision. A night ascent would have allowed the number and location of Confederate campfires to be determined. This would seem to be worth the risk that the balloon would be spotted against the dark sky.

The construction of the six pontoon bridges began early in the morning of December 11, 1862, under cover of fog and blowing snow. When the fog burned off, Confederate snipers began firing on the bridge builders. Work was halted while an artillery barrage battered the town. The snipers simply hid in basements until the barrage lifted, then emerged from the wreckage and resumed firing. Finally, Burnside sent volunteers across the river on boats to force them out and set up a bridgehead. The next day, as Union troops moved across the bridges to set up a mile-wide front, Lowe and the Allen brothers prepared their balloons.

Burnside issued his battle orders on the morning of December 13. It was to be a two-pronged attack. Gen. Edwin Sumner would attack Confederate units behind Fredericksburg. Gen. William Franklin would attack the Confederates south of town. Gen. Joseph Hooker's troops would be held in reserve. The instructions were very general: attack Confederate troops and take the range of hills behind the town. There were no specific objectives or tactical activities given.

The Union troops advanced under heavy fog. The Confederates could hear their bugle calls, the sound of the army marching and of gun carriage on the frozen roads. Lowe, floating above Burnside's headquarters on the far side of the river, was equally blind. Then, at about ten o'clock, a wind pushed the fog clear and the battle was underway. The whole of the Army of the Potomac was exposed to a withering barrage of artillery. The main battle was centered on the wide plain behind the town. The main Confederate defensive line was a sunken road topped by a four-foot stone wall. Behind this wall, which stretched for a quarter of a mile, waited six ranks of infantry in almost perfect protection. The Union troops began their attack on the wall at noon. Before the battle, a Confederate artillerist said that once he opened fire, not a chicken could live on the open ground between the town and the sunken road. He was nearly right. For the rest of the day, four divisions tried to take "that terrible Stone Wall." Their assaults left piles of dead and wounded but not one Union soldier came within a hundred feet of the wall.

During the battle, Lowe made repeated ascents with Union commanders. Lowe's primary function was to report the course of the battle to Burnside and his staff. Lowe simply yelled his observations to the ground. James and Ezra Allen apparently also operated that day although no details have survived. (James Allen, it will be remembered, had joined Burnside's Rhode Island regiment at the start of the war.) Lowe's balloon drew sporadic Confederate artillery fire during the morning, one shell passing quite close.

The final attack was a bayonet charge through the smoky twilight led by Lowe's friend and former commander Gen. A. A. Humphreys. As the division moved toward the wall, the survivors of the earlier assaults, lying scattered in the fields, grabbed at their feet and pants legs, trying to prevent them from throwing their lives away. The attack collapsed under fire and the battle was over.

Two days later, the survivors withdrew to a winter camp at Falmouth, leaving Lee in control of the battered town. Burnside accepted responsibility for the disaster and requested to be relieved. His replacement was Maj. Gen. Joseph Hooker.

The contribution of Lowe's balloons to the Battle of Fredericksburg was minimal. He was not allowed to make any flights before the attack. On the day of the battle, fog prevented any observations until ten o'clock. This left only two hours until the attack on the stone wall began. Also, Lowe's position on the east side of the river was a considerable distance from the lines.

A far more important reason for the Union defeat was Burnside's incompetence. He was incapable of seeing the tragedy taking place in front of the stone wall. At the height of the battle, General Hooker personally rode back to Burnside's headquarters to protest the order to continue the attack. The orders stood and Hooker's division soon littered the field with its dead and wounded. In the face of such blindness, any information Lowe provided was wasted.[35]

In the wake of Fredericksburg, the Balloon Corps saw little action. Lowe and the Allen brothers flew, weather permitting, to keep an eye on Confederate troop movements across the river. Also during the winter of 1862–63, Lowe experimented with hot air signal balloons. Ranging from 6 to 20 feet in diameter, they would use markings on the envelope and signal banners to relay messages. At night, red or green calcium flares would be used. The signal balloons were to be used by isolated cavalry patrols to relay signals to headquarters up to forty miles away. The tests were inconclusive due to the original balloons' shoddy construction and the refusal of the army to fund additional ones.

Lowe's flights were not always uneventful. In February 1863, he was operating near Falmouth when the balloon was fired on. The shells missed Lowe but one landed in a cesspool. David Hogan of the Thirteenth New Hampshire Infantry, on sentry duty nearby, was nearly buried by the smelly debris. Hogan was rescued unhurt if not unaffected.[36]

Although the early months of 1863 were relatively quiet ones for the Union Balloon Corps, they marked a resurgence of Confederate aeronautical activity.

During the summer of 1862, a second "silk dress" balloon was built in the Charleston-Savannah area. Its designer was Charles Cevor, a prewar balloonist. The balloon is believed to have had a volume of 7,500 cubic feet, the same as the first Silk Dress Balloon. Unlike the first two Confederate balloons, its construction was directly paid for by the Confederate Army. The final cost was $475.83, according to a list approved on August 21, 1862, by General Beauregard, the commander of the Department of South Carolina and Georgia. The balloon operated under Maj. D. B. Harris, Beauregard's Chief of Engineers. As its pilot, Cevor was paid $140 per month (Lowe received $10 per diem). His assistant, A. E. Morse, received $100 per month.

When the balloon was completed, Cevor and Morse first took it to Richmond. (This was around the time of the Second Battle of Bull Run and Antietam.) By November 21, 1862, they were back in Charleston. General Beauregard had been given command of the area in September. He quickly concluded the Union would soon be making an attack. Charleston was an important target for several reasons. As a major seaport, it was one of the Confederacy's links with the outside world. There was symbolism too—its harbor was protected by Fort Sumter, where the Civil War had begun. Beauregard soon bolstered the city's defenses, including defensive forts and extensive mining of the harbor. The Cevor balloon was part of this. Capt. W. H. Echols of Charleston's Office of Chief Engineer was ordered to pay any bills required to keep it aloft. Cevor's balloon was apparently quite active, as on February 16, 1863, he requested a charge account with the Charleston gasworks to ease the red tape that accompanied each inflation of the balloon.

The Union attack on Charleston began on April 7, 1863, with the shelling of Fort Sumter by ironclads. Although little damage was done on either side, it was clear the city would have to be taken by siege. Unfortunately, the records of operations by Cevor's balloon during that spring and summer have not survived. It is not known, therefore, what role the balloon played in the defense of the city.[37,38]

Chancellorsville and the End of Civil War Ballooning

Gen. Joseph Hooker had spent the spring rebuilding the morale and discipline of the battered Army of the Potomac. By late April, it was ready for another drive on Richmond.

For Lowe, the spring of 1863 was marked by setbacks that signaled the beginning of the end of the Union Balloon Corps. Jacob C. Freno, who had been fired as an aeronaut in December 1862 for gambling and spreading "treasonous rumors," swore out a complaint accusing Lowe of a number of crimes. These included stealing government property (including an entire balloon), payroll fraud, requisitioning army rations for himself and newsmen, and using government carriages to take his wife on sightseeing trips around Washington.

Lowe was able to show the charges were false and accused Freno of breaking into a warehouse and vandalizing the balloon *Constitution*. A warrant was issued for Freno's arrest, but he could not be located.

There were also major problems in the relationship between Lowe and the army bureaucrats in Washington. Paychecks for the Balloon Corps were often late and Lowe had trouble keeping the skilled ground crews needed to operate the balloon.

A more pressing problem was Lowe's shortcomings in the area of financial administration and inventory. Lowe frequently sent equipment and balloons to other commands without getting receipts. His claims for travel expenses were frequently based on verbal orders.

The beginning of the end came on April 7, 1863, when Capt. Cyrus B. Comstock, the chief engineer for the Army of the Potomac, was named officer in charge of the Balloon Corps. Unlike his predecessors, who had given the freewheeling Lowe a great deal of latitude, Comstock served notice he would exercise absolute control over the Balloon Corps. He ordered Lowe's pay cut from $10 to $6 per day, Clovis Lowe and John O'Donnell fired, and demanded an accounting of all property assigned to the Balloon Corps. It may have been his assignment was engineered by War Department officials seeking a confrontation with Lowe. Comstock certainly had little regard for the Balloon Corps ("an unsuccessful experiment") or Lowe ("acting without the knowledge or authority of anyone connected with the Army").

If a confrontation was sought, it was soon in coming. On April 12, 1863, Lowe submitted a long letter of resignation. He hedged it by saying that in view of the impending Union offensive, he would temporarily offer his services free. This was accepted. Although the end was near, the Balloon Corps still had one last battle.[39]

On April 27, General Hooker began his drive on Richmond. While Union cavalry swept around the Confederate rear, cutting supply lines, the main part of the Army of the Potomac would cross the Rappahannock and Rapidan rivers and position itself on Lee's left flank near the crossroads of Chancellorsville. Lee would be forced into a trap: if he headed for Richmond, the Union army could hit his flank; if he fought at Chancellorsville, the Union forces at Fredericksburg could break out and hit from behind. Lee saw the trap and began to move from Fredericksburg on May 1. In his balloon, Lowe saw the move and reported "heavy columns of the enemy's infantry and artillery . . . moving up the river accompanied by many Army wagons." General Hooker interpreted this as a retreat in the face of the impending attack. At the same time, Hooker lost his nerve. When the advancing units encountered Confederate skirmishers, Hooker abruptly broke off, the advance halted, and defensive lines formed around the Chancellorsville crossroads. This handed the initiative to Lee and Jackson. Hooker's forces were emplaced in a thick forest called the Wilderness, which reduced their firepower and artillery advantage.

On the morning of May 2, Lee sent Jackson on a long sweep toward the weak Union right flank. At one point, the column was spotted by Union outposts but Hooker believed these were fleeing units. At 5:00 P.M., as the Union troops were stacking their rifles and preparing dinner, Jackson's forces burst out of the tree line. The Union flank collapsed amid moonlit firefights. General Hooker ordered the Union troops at Fredericksburg to take the town and come to his rescue. The attack came the next morning, May 3. Lowe and the Allens, in the balloons *Washington* and *Eagle,* supported the attack. Gen. John Sedgwick's troops crossed the river at the town and at a point to the south. Outnumbered four to one, the 10,000-man Confederate holding force was pushed back. Sedgwick credited Lowe's reports with enabling him to attack the stone wall area with confidence, noting the intelligence "could not have been procured by any other means."

Meanwhile, the Confederate attack at Chancellorsville pushed the Union lines back. When Lee learned of the Fredericksburg breakout, he coolly split his forces again. Leaving a small force to keep the beaten General Hooker busy, the bulk of Lee's troops attacked Sedgwick's units on May 4, forcing them back. This done, the Confederates turned to again attack Hooker. He did not wait, withdrawing his forces back across the Rappahannock on May 6. He had been humiliated by a force half his size.[40]

The same day, Lowe's service with the army ended. He went to see Captain Comstock in hopes the salary issue might be resolved. It was not, Lowe asked to be relieved, and this was granted.

James and Ezra Allen continued to operate for some time afterward. Their balloon, the *Washington,* was in poor condition with numerous small holes and rotting seams. Worse, it was commanded by officers with little knowledge of ballooning. On May 30, the Allens were ordered aloft in near-gale winds. During his next flight on June 1, Ezra Allen had begun an ascent when a gust tore a 36-foot-long split in a seam. Ezra was barely able to make a safe landing. The army refused to order new balloons so the Allens had to make do. Yet the risks paid off. During the first week of June, the Allens spotted thick clouds of dust as the Army of Northern Virginia began another offensive. The Army of the Potomac headed after them. They met at the small crossroads of Gettysburg on July 1 through 3. By this time, the Union Balloon Corps had quietly dissolved.[41]

The Confederate balloon effort was also ending. The second "silk dress" balloon was lost in the spring or early summer of 1863 during the siege of Charleston. According to one version, it was blown free during a wind storm, drifted over Union lines, and was captured. In any event, it was put on display at the Patent Office in Washington and later cut up as souvenirs. A photo of a segment shows it was made of fabric squares. This suggests it actually was made of salvaged dresses rather than new material. Another casualty of the siege of Charleston was Langdon Cheeves. The builder of the first Silk Dress Balloon and father of the Confederate Air Force was killed in July 1863.[42]

Assessment

And so what were the accomplishments of the Union and Confederate Air Forces? Certainly Lowe and his fellow aeronauts provided information of value. E. P. Alexander, the Confederate artillery chief and pilot of the first Silk Dress Balloon, noted, "I have never understood why the enemy abandoned the use of military balloons early in 1863, after having used them extensively up to that time. Even if the observers never saw anything, they would have been worth all they cost for the annoyance and delays they caused us in trying to keep our movement out of their sight." Unfortunately, Lowe's information was rarely put to good use. The Army of the Potomac, in the first two years of the war, could be compared to a pride of lions led by sheep. There were many other problems—the early infighting, the turnover of command, the disinterest and hostility to the Balloon Corps within the army and War Department, as well as Lowe's ego and disregard for red tape. Fundamentally, the problem Lowe faced was that he sought to introduce a new idea—aerial reconnaissance—amid the hostile environment of war.

The Confederate aeronautical effort is also instructive. Whereas more than a dozen balloons flew for the Union at one time or another, the Confederates could only muster three. They were crude makeshift efforts built under trying conditions. They were symbolic of the Confederate war effort. With only a small fraction of the Union's industry and population, the South was forced to make do, then do without. One glaring shortcoming was the lack of portable gas generators. This meant Confederate balloons were tied to city gasworks.

The most valuable contribution was to the future—Lowe braving shell fire and the romantic legend of the Silk Dress Balloon would become part of the heritage of air power.[43]

The next decade saw several developments in the way of military ballooning. During 1867–68, James and Ezra Allen were employed as aeronauts by the Brazilian Army during the War of the Triple Alliance (1865–1870). This pitted Brazil, the Argentine Confederation and Uruguay against Paraguay and was ghastly even by twentieth century standards. When the war started, Paraguay had 250,000 males. When it ended, there were only 28,000. The Allens made numerous ascents during the siege of Humita on the Paraguay River. To counter their observations, the Paraguay Army used smoke screens.[44,45]

During the Franco-Prussian war of 1870–71, the French used balloons to maintain communications out of the besieged city of Paris. The first flight was made on September 23, 1870. The balloons were built in two railroad stations. When silk ran out, calico coated with linseed oil was used. A total of sixty-six balloons carried 155 people, nine tons of mail, carrier pigeons and other cargo. Eight balloons were lost. The flights' main purpose was to rally support in the provinces to relieve Paris. The last flight was launched on January 28, 1871. The same day, an armistice was signed.[46,47]

The experiences of the U.S. Civil War and the Paris airlift convinced European military officials of the balloon's value. During the closing decades of the nineteenth century, Great Britain, France, Germany, Russia, Austria-Hungary, Japan, and the United States all organized balloon units. These small groups would, in time, become the air forces of these nations.

In Great Britain, the first military experiments with balloons were authorized in 1878. The War Office allotted £150. The work was done at the Woolwich Arsenal under the command of Capt. J. L. B. Templer. Captain Templer was an aeronaut and owned the balloon *Crusader* (which thus became the first balloon used by the British Army). By the next year, a total of five balloons were in service.

Balloons were used during the maneuvers at Aldershot in 1880 and 1882 and were considered successful. Accordingly, in the fall of 1882, the Balloon Equipment Store was ordered to move to the School of Military Engineering at Chatham. There, a small balloon factory, depot and school was set up. Production of the balloons was literally a family affair: Mrs. Weinling, elder son Fred, daughters Mary Anne and Eugene, and youngest son Willie for a time held a monopoly on the manufacture of balloons for the British Empire. In 1884, the British made a major advance in balloon technology with the development of cylindrical tanks to hold compressed hydrogen. These were easier to handle than acid, iron, and a gas generator.

The first British military use of balloons came in the fall of 1884 when three balloons and a staff of fifteen noncommissioned officers and men were included in an expedition to Bechuanaland in southern Africa. The expedition was to expel a group of "filibusters" (a group of irregular military adventurers) who were raiding the territory. There was no fighting and the balloon detachment was limited to giving a native chief named Montsiou a brief ride. A second detachment was sent to the Sudan in February 1885. Most of the equipment had already been sent to Bechuanaland but the group was able to make several ascents which proved useful.[48–50]

After the two detachments returned to England, there was no attempt to maintain a regular balloon section; rather, it was an ad hoc organization of a few officers and men who believed in the future of balloons. Some training exercises with a captive balloon directing artillery fire were held and new equipment was tested. One such test involved small free balloons carrying cameras. A clockwork timer exposed the plates at regular intervals, then punctured the balloon to return it to earth.

By 1889, the point had been reached to decide whether balloons should become a regular part of the army. The test came during the summer maneuvers. A balloon detachment was part of a division commanded by Lt. Gen. Sir Evelyn Wood. It was attached to a unit sent in pursuit of a "flying column" of enemy troops encamped near the Frensham ponds. Sir Wood asked if there were any outposts at the rear of the enemy's camp. Lt. B. R. Ward made the ascent. Although it was nearly dusk and the terrain was not very open, he was able to spot pickets being set up on the near side of the enemy camp. There was no movement on the far side. He reported this and a night attack was successfully made.

Sir Evelyn Wood was favorably impressed and in 1890, a balloon section was established in the British Army as part of the Royal Engineers. Over the next few years, it had several homes while a permanent facility was being built at South Farnborough. (In time, it would become the Royal Aircraft Establishment, a major British flight test center.)[51]

By this time, nearly thirty years after Lowe's Balloon Corps had been dissolved, the balloon had returned to U.S. Army service. This was due to the vision of one man—Brig. Gen. Adolphus V. Greely. In 1891, he had been appointed Chief Signal Officer of the Army. One of his first actions was to send Lt. William A. Glassford to France for a year's study of ballooning. Glassford returned in 1892 with a balloon and set about organizing a Balloon Service. He enlisted William Ivy, a famous aeronaut who performed under the stage name "Ivy Baldwin," as a sergeant and put him in charge of the balloon. The next year, the balloon, named the *General Myer,* was put on display at the Chicago World's Fair. In addition to making several hundred ascents, Glassford also tested use of a telephone for balloon-to-ground communications. This was the first time this had been done. Use of a telephone permitted both faster and more detailed information to be sent than with a telegraph. The balloon *General Myer* lasted about three years before it was too rotted to fly. Sergeant Ivy and his wife sewed together its replacement—a 14,000-cubic-foot silk envelope.[52]

By the start of 1898, the United States was becoming increasingly concerned by events in Cuba. The island, the last remnant of Spain's once vast South American colonies, was being racked by a rebellion. The U.S. was shocked by newspaper accounts of Spanish cruelties in trying to put down the revolt. On February 15, 1898, the battleship USS *Maine* exploded and sank in Havana Harbor. Although subsequently traced to an internal explosion, both public and "Yellow Press" were quick to blame the Spanish authorities. President William McKinley gave Spain an ultimatum to leave Cuba by April 20. This was refused, and the Spanish-American War began.[53]

The army's sole balloon was shipped to New York and then to Tampa, Florida. Lt. Col. Joseph E. Maxfield of the Signal Corps was ordered to set up two balloon companies (the personnel were to be taken from the nearest infantry units). When Maxfield arrived at Tampa, he found the balloon and ground equipment scattered all over the railroad yard, no officers, no men, and orders to proceed immediately to Santiago, Cuba. In fact, it took weeks to round up the equipment.

When he finally sailed, he had only three officers, twenty-four enlisted men, no rifles, ammo, or mess kits, and only part of the balloon equipment.

Nor did their troubles end when they disembarked in Cuba on June 28. Maxfield and Ivy discovered they had no gas generator, acid, or iron filings. There was only enough compressed hydrogen in cylinders for one inflating. Worse, the tropical heat had softened the balloon's varnish, sticking the envelope together. Ivy carefully separated the fabric, sewed up the tears, and had the balloon, called the *Santiago*, in the air on June 30.

Three flights were made that day: the first by Ivy and Maxfield, the second by Maxfield and Lt. Col. George M. Derby, and the third by Lt. W. J. Volkman and Gen. Ignacio M. del Castillo of the Cuban rebel army. The flights confirmed the presence of the Spanish fleet in Santiago Harbor.

That evening, Gen. William Shafter put his chief engineer, Col. George Mc C. Derby, in command of the balloon unit and ordered it moved to El Poso Hill. It would provide information for the attacks on Spanish positions at El Caney and San Juan Hill.[54] The next day, July 1, the attack on San Juan Hill began. Maxfield, Colonel Derby, and Ivy made the first ascent to observe troop movements at El Caney and on the roads leading to San Juan Hill. Derby then ordered the *Santiago* moved to the front line. Maxfield objected, saying the balloon would be hit by ground fire. Despite this, the balloon was moved to a grove of trees only 650 yards away from Spanish positions on the lower slopes of San Juan Hill. As the balloon, with Derby and Maxfield aboard, ascended, the tether and telephone line became tangled in the trees and the *Santiago* could climb no higher than 300 feet. Despite the low altitude, the aeronauts were able to spot a hidden trail and ford which allowed the U.S. troops to spread out. Artillery fire was also directed against Spanish positions.

Yet the *Santiago*'s usefulness was short-lived. The Spanish officers recognized the danger and yelling, "*Matenlo! Matenlo!*" ("kill it, kill it"), ordered the balloon shot down. The short range and low altitude made the *Santiago* a sitting duck for everything from small arms to heavy artillery. Several times, rifle bullets tore through the basket and silk envelope. Maxfield finally ordered the balloon down, but it was too late. As one observer later wrote, "The balloon was dying, dying a gigantic and public death before the eyes of two armies. It quivered, sank, faded into the trees amid the flurry of battle."

The Spanish guns continued to fire at the balloon's location, causing heavy casualties among the U.S. troops in the area. It was clear the U.S. position was untenable: either the troops would have to take the hill or withdraw. The Rough Riders, led by Lt. Col. Theodore Roosevelt, and the all-black 10th Cavalry moved up the hill. When the fighting stopped at 4:30 that afternoon, the U.S. held the high ground and the battle for Cuba was all but over. Few had good words for the *Santiago*'s contribution to that "Splendid Little War." In retrospect, this was due more to command errors (placing the balloon too close to the front lines) rather than a failure by its observers or ground crew. The *Santiago* also held the unwanted distinction of being the first combat balloon damaged by enemy action.[55,56]

World War I

During the remaining years of the nineteenth and the early years of the twentieth centuries, balloons saw action several times. The first major use of balloons since the Civil War was the Boer War of 1899–1902. Four balloon sections were used in the war. The first section was at the battle of Magersfontein where the observer called down artillery fire on enemy ponies hidden in a gulley, killing more than 200. Another section was with the besieged British units at Ladysmith. The balloon directed fire during the battle of Lombard's Kop, but, in time, the gas ran out and the balloon could no longer be used. A third unit, put together at Cape Town, was part of the relief column marching toward Ladysmith. A final section was with the British units at Kimberley. There were, of course, the familiar problems: high-level indifference, supply problems, and unfamiliarity of artillery units with the signaling methods.[57]

During the Russo-Japanese war in 1904, both sides used balloons.

The Russians had to improvise: when the balloon materials were captured, a Czarist officer built a balloon from bedsheets coated with flax oil. The French also used balloons to scout Muslim rebels in the Moroccan campaign of 1907–1908.[58]

It was also at this time that the first technical advance in balloon reconnaissance since its origin in the French Revolution was made. The balloons used up to this point were spherical. This was ideal for a free-floating balloon, but when tethered, this shape caused it to twist in wind gusts. In 1894, Major Von Parseval, a German airship designer, and Captain Von Sigsfeld changed the shape to a cylinder. To stabilize it, two fabric horizontal stabilizers were fitted to either side and a tubular "air rudder" curved around the rear and underside of the balloon. The balloon would turn into the wind. Only the forward section was filled with gas; the rear portion and air rudder were kept inflated by the wind. The new balloon was called a *Drachen* (Dragon).

The new balloon was a German secret but French and Belgian intelligence acquired drawings. The French modified the *Drachen* by replacing the air rudder with three large stabilizing fins. It was called a *Cacquot* and the French and Belgians had some in the early years of the twentieth century.[59] Whatever its official name, the balloon's distinctive shape led to it being called a "sausage."[60]

Despite becoming a regular part of European armies, military balloonists still faced many of the same problems Lowe had known. In the German army, for instance, a series of service manuals were issued for balloon detachments between 1890 and 1914. After the October 1903 manual, however, there were no basic changes in text, reflecting a lack of official interest. Moreover, the role of the balloon was narrow—the observer was to spot the deployment or approach of enemy troops. Artillery direction was considered only in terms of classic fortress warfare. After airplanes made their appearance, the manuals were silent on any threat they might pose to the balloons or defensive measures to be taken.

In the United States, official disinterest was more direct. The army budget had only enough money to inflate the balloon once per year. Ivy, believing there was no future for him in the army, left in 1900.[61]

In Europe, the stability which had lasted since the end of the Napoleonic Wars was breaking down. France, bitter over the humiliation of the Franco-Prussian War, wanted revenge. Germany, feeling both ambitious and insecure, became increasingly bellicose. To the east, Imperial Russia, a decaying feudal autocracy beset by internal revolt, and the declining Austro-Hungarian Empire vied for influence over the weak independent states of the Balkans. The years between 1905 and 1914 saw a series of crises: the First Moroccan Crisis, the Bosnian Crisis, the Second Moroccan Crisis, the first and second Balkan wars. Each time, diplomacy was able to keep them localized but nothing was really settled. A European war seemed inevitable, only an incident away. Or a few shots.

On June 28, 1914, a Serbian nationalist and member of the Black Hand terrorist group, named Gavrilo Princip, killed Archduke Francis Ferdinand and his wife at Sarajevo. The Austrians seized the killing of the heir as a pretext to crush the nation of Serbia and establish their dominance of the Balkans. On July 28, the Austro-Hungarian Empire declared war on Serbia. Imperial Russia declared war on Austria, then Germany declared war on Russia and France, and finally, on August 4, Great Britain declared war on Germany. World War I had begun.

The German battle plan (the Schlieffen Plan) envisioned sending nearly the entire army through Belgium in a long sweep around Paris. The French Army would be destroyed in six weeks. The Germans could then turn their attention to Russia. It would be a short war.

At first, the German sweep went well, but in early September, a gap developed in the German lines and the French counterattacked along the Marne River. With the German advance halted, each side tried to outflank the other in "the race to the sea." By mid-October, a line of trenches stretched from the North Sea to Switzerland.[62,63]

Observation balloons proved ideal for trench warfare. The observer could watch the enemy positions for hours, becoming familiar with the normal routine. Any changes—troop movements or new batteries being emplaced—could be spotted and reported to intelligence officers on the ground by telephone as they happened. The observers could also use very long focal length cameras to take oblique photos of the enemy trenches. (Photography from balloons had been tried even before the Civil War but this was the first operational use.)

The early months of the war showed several shortcomings, however. The German manuals indicated an observer could only see about four and a half miles. It was soon found this was due to inferior field glasses; when better quality ones were issued, the oberver's range nearly doubled to eight miles. It was also discovered the balloons were too small—despite their sausage shape, they still swayed in high winds. In early 1915, larger, higher-flying balloons were produced. These gave both a greater visual range and a more comfortable ride.[64]

In April 1915, the Germans began an offensive at Ypres, Belgium. This set the pattern for the next three years—a spring offensive on the Western Front as both sides tried to break through by hurling increasing masses of troops and shells against the trench lines. The battles of World War I followed a stereotyped pattern. The assault would begin with a massive artillery bombardment along a narrow front. In 1915, this would last a day or two; by 1916, this would last a week. By 1917, the French would fire six million shells along a twenty-mile front. This vast use of firepower was necessary because the trench lines were doubled and tripled in depth, the machine gun nests were concrete-lined, and command posts were safe against all but a direct hit.[65]

The observation balloons would first spot the targets, then direct fire against them, and finally assess the damage. A primary target was enemy artillery batteries. These attempted to disrupt the barrage by counter battery fire (i.e., shelling the enemy artillery to prevent them from firing). The balloon observer would plot the flashes, then call down artillery fire on them. Even the presence of sausage balloons acted as a deterrent—the balloon could remain aloft nearly constantly; if the artillery units wanted to avoid detection, they would have to remain silent. The only time they could fire was when the balloon was down to change observers or during bad weather. Another target was to blast gaps in the barbed wire tangles, often 100 feet wide, in front of the trenches.

Once the "softening up" was completed, the troops would go "over the top" and move across "no-man's-land" toward the enemy trenches. During the assault, the sausage balloons would observe the progress of the attack (troops carried fabric panels, flares and mirrors), adjust the covering barrage as the line moved forward, and note the location of enemy troops, strong points, and artillery units. They would warn of enemy counterattacks and direct artillery against them.[66]

Aircraft (or, as they were then called, aeroplanes) were also being used for reconnaissance. The relative advantages of balloons and aircraft were summerized in a British report in May 1915:

> The balloon appears to have been the better for the purpose of reporting the general situation and the general artillery activity. Both by day and night the observer was able to keep the Artillery Group Commander informed as to the situation, whence hostile shelling was coming, what places were being most heavily shelled, the centres of greatest activity, the presence of gas, and the rough direction of its movement. As regards ranging, the aeroplanes were the more successful, and conducted shoots under weather conditions which ren-

dered observation for the balloon impossible. Aeroplanes located many more flashes than the balloon during daylight, but none at night. The balloon was able to report the direction of flashes at night, and in some cases to identify the battery owing to the observer's intimate knowledge of the ground. The advantage of the telephonic communication of the balloon over the wireless of the aeroplane was very apparent.[67]

By the fall of 1917, experiments were being conducted by the British in which balloons and aircraft worked together, combining their relative advantages. The balloon observers did the initial ranging on the target. During intense artillery bombardments, several different batteries might be firing at a single target. Because the balloon observer was in telephone communication with the chart room, he would know the moment a particular battery's shell would hit. He could then pick it out among the various shell bursts. (An aircraft did not have such instant two-way communications and so had difficulties.) Once the shells were landing close to the target, an aircraft would take over and make the final corrections. As it was directly over the target, the aircraft had a better view. Once the shells were hitting the target, the balloon observer would take over again until the target was destroyed. The advantage of this system was that it minimized usage of aircraft and pilots.[68]

Thus, both the Allies and German commanders had at their disposal well-functioning aerial reconnaissance networks the likes of which Lowe could not have dreamed of during the Civil War. Yet despite this information, the Western Front was soon locked in a bloody stalemate. The preassault bombardment, in which balloons had a key role, also showed the enemy where the attack would come. Reinforcements could be moved in to back up the defenders. When the assault forces climbed out of their trenches and moved across no-man's-land, it was in the face of withering machine gun fire. The casualties were appalling: during the battle of Verdun, which began in February 1916, 700,000 French and German soldiers died. This is the equivalent of killing the young males of a medium-sized town each morning and afternoon for ten months.[69] The result was a futile see-saw across the same shell-torn ground. Advances were measured in the hundreds of yards along a front a mile or so wide. For each of those square yards, a human being died. The story was the same at the Somme in the summer of 1916, and at Passchendaele in July–November 1917.

War in the Air

During the Civil War, Lowe and his balloonists were fired on many times, yet escaped unharmed. The observers of World War I had no such immunity from the carnage down below. The balloons and observation planes were so valuable it was critical they be destroyed. One way was to fire artillery shells in hopes of either hitting a balloon or destroying the winch and cutting it adrift. Another was to send aircraft to shoot it down.

Soon after the war began, pilots and observers began carrying rifles and pistols aloft to take pot shots at enemy aircraft. Sausage balloons fixed on their tether lines and filled with flammable hydrogen made tempting targets. One early attempt saw two French pilots take off armed with a musket and six rounds of incendiary ammunition. Their plane spiraled down on a German balloon floating at 3,000 feet. The "gunner," Lt. Jean Moinier, blasted away but the smooth-bore gun was too inaccurate and no hits were scored. The aircraft did not pull out until it was 300 feet off the ground. The Germans fired away with cannons, machine guns, rifles, and pistols. Their plane was filled with holes but they made it back.[70]

The first balloon kill was made by a French pilot named Captain Happe. His aircraft was a Maurice Farman pusher. It was so overloaded with bombs it could not climb above 3,000 feet or make more than a slow turn, yet he flew three missions a day. On January 10, 1915, acting without orders, he decided to attack a German balloon near Nieder-Marschwiller. He bombed the balloon, destroying it, but his own plane was so badly damaged by the blast it barely made it back.[71]

Such makeshift efforts soon gave way to fighters—aircraft armed with machine guns and specifically designed to destroy other aircraft. Some of these fighters also carried the first air-to-air rockets. They were developed by a French pilot named Lt. Y. P. G. Le Prieur. The rockets were "Fourth of July" skyrockets stabilized with a long stick. They carried an incendiary warhead with a sensitive impact fuse which exploded on contact with the balloon's fabric. The rockets were mounted on the outer interplane struts and were fired electrically either in pairs or a full salvo.

The first use was made on May 22, 1916, during the battle of Verdun. Several French aircraft attacked German sausage balloons to clear the way for a counterattack on Fort Donaumont. Five German balloons went down in flames.[72]

Although several kills against both balloons and aircraft were scored, the rockets proved unreliable, often veering off course. Improved incendiary ammunition soon replaced the rockets.

Although many fighter pilots attacked balloons, some specialized in their destruction. A. W. Beauchamp-Proctor, a British pilot, destroyed sixteen balloons out of his final total of fifty-four. A German pilot,

Heinrich Gontermann, shot down eighteen sausage balloons along with twenty-one aircraft. Ironically, both died in accidents: Beauchamp-Proctor in 1921 while practicing for an RAF aerial pageant, Gontermann in October 1917 when his Fokker Dr.1 triplane broke up in flight.[73,74] Among French pilots, Leon Bourjade and Michel Coiffard were leading "balloon busters." Coiffard destroyed twenty-eight balloons and six aircraft before his death in October 1918.[75] By this time, the most famous balloon buster had made his brief but violent passage through the skies of France—Lt. Frank Luke.

At first glance, a sausage balloon would seem the easiest of targets. Indeed, one French pilot, Robert Waddington, destroyed a balloon with only *six* rounds. Reality was different. Artillery units had machine gun squads as protection against infantry attack. When planes began to attack balloons, they became antiaircraft units. Soon sausage balloons were heavily defended "flak traps." Any attacking aircraft had to run a gauntlet of ground fire and defending fighters. The standard procedure was to take off at dawn, climb in the direction of the sun, then turn and dive on the balloons with the sun at the pilot's back. The fast dive and use of the sun as cover hopefully gave the element of surprise and threw off the gunner's aim. After making the firing pass on the balloon, the plane would pull out at low altitude and head for home. Frequently, the plane would be riddled with holes. Often it would be shot down.[76]

For the balloon observer, there was nothing more frightening than the call: "hostile airplane overhead." Within a matter of seconds after the balloon caught fire, it was transformed into a flaming comet, plunging toward the ground. The radiated heat from the burning gas bag was so intense, the observer's clothing caught on fire. Yet almost alone among World War I aviators, the balloon observers had an alternative to death by fire or jumping. Very soon the baskets were fitted with parachutes. The top of the open parachute was attached by a cord to the gondola. The shroud lines were attached to a harness the observer put on before leaving the ground. When danger threatened, the observer would simply jump over the side, his weight would break the cord, and he would float to earth. Improvements were soon being made. Because it was uncomfortable to wear the chute constantly, some observers attached the shroud lines to a ring. This ring could then be attached to a hook on the observer's harness. Although more comfortable, this carried the risk that the observer, panic-stricken by the sight of his balloon erupting in flames, would hurl himself over the side without first hooking the ring onto the harness. Many German observers owed their lives to a woman stunt jumper, Kaethe Paulus, who helped develop improved parachute designs. The British and French added a further refinement. Instead of allowing the parachute to hang free, it was packaged in a cone-shaped container attached to the outside of the basket. (The back-pack parachute manually deployed by a rip-cord was invented by Leslie L. Irvin in 1919.)

Balloon observers were quick to use the new parachute. Some jumped at the sound of an engine or machine gun in the distance or upon sighting an aircraft. If the balloon caught fire, the burning debris could easily set the observer's parachute on fire, sending him plunging to the ground. It was best not to hesitate.

Although the parachute was standard equipment for balloon observing, very few aircraft pilots (mostly German) would carry them.[77]

America Enters the War

From the middle of 1917 through the first few months of 1918, there were several turning points in the war. In March 1917, internal revolt forced the Russian czar to abdicate. During May and June, large segments of the French Army mutinied, refusing to go on the offensive. That same summer, units of the German Navy also mutinied over food and living conditions. In November, Lenin and the Bolsheviks overthrew the Russian government. Now facing civil war, the Communists signed a separate peace with Germany in March 1918. The Treaty of Brest-Litovsk gave the Germans eastern Poland, the Ukraine, Finland, and the Baltic states. More importantly, it allowed the Germans to shift the bulk of their forces in the east to the Western Front. In March 1918, German Gen. Erich Ludendorff launched an offensive aimed at driving a wedge between the French and British armies. By July 1918, German troops had pushed the Allies back some forty miles (the first significant movement of the lines since September 1914) and were only thirty-five miles from Paris.

The German advance came too late, for on April 6, 1917, the United States had declared war on Germany. By August 1918, some two million U.S. troops were in Europe. By this time, the German offensive had spent itself. Their reserves gone, the Germans were forced back toward the border.[78]

With the entry of the U.S. into the war, development began on a balloon bomber. Working on the project was Dr. Robert Millikin. During the 1930s, he would do basic research on cosmic rays, a field in which balloons would play a critical role. The balloon bomber was intended to attack German cities. As with several other far-sighted projects to build pilotless flying bombs, it did not go into action. Millikin's balloon bomber sank into obscurity. The idea's time had not yet come.

In addition to ground forces, air units were also sent. One of these was the 27th Aero Squadron; among its pilots was the premier American balloon buster—Lt. Frank Luke. Luke did not fit the popular image of a World War I pilot. He was moody and rarely mixed with the other pilots, preferring to be alone. Moreover, he had a record of insubordination and hostility to authority. The other pilots despised him. This became worse on August 16, when he claimed his first "kill"—it was not confirmed and his squadron mates who doubted the story considered him a liar.

Virtually the only pilot who could stand him was his wingman, Joseph Wehner. Both were quiet, withdrawn, and were of German descent. The two outsiders became a balloon-killing team. Luke would dive on the balloon while Wehner provided "top cover" to fend off any German aircraft.

Luke's first confirmed kill was made on September 12 when he destroyed a German balloon near Marrieulles. To ensure his word was not questioned, he landed at an American balloon company that had seen the action and had them sign as witnesses. To underline the danger of attacking balloons, his Spad was so full of holes it had to be scrapped—the first of five. For the next seventeen days, Luke made an average of one kill per day.

On September 14, Luke and Wehner were again on the prowl. Luke destroyed two balloons while Wehner shot down a German Fokker. A witness to the fight, Lt. Leo Dawson, said later: "If anybody still thinks Luke is yellow, he's crazy. He's not yellow; he's stark, raving mad. He went by me on that attack like a wild man. I thought he was diving right into the balloon. Then after it was blazing, I saw him take another swoop down on it!" Luke and Wehner were not yet satisfied; they told the ground crews to fuel their Spads for another flight. Capt. Alfred Grant, commanding officer of the 27th Squadron, ordered Luke to stay on the ground. Wehner went out alone to attack a German balloon near Waroq. A few minutes before he arrived, French pilot René Fonck destroyed it. Undaunted, Wehner attacked eight German planes that were pursuing an observation plane, downing two of them.

This was only the start; over a period of five days, Luke shot down eight balloons. One evening, Luke put on a show for Capt. Eddie Rickenbacker, Gen. Billy Mitchell, and 1st Pursuit commander Harold Hartney. Luke pointed out two German balloons, then took off, destroyed them within four minutes, as he had predicted, then returned to the airfield.

The violent pace took its toll. On September 18, Luke and Wehner each shot down two balloons. As Wehner pulled up, he saw a formation of German planes about to attack Luke. Wehner fired a flare as warning but Luke did not see it. In desperation, Wehner attacked the Germans, saving Luke at the cost of his own life. After Wehner went down, Luke turned on the German planes, destroying two of them. Almost out of gas, he broke off. On his way home he saw three French Spads attack a German observation plane at long range. Luke sped past the French planes, closed on the observation plane and shot it down. He had made five kills in less than ten minutes and was America's leading "ace."

The loss of his friend devastated Luke and he became increasingly erratic. Between missions, he brooded and twice went AWOL to spend the night with friends at a French squadron nearby.

At this same time, the Allies were preparing to launch their final offensive in the Meuse River–Argonne Forest area. Because of poor weather, the Germans had to rely on balloons for observations. They were considered a threat and their destruction was planned as part of the offensive's opening. Before dawn on September 26, the Allied barrage lit up the day. As the attack began, a selected group of pilots went after the German balloons, destroying six of them in less than an hour. A total of twenty-one were destroyed during the first five days.

Luke made his last combat report on September 28:

> I flew north to Verdun, crossed the lines at about 500 meters and found a balloon in its nest in the region of Bethenville. I dove on it firing both guns. After I pulled away it burst into flames. As I could not find any other I returned to the airdrome. One confirmation requested.

The next day, Luke was indefinitely grounded by his command officer. Luke defied the order and took a Spad. He landed at a forward airfield to refuel, then took off with an arrest order close behind. At sunset, he dropped a note to the U.S. balloon headquarters at Souilly, telling them to watch three German balloons. He then attacked and destroyed the balloons at Dun-Sur-Meuse, Briere Farm, and Milly. He had apparently been wounded during the attacks on the second and third balloons. Despite this, he strafed a group of German soldiers in the village of Murvaux, killing six of them. His plane was too badly damaged and he landed nearby. Luke was surrounded but refused to surrender, pulling his .45-caliber revolver and firing until a German rifle bullet killed him. In just over two weeks, he had destroyed fourteen balloons and four airplanes. He had lived as a warrior and died the same way.[79,80]

Ironically, on September 29, the same day Frank Luke died, General Ludendorff told a stunned German government the only way to prevent the Allies from reaching the border was to make an immediate peace.[81]

The U.S. Balloon Service in World War I

Like ground and air units, the U.S. Balloon Service was in action by the late summer of 1918. The plans were extremely ambitious. Three stateside balloon schools were to produce a total force of 14,467 officers and men. These would provide sixty-nine balloon companies. A total of 500 balloons would be produced. (Actual numbers proved far lower.) Once in France, they underwent further training under actual wartime conditions. A total of 157 officers graduated by the end of the war. Additionally, 174 machine gunners, 68 winch operators, 63 chartroom clerks, 58 telephone experts and 55 radio operators graduated.

Once in action, the observers quickly learned the dangers of combat ballooning. During a fifteen-day period during the Meuse-Argonne offensive, American observers made thirty parachute jumps and lost twenty-one balloons (fifteen to fighters, six to ground fire). The first American balloonist to die in action was Lt. C. J. Ross in October 1918. He was directing an artillery barrage on a cloudy day when a squadron of German fighters appeared out of the clouds and set the balloon on fire. Lieutenant Ross's companion in the basket had difficulty getting out and Ross delayed his jump until he was clear. Ross's parachute was ignited by burning debris and he fell to his death.

Most parachute jumps ended in happier ways. Indeed, balloon observers developed a kind of "reverse ace" status—rather than how many planes they had shot down, it was based on how many times *they* had been shot down. Lt. George D. Armstrong was shot down three times, the second and third times on October 6, 1918, within a period of thirteen minutes. Between September 17 and October 6, Lt. James A. McDevitt jumped four times (the second on October 5 and the third and fourth times on October 6).

The unofficial American balloon ace was Lt. Glenn Phelps. His first jump came on July 15 when he and another observer, Lt. R. K. Patterson, were directing artillery fire. As they worked, shells began bursting nearby; as they came closer, the two bailed out. Once on the ground, they learned this was friendly fire, trying to chase off three enemy planes. A half hour later, the two were back in the air.

Things remained quiet for the next several hours until Phelps and Patterson noticed five planes approaching them from the Allied side of the line. They thought they were friendly, an error which became clear when incendiary bullets started hitting the balloon and basket. For a second time, Phelps and Patterson took to their chutes. As Phelps descended, the empty basket fell past him, trailing burning debris.

Phelps's next jump came three weeks later when his balloon was attacked and set on fire by eleven enemy fighters. Jump number four came in late October when a single German plane fired on his balloon. This time the balloon did not catch fire. Phelps was preparing to go up in it again when he found it had been hit more than 100 times.

Phelps' fifth jump was made on November 10, 1918. This time it was two American planes that set his balloon aflame, their pilots believing it was German. Once more he landed safely.

It was during the final weeks of the war that the U.S. Balloon Service reached its greatest strength. During the week of October 30, seventeen balloon companies at the front flew a total of fifty-four hours.[82,83]

Even as the Allied armies advanced, Imperial Germany was disintegrating from the inside. On November 4, the sailors at the German base at Kiel mutinied. This quickly spread to the cities. On November 9, Kaiser Wilhelm II abdicated and went into exile in Holland. At 5:20 A.M. on November 11, 1918, a delegation from the German government signed the Armistice. Fighting was to end at 11:00 A.M. And so, at the eleventh hour of the eleventh day of the eleventh month, a silence fell across a battered landscape. As a British army communique noted: "All along the Front, the Balloons are down."

So then, what of the first 130 years of balloon reconnaissance?

The first century of that history was one of false starts. The Compagnie d'Aérostiers contributed to French victories, yet high-level opposition ended the experiment. The military balloon activities during the first half of the nineteenth century were scattered and represented dead ends. The story of the Compagnie d'Aérostiers was repeated during the Civil War. In this case, the causes were more complex: infighting between the aeronauts, the turnover of Union commanders, and official hostility. The net result was each generation of combat aeronauts had to start from scratch. They could draw nothing from their predecessors except inspiration—certainly nothing in the way of practical experience.

It was not until the end of the nineteenth century that reconnaissance balloons became part of the world's military forces. Yet, even then, these early air forces suffered from lack of money and equipment. In a way, this could be expected. For all of history, war had been two-dimensional. The balloons meant the addition of a third dimension. Given the normal struggle for men and resources, the visionary claims of the balloonist would easily fall on deaf ears.

It was not until World War I that balloon reconnaissance came into its own. Above the blood-stained trenches, balloons became part of a well-functioning intelligence-gathering network. Yet it was too late. Airplanes had been developed. These made the skies too dangerous for tethered balloons to long survive.

2

Outward and FUGO

Disillusionment soon followed the armistice. A generation of European youth had been consumed in the pointless slaughter of the Western Front. The political, social, and economic stability of Europe had been damaged. Inflation and depression fed uncertainty and discontent. In the streets, extremists of the Left and the Right battled for power. Fascists took over in Italy, Germany, and Spain. In Russia, tens of millions, caught up in Stalin's purges, went to the camps and their deaths. Everywhere, the old values of freedom, democracy, and the individual seemed in retreat.

This same instability also affected Imperial Japan. The Great Depression hit in the mid-1920s, leaving millions of industrial workers unemployed, and reducing farmers to eating roots and bark. In the battle for power, the right wing Ultra Nationalists emerged as the dominant political group. The Ultra Nationalists, many of whom were army officers, saw Japan's salvation in expansion overseas and the eradication of Western ideas at home.

By the 1930s, events were moving toward war. On September 18, 1931, the Japanese Army invaded the Chinese province of Manchuria and set up a puppet state. At home, Ultra Nationalists assassinated Japanese politicians suspected of liberal views, while the "Thought Police" cracked down on any opposition. In July 1937, the Japanese again attacked China. They took the cities of Peiping, Shanghai, Nanking, Hankow, and Canton in a brutal campaign that saw indiscriminate murder of Chinese civilians.

In Europe, Nazi Germany was on the march—occupying the Rhineland, forcing a union with Austria, and taking Czechoslovakia. Finally, on September 1, 1939, Germany invaded Poland, beginning World War II.

As war raged in Europe, Japan's aggression brought it increasingly into conflict with the United States. In 1939, the U.S. embargoed scrap iron; then, following the Japanese move into French Indochina in July 1941, the U.S., Great Britain, and the Netherlands cut off the oil needed to fuel Japan's war machine and demanded they withdraw from the conquered areas.[1,2]

The only obstacle to Japan's domination of the Pacific was U.S. naval power. Japan's military leaders made the ultimately suicidal decision to eliminate that obstacle. The December 7, 1941, attack on Pearl Harbor was a singular victory. In less than two hours, the U.S. Pacific Fleet was destroyed.

Amid this colossal struggle, there would appear two programs to develop bomb-carrying balloons. Both, ironically, had similar targets—forests—and shared an affinity for power lines. One was a short-range system that had little impact. The other was the first intercontinental weapon, and would have consequences lasting long after the war that spawned it.

Outward

The British balloon bomber program, called Operation Outward, had its start in 1937. Although outmoded for reconnaissance, barrage balloons had an important role in air defense. A bomber, trying to attack a target protected by them, risked having a wing cut off by the steel cable which anchored the balloon to the ground. There was concern, however, about the effect a runaway balloon's steel cable would have if it hit a power line in the National Grid. Accordingly, the Air Ministry carried out experiments in 1937. It was found that power would be cut for about six hours plus another two hours for every additional damaged cable in the area. The emphasis at this time was on assessing the danger from "friendly" balloons, rather than on using the technique against an enemy.

The idea of balloon attacks on Germany appeared during the first winter of the war. The balloons would be launched from France and drift east over Germany, carrying incendiaries or high-explosive bombs. Although, like all free-flying balloons, they were at the mercy of the wind, a unique refinement was added. Each balloon carried a small transmitter and its position could be plotted using direction-finding equipment. Once the plot showed it over a suitable target area, a radio signal would be transmitted and the balloon would drop its bomb. This system allowed some degree of control, rather than just scattering the bombs at random.[3]

On May 14, 1940, before launches could begin, the German Army invaded France. The fast-moving armor destroyed the French Army and drove the British off the continent. The French surrendered on June 22. This was followed, on July 10, by the first German air raid on England—the Battle of Britain had started. As the summer dragged on, the attacks increased, as the Germans tried to destroy the RAF in preparation for the invasion.[4] In early September, the attacks shifted to London. For fifty-seven nights, from September 7 to November 2, the Luftwaffe bombed and burned the city.[5]

It was against this background that an incident occurred which highlighted the possibilities of balloon attacks. On the night of 17–18 September 1940, a gale broke free a number of barrage balloons and swept them across northern Europe. The aerial of the Swedish international radio station was knocked down. Power lines were damaged and the electrical railroad was interrupted. Similar damage was done in occupied Denmark. About five balloons reached Finland. A report on the confusion and havoc they had caused was given to the War Cabinet. Churchill made a note on his copy: "We may make a virtue of our misfortune WSC 23.9.40."

In response, the Chiefs of Staff Committee asked the Air Ministry for an assessment. Their report was negative, reflecting a fear the Germans would respond in kind.[6] It said that the German grid system was primitive and thus not a good target. The British network was more vulnerable. It was also noted the Germans controlled a much longer coastline and so could launch balloon attacks under more varied wind patterns than could the British. It would also involve large quantities of materials during a time of shortages. The Chiefs of Staff, therefore, rejected the idea.

It might have ended there, except the Board of Admiralty was interested in the idea. The project was assigned to the Director of Boom Defences (who was responsible for antitorpedo and submarine nets used for harbor defense). This was not as completely illogical as it sounded. During the Battle of Britain, the Boom Defence Department had proposed free-flying balloons with trailing wires as a defense against bombers.

The Admiralty's assessment was more upbeat. The balloons had the advantage of silence. They were also easy to produce and posed a major threat to the Germans. Also, with no crew aboard, British casualties were avoided.

The balloons would carry incendiaries—6-lb socks filled with flammable material. These would burn from both ends for about fifteen minutes. Because the "bomb" was flexible, it could wrap around a branch. Two or three socks would be carried by each balloon. Large areas of Germany were covered with forest and heathland. The trees were primarily pines which would burn easily most of the year. This would tie down large numbers of men in fire watching. (In England, the forests were small and the trees lost their leaves in the fall, both of which lessened the fire risk.)

The upper-air winds were also favorable. Above 16,000 feet, winds blew in the correct direction 55 percent of the time. Conditions were favorable for German launches only 38 percent of the time.

Finally, to avoid any excessive demands on the Air Ministry's supply of hydrogen, coal gas would be used to inflate the balloons. Launch sites would be at the Boom Depots at Harwich and Dover.

The Air Ministry rejected the proposal (although the Minister of Aircraft Production appears to have been the real opponent of the project). The specific objections were: the balloons were not likely to be effective, too many balloons, people and materials would be required, hydrogen was in short supply (the proposed use of coal gas was ignored), the balloons posed a danger to British aircraft, and the risk of German counterattacks was too great.

It was now the Admiralty's turn in this paper battle. Production of 5,000 balloons per week would take only 6 men and 190 women. Also, there was more hydrogen being produced than could be used—there would be no shortages. In answer to the final objection, the Admiralty went to the Central Electricity Board for an assessment of the relative vulnerabilities of the two countries. A report prepared by C. W. Marshall found that frequent short circuits could damage a power network and that immediate action would have to be taken. It would take the Germans five seconds to clear such faults. In this time, serious damage to a power station could occur. The CEB could do the same in one second with no damage to British power stations.

In September 1941, the Chiefs of Staff were asked by the Admiralty to authorize production of 5,000 balloons with attacks to begin on November 15, 1941. The Air Ministry asked for more tests, which were performed in January 1942, around Lynton in North Devon. These were successful and preparations began in earnest.

The program was given the code name "Outward" and the first launch site was set up at Harwich at Landguard Fort on the point at Felixstowe. The launches were scheduled to begin on March 11, 1942.

Attacks Begin

The first Outward balloons were launched from Harwich on March 20, 1942. The balloons were inflated in the open and then released when the wind direction was right. The first confirmation that the balloons were reaching their targets came on March 23, when the BBC monitored a Hungarian broadcast from Budapest warning that balloons carrying chemicals were landing and should not be touched and the police or military should be notified. The Swiss, unfortunately, made the same announcement.

On April 15, the *Daily Express* carried a garbled account claiming a new type of incendiary bomb had been dropped over the Rhineland and started a big fire at Tilsit in East Prussia. Soon after, the *Daily Mail* carried a report (apparently based on Swedish newspaper accounts) that bombs filled with liquid phosphorus had been dropped by parachute and caused "grave damage" to forests near Berlin. More important confirmation came from intercepted air-to-ground messages from fighters trying to shoot down the balloons. The Admiralty estimated the wear and tear on the German fighters alone was greater than the thirty-five shillings each balloon cost.

The problems between the Admiralty and the Air Ministry continued. In June, despite the fact a liaison arrangement with the RAF had already been established, the Air Ministry raised concerns that the balloons might damage British aircraft. An arrangement was made so the Air Ministry could ask the Admiralty to halt launches when Bomber Command raids were scheduled.

In July, operations expanded with the opening of a second launch site at Oldstairs near Dover. It operated from a subdepot of Boom Defence at Walmer and was code named "Salvage."

The same month saw Outward's greatest success. On July 12, 1942, a balloon hit a 110,000-volt power line near Leipzig. The overload switch at the Bohlen power station was slow to operate and the generators were thrown out of step. One burst into flames, destroying the station. The damage was estimated to be £1 million.

For the next two and a half years, the balloons continued to be launched, interrupted by frequent requests from the Air Ministry to suspend operations. (All launches had to be made during daylight, and two hours notice was required before launches could begin.) Outward was greatly assisted by the cooperation of the Chief of Balloon Command, Sir Leslie "Sausage" Gossage. He kept the navy supplied with hydrogen from Balloon Command. Without his help, Outward would have faded away. Another person who played a large role in its success was the Director of Naval Meteorological Services, Capt. L. G. Garbett. Only once did the balloons drift back over England. However, as Outward was a free balloon, some landed in neutral Sweden and Switzerland. On January 19–20, 1944, lighting on the Swedish railroad in the Lund/Halmstad/Falkenberg area was knocked out by the balloons and two trains collided at Laholm.

The approach of the D-day invasion spelled the end of Outward. In April, 1944, the Air Ministry asked for a complete halt of operations lest the balloons interfere with the large numbers of aircraft attacking targets in occupied France. Ultimately, a compromise was reached. A "trickle system" was used with one balloon released every ten minutes. Finally, on September 4, 1944, the last Outward balloon was launched. By this time, the British 21st Army Group was in Belgium and in the "line of fire."

Outward Assessed

A total of 99,142 Outward balloons were launched: 53,543 carried incendiaries, the other 45,599 were fitted with trailing wires. This was accomplished with only 6 Naval and Royal Marine officers, 7 WRNS officers, 80 Royal Marines, and 140 Wrens. The total cost was £220,000.

In military terms, Outward was only a small part of the air offensive against Germany. Despite the huge number of balloons, when compared to the nightly mass bombing raids of Bomber Command, it is clear Outward was only a sideshow. The program did pay for itself, economically. The damage done to the Bohlen power station was four times greater than the entire cost of the program. Also, the harassment value of the balloons should not be overlooked.[7] Among the negative aspects were the internal fighting between the Admiralty and Air Ministry, as well as the damage to relations with Sweden and Switzerland caused by wayward balloons.

In terms of technology, Outward was simply a more advanced version of the balloons used to attack Venice in 1848–49. The other balloon bomber program would be very different.

Early Japanese Balloon Weapons

Japanese work on balloon weapons dates to 1927. In the early 1930s, after the Manchurian invasion, they examined a number of ideas for harassing the Russians across the Amur River which formed the Sino-Soviet border. One project, called SEGO, was a propaganda balloon. A 13-foot envelope could travel 62 miles and drop leaflets and banners. The Japanese also studied SEGO's ability to carry a bomb as large as 66 lb, which would be dropped by a time fuse. Range and accuracy were to be similar to the German "Big Bertha" used to shell Paris in World War I.

Balloons were also examined as a means of transporting airborne troops. Practice ascents and descents were made. The plan which finally emerged was to attach each soldier to a 19.7- to 23-foot balloon. He also held on to another 16.4-foot balloon. When the soldier reached the drop zone, he would release the larger balloon and drift down on the smaller one.

Work on balloon weapons tapered off in the late 1930s.[8,9] However, interest resumed in the summer of 1942 during the Battle of Guadalcanal. A conference was held, seeking ways to interfere with American aircraft using Henderson Field. It was mentioned the army's Noborito Lab was working on the old SEGO project. Tech. Capt. Teruhiko Takeda explained the 13-foot balloons would trail long lengths of piano wire attached to a grenade. Large numbers of these balloons would be launched as U.S. fighters took off. The fighters would hit the wires, the grenades would explode and damage or destroy the aircraft. Captain Takeda was placed in charge of a fifteen-man development team. By the time the balloons were ready, however, the situation on Guadalcanal had deteriorated and the mission was canceled.

By the end of 1942, with the Doolittle raid on Tokyo and the Japanese defeats at Midway and Guadalcanal, the tide of war was shifting. In response, the Japanese began looking for ways to carry the war to the U.S.

mainland. This was a problem, however. During the early months of the war, Japanese submarines had shelled shore targets. The submarine *I-25* had also twice launched air strikes on Oregon forest, using a collapsible float plane carried in a watertight hangar. Japanese submarines were now needed to resupply the increasing number of cut-off island garrisons. There were none to spare to send across the Pacific for harassment. The defeat at Midway both crippled Japanese carrier power and removed any possibility they could take Hawaii, removing any threat to the West Coast from that quarter. Finally, the Japanese aviation industry was unable to build large, long-range aircraft. Thus, the attack would have to be made by balloon. This offered the possibility of a massive attack, able to do real damage, rather than pinpricks. It would panic the American people and force the U.S. to divert men and effort to home defense.

The program was approved in September 1942. Reflecting the mutual hatred between the army and the navy, each conducted separate balloon research programs.[10]

The navy project, based at the Sagami Naval Arsenal, was a study of upper-air currents. Lt. Cmdr. Kiyoshi Tanaka, a scientist and naval ordnance engineer, was project director. The Central Meteorological Department made ground-based measurements. The primary emphasis was on balloons carrying radio transmitters. Precise tone signals indicated weather data and systems function. By 1943, a number of balloon projects were underway. In March, a 19.6-foot balloon with a design range of 1,863 miles was developed. It subsequently flew 621 miles between the west and east coasts of Japan. The balloon could stay aloft for over thirty hours at an altitude of 26,247 feet. The navy, encouraged by its success, began adapting the balloon for submarine launching. The submarine would surface at night about 620 miles from the U.S. coast. The balloon would be inflated on deck and an automatic altitude control system and an 11-lb bomb were attached. Flight time would be about ten hours. The bomb would be released by a timer. The probability of success was considered quite good, providing the flight took place only in daylight *or* only at night. Gas expansion and contraction from temperature changes would cause problems over longer flight times. Two hundred of the balloons were manufactured. Commander Tanaka went to Tokyo to ask for the use of the submarines *I-351* and *I-352* to carry the balloons, hydrogen-generating equipment, and launch crews on operational missions. The demands on the Japanese submarine fleet remained too great and the project had to be abandoned.[11,12]

In early 1944, the Japanese Navy began flying a more advanced 29.5-foot diameter balloon. Called the "B-type," it used a rubberized silk envelope and was dark gray in color. On February 28, a B-type balloon covered 5,000 miles in forty hours. The B-type balloon's payload was one or two transmitters. Radio signals from the balloons were received by direction-finding stations in Japan. Triangulation indicated the balloon's position. Plotting the balloon's movement indicated the speed and location of wind currents. The radios also transmitted data on temperature, air pressure, and altitude. The balloon's internal gas pressure and ballast drops were also reported. The B-type maintained its altitude automatically. When it descended below a preset altitude, an aneroid switch closed, firing a small black powder charge, releasing a sandbag. Usually, eight sandbags were carried, each weighing 6.6 lb.

The results from the early flights were encouraging and in May, 1944, a contract was placed with the Fujikura Rubber Company. At the same time, the navy was ordered to combine its efforts with that of the army. Commander Tanaka was placed under the direction of Maj. Gen. Sueki Kusaba. This was not the end of the navy program, however. A small group of navy scientists with the knowledge and support of high navy officers planned a "private" attack on the U.S. The work took place at a technical lab above the village of Nishiki. Its cover was as a subdepot of Sagami Naval Arsenal. This was to keep the secret from the army, not the U.S.

The balloons were 6.6–9.8 feet in diameter and made of rice paper coated with polyvinyl and alcohol. A small aluminum gas relief valve was fitted. Each balloon was armed with 100 tube bombs only 0.4 by 4 inches long. Each tube was divided into three compartments filled with acid, zinc, and alcohol. The balloons would be launched at dawn from a submarine 400 miles off the coast. They would rise to about 24,000 feet and drift east. Maximum flight time was only eighteen hours, as they carried no ballast. Gradually, the balloons would descend and when they reached 9,000 feet, the bombs would be dropped. When each tube hit the ground, its glass cap would break and the chemicals would mix and ignite.

In May 1944, the submarine *I-54* was ordered to Etajima Shima for modifications. Hydrogen accumulators were fitted in the engine room, a pipe network was added to the aft deck for filling the balloons, and the hangar was converted into an arsenal for the bombs. After several days of work, crews boarded the submarine for practice launches. The *I*-55 was also modified. The attack was to take place during the summer of 1944. In June, however, U.S. Marines attacked Saipan and the two submarines were needed for other assignments. The equipment was removed and the navy's plans were finally ended.[13]

FUGO

The army balloon program was designated "FUGO." This was not a code name. Rather, "FU" was the thirty-second character of the Hiragana Syllabary. "GO" represents numbers in a series—thus, "Project 32." "Fu" is also the first character of the Japanese word for balloon, *fusen.*

The army's research concentrated on materials, control devices, weapons, and launching methods. Two major problems were the cold temperatures and the low atmospheric pressures at high altitudes. Japanese army equipment was designed to operate at temperatures as low as −22°F. At 33,000 feet, however, the nighttime temperatures dropped to −58°F. This, combined with atmospheric pressures one quarter that of sea level, adversely affected a wide range of materials. Rubber and springs lost their elasticity, batteries' electrical output was greatly reduced and the reliability of ballast-dropping charges decreased under these conditions. Considerable development work was done on high-altitude explosives, low-temperature batteries, and use of solar heating and insulation for temperature control.

During the winter of 1943–44, the army flew some 200 of the 6-meter paper balloons originally developed for the navy's first planned attack on the U.S. Instead of bombs, they carried radio transmitters. The test flights indicated the need for a pressure relief valve. During the day, the sun heated the hydrogen, causing it to expand. This increased the balloon's internal pressure to the bursting point.

The flights, along with ground observations from Japan and reports from ships and islands, provided data on wind-flow patterns across the whole of the Pacific Ocean. This was critical to the success of the army project. Whereas the navy projects envisioned launches from submarines a relatively short distance off the U.S. coast, the army's plan was more ambitious. The balloons would be launched from the east coast of Japan, then cross the Pacific before releasing their bombs over the U.S. It was necessary to know the best altitude for the balloons, the time of strongest winds, how long a flight would take to reach the U.S., and what the dispersion of the balloons would be. The key was the jet stream—a river of air, flowing west to east, high above the northern Pacific, at speeds of 120 to 185 mph. It is strongest in the winter months, between November and March. During the summer, it reverses direction. (For several weeks in the spring and fall, the stratospheric winds nearly stop.)[14] U.S. meteorologists had only a limited knowledge of the jet stream, believing high-altitude winds reached only 30–60 mph.[15]

By the spring of 1944, the data indicated the balloons could reach the U.S. riding the jet stream. Work was consolidated under army control. A meeting on the FUGO was held in May at the Weapon Administration Bureau in Tokyo to review the remaining problems. Maj. Gen. Kusaba briefly described its current status, then spent four hours discussing the project with representatives of several technical institutes. The review was encouraging, and the army's Noborito Research Institute received a two million yen budget (about $460,000 at prewar exchange rates).

This marked the start of an intensive research and development effort to get FUGO ready for the coming winter campaign. As a first step, 10,000 paper A-type balloons were ordered. Tests of the components' abilities to withstand cold were made between May and August and used nearly all the dry ice in Tokyo.

Test flights were also made. Prototype FUGOs were fitted with radios that reported systems function. One of these flights was made on August 29, 1944. Launch came at 7:29 A.M. In less than an hour, the balloon reached 21,327 feet. Its climb rate slowed and it reached 26,248 feet after two hours. It stayed at this altitude until sunset, when it began a slow climb. After about three hours, it reached 32,810 feet. The balloon remained at this altitude throughout the night, and the next day an automatic ballasting system compensated for the cooling and heating of the gas. At sunset of the second day, its altitude varied slightly; then the balloon began a fast climb to 39,372 feet. Although radio reception was poor during the second night and into the third day, it appears the balloon remained between 36,091 and 39,372 feet. Forty-eight hours into the flight, contact resumed. After fifty-three hours, the balloon had dropped seventeen bags of ballast (the radio's frequency changed as each bag was dropped). Nineteen remained; over the next three hours, eight more of these bags were dropped. Soon after the third sunset, contact was lost. The balloon had flown 58 hours, 14 minutes. This was sufficient time to reach the U.S. on the winter jet stream. Enough ballast remained for another forty-eight hours.[16]

The navy's B-type balloons were also used during this period for weather studies. Phase I took place between August 17 and 31 and involved six launches (nineteen B-type balloons had been launched earlier). The six balloons transmitted between two and twenty-two hours. These flights revealed a flaw. The glued seams split when the balloons' internal pressure rose too fast when too much ballast was dropped. Half burst in this manner. The flights were halted and the balloons were returned to the Fujikura Rubber Company for regluing and addition of pressure relief valves.

Ironically, despite the failures, the navy had reached the U.S. In August, one of the balloons landed near Yerington, Nevada. A cowboy, Sam Ellison, found it caught in cottonwood trees. He and Charles Ragsdale, the ranch owner, pulled it free and tied it to a fence. Ragsdale called the military but no one expressed interest. He deflated the balloon and later cut it up to dam a small creek for a cattle pond (the fabric was waterproof).

The B-type balloon flights resumed with four flights between September 29 and October 9. Balloon #26, launched on September 29, transmitted for a record eighty-seven hours. The third phase had five flights between October 29 and November 5. Balloon #32, launched on November 2 (Japanese time), was recovered in the ocean off San Pedro, California, on November 4, 1944. It had crossed the Pacific in two days and twenty hours.[17]

The balloons' production plan had been established by the end of July and army personnel had begun instruction at each workshop. By October, all the workshops were trained and production was underway on a rigid schedule lasting five months. The last of the 10,000 balloons were to be delivered at the end of February 1945. Thousands of Japanese were working on FUGO, but they were not told what the balloons were for. Those who did hear that it was to attack the U.S. did not believe it. The mission's nature was its own security.

The FUGO's odyssey began in hundreds of Japanese homes where the paper for the balloons was handmade from tree bark. It was peeled, beaten flat and washed at least fifty times. The finished paper was delivered to the army in 1,000-sheet lots. These were sent to seven manufacturing facilities in Tokyo. About 600 sheets were needed for each balloon. The work was done by teenaged high school girls. Because the paper was easily damaged, they were told not to wear hairpins, to cut their fingernails short, to wear socks even in the summer heat, and to use gloves. This was made more burdensome because shifts in Japanese war industries were often twelve to sixteen hours long. The first step was to laminate four layers of paper together. The glue was made from powdered arum root (a kind of potato). Coloring was added to show how evenly the glue was applied. The powder was edible and, because of the severe food shortages in Japan, the girls often stole it. The laminated sheets were dried in a heater, washed, and then treated to prevent them from cracking from the high-altitude cold.

Next, the laminated sheets were inspected for flaws. The paper was laid on a floor of frosted glass that was backlit. Under the light, the paper became translucent with a bluish color from the glue. Areas with too little glue appeared lighter in color. Weak spots were marked with chalk and patches were applied. The paper was trimmed and the balloon panels (called gores) were glued together, the top hemisphere first, followed by the lower half with the relief valve. Once finished, the two halves were glued together and a scalloped band was added. The nineteen shroud lines were attached to this band.

The complete A-type balloon was 32.9 feet in diameter and had a volume of 19,000 cubic feet. Large theaters and sumo wrestling halls were used for assembly and leak tests, among them the Nichigeki music hall, the Toho theater and the Kokugi-Kan wrestling hall. All objects on the floors and walls were wrapped in paper (to protect the balloons from abrasions. It was difficult to spot such damage once the balloon was finished.).

After a balloon was completed, it was inflated with air and sealed. After twenty-four hours, it was checked for leaks. Those which passed were coated with a lacquer made from the fermented juice of green persimmons. The balloons could then be sent to the launch sites.

Three launch sites were established: Nakoso (six launch stations), Otsu (nine launch stations), and Ichinomiya (six launch stations). All were on the east coast of Honshu and were relatively close to Tokyo.[18] The short rail links allowed easier movement of the mass of supplies needed. Thirty hydrogen cylinders were needed to fill each balloon. The Otsu site had its own hydrogen-generating equipment. The hydrogen was generated by mixing caustic soda (NaOH), ferrosilicon (Si), and water. It required more than 2,000 tons of caustic soda to fill 4,000

FUGO balloons. The locations of the sites also provided security for the project. All were in sparsely populated areas and farmers and fishermen were ordered out of the area.

The FUGO was, despite its appearance, a complex device. Suspended from the shroud lines was the gondola, a 32.5-inch diameter aluminum ring to which the sandbag ballast and bombs were attached. Sitting on top of the ring was a platform that held the automatic altitude control system and the battery. The altitude was controlled by four aneroid barometers in a wooden box. Power was supplied by a 2.3-volt lead acid battery placed in a double-walled celluloid box. During the day, it was kept warm by solar heat; at night, an antifreeze liquid protected it from the cold.

This automatic control system was the key to the FUGO's successful operation. To ride the jet stream, it would have to remain between 30,000 and 38,000 feet. If it descended below this, it would "fall" out of the jet stream and not be able to reach the U.S. before the ballast was exhausted. Normally, the balloon's altitude would vary widely. During the day, the gas would be heated by the sun, causing the balloon to rise. The increased pressure would be vented out the relief valve and the gas would be lost. At night, the remaining gas would cool and the balloon would descend. The cycle would repeat—losing gas by day, descending at night.

The system operated as follows: when the balloon descended to a preset level around 30,000 feet, the aneroid switch closed, firing small explosive charges (called blow plugs). This would drop a sandbag. A two-minute time delay was built into the system to allow the balloon to climb before another sandbag would be dropped from the opposite side of the ring. If the aneroid switch was still closed, this continued until the balloon was above 30,000 feet. Typically, thirty-two sandbags were carried. Assuming an early morning launch, the last sandbag would be dropped during the afternoon of the third day when the balloon was over the U.S.[19]

The bombs would now be dropped. The load varied from two to six bombs. Normally, four 5-kg Type-B incendiary bombs and one 15-kg Type-C antipersonnel bomb were carried. (On some flights, a 12-kg Type-A incendiary was carried, rather than the antipersonnel bomb.) The 5-kg incendiaries were cylindrical and resembled long tomato juice cans. The 15-kg antipersonnel bomb's casing was made of "shrapnel rings" and had a lethal radius of 150 feet. The 12-kg incendiary bomb held three thermite "fire pots" and had a danger zone similar to the antipersonnel bomb. The 5-kg incendiaries hanging on the ring would be dropped first. The 15-kg antipersonnel bomb was suspended from the center of the ring and was dropped last.

FUGO's target was the forests of the Northwest. The goal, as with all Japanese attacks on the U.S., was to start widespread fires, generate panic, and divert troops to home defense.

To heighten the psychological impact, the FUGO would then self-destruct. When the last bomb was dropped, two fuses would start to burn. The first, a 2-minute-49-second fuse, detonated a block of picric acid, sitting on top of the altitude control box, which blew the ring apart. A second 1-hour-22-minute fuse ignited a small package of magnesium flash powder attached to the hydrogen-filled balloon. In theory, each balloon could cause multiple fires and casualties, then destroy itself, leaving only a few bits of metal, burned paper, and no explanation. (As a further security measure, only letters and numbers were used on the parts, not Japanese characters.)[20,21]

It was now November. The balloons, hardware, bombs and hydrogen were at the launch sites. High above, the winter winds blew strong. It was time to send FUGO to war.

Attacks Begin

The first FUGO was launched on November 3, 1944 at 5:00 A.M. In the predawn darkness, it climbed upward, the silence disturbed only by the rustling of paper, finally becoming lost in the early morning sky. It headed east toward America. The plan envisioned up to 15,000 balloons launched between November and March. However, the plan faced problems from the winter weather. It was difficult and dangerous to fill and launch the balloons on windy days. Low winds occurred on only three to five days a week and then for only a few hours each day, before the onshore breezes began at sunrise and sometimes in the early evening. There could also be no rain, snow or even clouds. Water would gather on the balloon, then freeze. The added weight would prevent it from reaching the jet stream. The best time to launch was just after the passing of a high-pressure front. Conditions were unfavorable if a high-pressure front was approaching or a low-pressure front had just passed. There were only fifty days in which launching was possible. It took thirty minutes to an hour to prepare each balloon. During each of the favorable days, the stations would have to launch 200 balloons.

A further problem was supply and transport of the hydrogen tanks. Only 8,000 tanks of the 20,000 needed were on hand by late December. The shortages cut back the number of launches. A total of 150 per day was planned; about 30 was the actual figure. The estimated total was 700 balloons launched in November and 1,200 in December.[22]

The U.S. was slow to realize the danger approaching on the winds. On November 14, 1944, Coast Guardsmen spotted a FUGO landing in the sea five miles west of the Hawaiian island of Kailua. A boat recovered the paper envelope, shroud lines, and gondola. The Naval Research Lab examined the debris and concluded from the automatic ballast system that it may have flown from Japan. Its purpose was believed to be weather data or aircraft detection, rather than carrying incendiaries. Transportation of insects or germs was considered "in the realm of possibility."

The first "incident" on U.S. soil occurred on December 6 near Thermopolis, Wyoming. Three men and a woman at the Ben Coe coal mine heard a whistling noise, then an explosion, and saw smoke in a draw near the mine at 6:15 P.M. Mountain War Time. They also reported seeing a flare in the sky and a parachute. Sheriff Ken Moyer searched the area that night and the next day and found fragments of a bomb. It was one and a half miles from the mine and fifteen miles from the town. The fragments were identified as being from a Japanese 15-kg antipersonnel bomb.

The second incident occurred on December 11 when two woodcutters, O. B. Hill and his son Owen, found a balloon and shroud lines in the woods seventeen miles from Kalispell, Montana. The balloon had landed sometime between November 11 and November 25. An inspection tag indicated it was completed on October 31. The FBI, Army, Navy, and Air Force were all notified. In the next two weeks, fragments of balloons were found in Manderson, Wyoming (December 19), Marshall, Alaska (December 23), and Holy Cross, Alaska (December 24).

On the last day of 1944, Larry Miettunen was driving about seven miles from Estacada, Oregon, when he saw what he thought was an upside-down parachute in a tall Douglas fir. With the help of Dave Horner, he cut the tree down and recovered the FUGO. The wreckage consisted of the balloon, shroud lines, burned fuses, and one-quarter of the gondola ring (presumably, the gondola self-destruct system exploded but not the balloon charge). It was taken to the Estacada high school and spread out on a tennis court for examination. The balloon was estimated to have landed between December 27 and 31.[23]

Although the U.S. had now recovered several FUGOs, their purpose remained unclear. Some local military authorities thought the Kalispell balloon might have come from a Japanese relocation center or a German POW camp. The Naval Research Lab still felt they might be weather balloons or antiaircraft barrage balloons that escaped and drifted across the Pacific. They also mentioned the possibility the balloons were launched from submarines or even carried personnel.[24,25]

During the first two weeks of 1945, the picture became clearer and more ominous. On January 4 at 5:40 Pacific War Time, a Mrs. Cyr was pulling into the driveway of her home on South Peach Street in Medford, Oregon. A 5-kg incendiary came whistling out of a dark overcast sky. It landed near the barn, exploded, and blew a four-foot diameter crater in the ground. Thirty-five minutes later, near Sebastopol, California, north of San Francisco, a FUGO balloon landed in a snow-covered field. The envelope skirt, shroud lines, remains of the envelope destruct unit, damaged ballast gear, burned fuses, and part of four 5-kg incendiary bombs were recovered.

The next day, January 5, the gun crew on a merchant ship off Kodiak, Alaska, shot down a balloon. The first shooting down of a FUGO over the continental U.S. occurred on January 10. A balloon was spotted floating above Crater Lake and a Lockheed P-38 Lightning fighter was scrambled. The P-38 fired on the FUGO as it drifted above Lakeview, Oregon. It scored several hits but the balloon did not catch fire. Rather, the hydrogen leaked out and the balloon began to descend. The P-38 continued to fire as the balloon dropped lower and lower over the Tule Lake region of northern California. It finally came to rest in a tree in the Modoc National Forest, about thirty miles west of Alturas, California. The Explosive Disposal Team had to be guided through the mountainous, logged-over area by a forest ranger in a Navy biplane. Despite its encounter with the P-38, damage was limited to holes in the balloon.

The dimension of the threat facing the U.S. was summed up in a classified report on the Sebastopol balloon:

> It is now presumable that the Japanese have succeeded in designing a balloon which can be produced in large numbers at low cost and which is capable of reaching the United States and Canada from the western Pacific carrying incendiaries and other devices . . . .

It must be assumed that a considerable number are coming over . . . . It is to be expected that the number will increase and when the dry season arrives considerable damage will result unless effective countermeasures are developed.[26]

Countermeasures

The U.S. efforts to meet the threat were on several levels. Air defense of the West Coast was the responsibility of the Fourth Air Force, headquartered at Hamilton Army Air Field near San Francisco. It lacked the means for adequate defense, however. By late 1944, nearly all the early warning radar stations had been placed on caretaker status. The Ground Observer Corps had been disbanded and the Information and Filter Centers had been closed down. There were no aircraft on ground alert. The Fourth Air Force's primary activity was the training of replacement pilots.

This situation would have to be reversed. A plan was discussed on January 17, 1945, to reactivate elements of the air defense network (radars, ground observers and control centers). A fighter-training group would be positioned in each of the vital areas. Units in an advanced state of training would be used. It was envisioned they would stand a two-week or one-month alert.

The FUGOs were a difficult target. Since the start of World War II, air defense had been based on the use of radar to track the target and guide the interceptors. The FUGOs, however, were poor radar reflectors. Also, their operating altitude of 30,000 to 38,000 feet was near the maximum ceiling of propeller-driven fighters. The most significant warning was from transmitters fitted to some of the balloons so the Japanese could track them. The first signals were picked up on December 6, 1944. The signals could not be used for interceptions, however, because they faded before the balloons reached the coast. Further, only a few carried the transmitters. A direction-finding network was established but very few accurate tracks were obtained.

The Fourth Air Force's first attempted interception was made on December 19, 1944, ironically, before the nature of the balloon threat was fully understood. Four fighters were directed by the Los Angeles Control Group to search the Santa Monica area for a reported balloon. They could not find it.

Two other plans were developed to cope with any balloons that got through. The first, the "Firefly Project," was aimed at limiting the threat of wild fires. Stinson L-5 and Douglas C-47 aircraft and about 2,700 soldiers (200 of them paratroopers) were stationed in danger areas to fight forest and grass fires. There were also fears the balloons might be used to carry germs. To cope with this, the "Lightning Project" was organized. Recovery crews were supplied with protective suits and long-handled tools for use in examining the balloons. Health and agricultural officials, veterinarians, 4-H clubs and agricultural colleges were discreetly told to watch for any strange livestock or crop diseases. Decontamination chemicals and sprays were also stockpiled in western states.[27]

A major concern was the public's reaction to this new weapon. The national mood was far different from the dark days following Pearl Harbor, when a Japanese invasion of the West Coast seemed a real possibility. Would the knowledge that in the sky above, silent and unseen, balloons were randomly dropping bombs onto homes, factories and forests, bring the fear back? Would the realization that, for the first time in living memory, the U.S. was under direct continuous assault by a foreign power generate the panic the Japanese sought? There was also the potential for disruption of war industry production. The European experience was that following an air raid, worker absenteeism due to illness increased significantly.[28]

There was another consideration. If the Japanese learned the balloons were reaching the U.S. and causing damage (even if minor), this would encourage them to increase the attacks. The only press mention of the balloons were local newspaper accounts and January 1 articles in *Time* and *Newsweek* on the Kalispell balloon.[29,30] It was concluded that the best defense against panic was silence, so on January 4, 1945, the same day as the Medford and Sebastopol incidents, the Office of Censorship requested all newspapers and radio stations to withhold any mention of the balloons. The goal was to prevent any reports from reaching the press of neutral countries and being picked up by Japanese intelligence. (In late December, the Chinese newspaper, *Takungpao,* had carried a report.) This voluntary censorship, however, made it difficult to warn people of the danger.[31] The only subsequent article was in the January 15 *Newsweek.* It stated that three balloons had been found, that they must have been launched from submarines as they had a range of 200 to 400 miles, and may have carried saboteurs.[32] After this, there was only silence.

Further Incidents

In reality, the situation was far from quiet. During January, about 2,000 balloons were launched, almost double the December total. On the other side of the Pacific, the number of incidents also picked up. On average, a new balloon or debris was reported every other day.[33]

February's total of about 2,500 balloons was only a modest increase from the previous month. In the forest, plains and deserts of North America, the story was far different. No longer were FUGOs coming in ones or twos. Rather, they were coming in waves. There would be a few days of no or only one balloon, a sudden increase, a peak, then a drop-off. Each wave lasted two or three days. More ominously, each wave's peak was higher than the last. The month's fourth wave began on February 21 when four balloons were reported. This included a balloon landing near Ephrata, Washington, losing three sandbags and then ascending and disappearing and a FUGO being shot down near the U.S./Canadian border.

The incidents increased the next day when twelve reports came in, among them, a balloon landing near Kirby, Wyoming, its battery having discharged when the antifreeze leaked out; a balloon seen exploding in midair near Powell, Wyoming; and fragments found near Chase, British Columbia, Ellsworth, Nebraska, and Porcupine Plain, Saskatchewan.

The most unusual of the day's events was the capture of a balloon by a sheriff near Tremonton, Utah. Box Elder County Sheriff Warren W. Hyde received a call from Floyd Stohl reporting a balloon on his ranch. Sheriff Hyde drove out to the landing site to watch over the balloon until the FBI and military could arrive. When Sheriff Hyde reached it, the balloon, warmed by the weak winter sunlight, had started to drag across the ground. With ballast gear bouncing off sagebrush, it crossed over Blue Creek Divide and entered a small canyon with the sheriff in hot pursuit. He was able to grab hold of it. The balloon was caught by the wind and took off with Sheriff Hyde dangling in the breeze. It flew across the canyon, landing on the rim. Hyde attempted to tie it down but again the wind carried the balloon across the ravine. Once more the sheriff tried to secure it but failed and he was again carried into the air. For 55 minutes, this struggle continued. Finally, the balloon landed near the only chokecherry bush in the draw and Hyde was able to loop a rope around one of its roots. Sheriff Hyde was later honored at a ceremony attended by the governor and military and civil defense officials.[34]

The number of incidents began to decline as the wave passed. Unlike earlier waves, however, the total did not drop back to zero but continued at the rate of one or two per day until the month's final wave (three on February 27 and four on February 28).

Although it was tempting to think these waves represented the pattern of launches (i.e., an intensive series lasting several days, followed by a similar period of low activity due to bad weather and/or supply problems), the truth may be more complex. In only a few cases was the balloon shot down, seen to explode in midair, land or were the explosions of bombs heard. In many cases, only burned envelope fragments were found which may have been on the ground for days or weeks.

The balloon offensive was intended to be a year-round effort. During the winter months, however, the Northwest forests were covered with deep snow and were largely invulnerable to incendiaries. But during the summer (July through September), the forests would be tinder dry. The summer jet stream, however, was too weak for the FUGO balloons to reach the U.S. Subsequent attacks would, accordingly, use two other types of balloons. The remainder of the 300 rubberized silk 9-meter B-type balloons would be fitted with bombs. The second was a larger version of the paper A-type balloon. It was 49 feet in diameter (the FUGO was only 33 feet). The 15-meter paper balloon had a higher altitude and could carry a heavier bomb load. One difference was in the vent system. The Japanese could not develop a gas valve in time. Instead, a large air tube was used. As the internal pressure increased, the gas bubble would be forced down the tube until it was finally vented. The tube's length, about 100 feet, prevented a too rapid loss of gas. Test launches were made in preparation for the summer offensive. Two experimental 15-meter balloons were flown. Also, three more B-type balloons were launched in February, 1945. They had gas relief valves and radio transmitters but no bombs. One was recovered at sea on April 23, west of Queen Charlotte Islands, British Columbia.[35]

The launch sites continued a maximal effort. During March, some 2,500 balloons were launched—the same as in February. A custom had developed among the launch crews. Just before takeoff, the soldiers would place their personal Samhara, an amulet carried for protection against accident, in a fold of the balloon. The high launch rate posed dangers for the crews. The 8,100 cubic feet of hydrogen in each balloon was highly flammable. Moreover, balloon envelopes, stacks of bombs, and hydrogen tanks crowded the launch site, posing the risks of fires and explosions. Two or three hydrogen fires per day occurred. When a fire was spotted, the rubber hose filling the balloon would be crimped off, the valves closed and buckets of sand would be thrown on the fire.[36,37] Another potential danger was the wind blowing the balloons back over Japan after launch. Only two such incidents occurred, both on March 13, 1945 (24 hours after launch) and no damage resulted. A more important concern was the possibility the FUGOs would stray into Soviet airspace, causing an international incident. This was one reason sites in northern Japan were not used. As additional insurance, antiaircraft guns would fire on any balloons drifting toward Sakhalin Island.[38,39]

The high launch rate was reflected in the level of incidents on the other side of the Pacific. March began quietly; there were only a few scattered reports between the 1st and the 9th. Then, on March 10, eleven incidents were reported.

It was also on March 10 that the Japanese balloon offensive inflicted its most significant damage to the U.S. war effort. Out of a rainy afternoon, a balloon drifted at low altitude across the Yakima Valley in Washington state. At 3:23 P.M., it struck the main power lines from the Bonneville dam and shorted them out. Thirty miles to the east, the power line led to a place called the Hanford Engineering Works.[40] It was one part of the Manhattan Project—the secret crash effort to develop the atomic bomb. Hanford produced the artificial element, plutonium. Inside the B reactor, uranium was irradiated, converting some of it into plutonium. The irradiated uranium was then moved to the two chemical processing facilities, the B and T plants, where the plutonium was separated out. It was then sent to Los Alamos for final refinement. Hanford was completed in September, 1944, but several months were needed to clear up problems. The first plutonium was not shipped until late January, 1945.[41] The amount of plutonium produced during early 1945 was very small and was used for experiments. It was so scarce that hourly allotments were made. The full-scale production needed for the bomb itself would not begin until May.[42]

When the balloon shorted out the electrical power, the B reactor immediately shut down. Plutonium production was interrupted for three days, until the Hanford reactor was brought back to full capacity. Only a few people involved with the Manhattan Project were told the reason for the loss of power. This was not Hanford's only run-in with the balloons. The same day, two security guards and two M.P.s at the Yakima Road barricade west of the Hanford Works shot down another balloon. It was later found near the ghost town of Cold Creek, just outside the Hanford boundary.[43]

There is irony in the Hanford incidents. The FUGOs were unguided weapons, driven by the shifting, uncertain winds. Yet they had struck at a facility that represented the greatest single threat to Japan. In war, as in all human activities, luck plays a role.

The events of March 10 were only the prelude to an avalanche of balloons, lasting through the end of the month. This was not the isolated, neat waves of February; rather, the peaks and valleys came close together. More importantly, even on the "slow" days, the number of balloons was often higher than on the peak days of February. The greatest number of reports came on March 13, with eighteen balloons. The numbers fluctuated from day to day (seven on March 18, four on March 19, and ten on the 20th).

Behind the numbers was a story repeated time after time. It began with an ordinary citizen, going about his business, far removed from the war, suddenly finding a balloon. There might only be envelope fragments, pieces of ballast gear or bomb fragments. Sometimes, however, complete balloons were recovered. One FUGO, found near Volcano, California, on March 22, was still partly inflated. It stood some twenty feet tall, looking like some alien mushroom. The most spectacular discovery was the Grimes, California, balloon. It was found by a motorist driving through the Sacramento Valley in the predawn hours of March 14. The balloon had become tangled on a power pole. The gondola and its payload of one 12-kg and one 5-kg incendiary bomb were suspended some fifteen feet above the ground. The gondola was muddy, as if it had been dragged across wet ground. The shroud lines were stretched over the wires to the deflated balloon which lay across the road.[44]

A discovery would be reported to the local sheriff and very soon after, FBI and Army personnel would descend on the site. An ordnance disposal officer would disarm any bombs. Sometimes the balloon would be examined by men wearing protective suits and using long poles, looking for any signs they were carrying germs. The area was searched for any additional debris. The balloon would be packed up and anybody who knew of the incident was told to say nothing about it.

Most of the incidents were occurring in a triangular area encompassing western Canada, Washington, Oregon, and northern California and extending east through Idaho, northern Nevada, Montana, Wyoming, South Dakota and Nebraska. Some, however, landed farther afield. The farthest east any incident occurred was Farmington, Michigan, a suburb west of Detroit. On March 25, fragments of a 5-kg incendiary were found. At the other extreme, envelope fragments, shroud lines, ballast gear, a battery and two exploded 12-kg incendiaries were found near Desdemona, Texas, on March 23 (this is the only balloon known to carry two such bombs). Additionally, three FUGOs were found in Mexico.

The increasing number of balloons was serious for another reason—it was now spring. The snow was melting in the forests of the Northwest. Soon they would be tinder dry and ready to burn. Air defense against the balloons remained difficult. Only eleven were shot down during March. The most unusual interception of a balloon occurred on March 22. Three Bell P-63 King Cobras were scrambled from Walla Walla AAF in pursuit of a balloon. They chased it from Redwood, Oregon, into Nevada where it began to descend. The balloon landed in the hills outside Reno. One of the pilots landed, intending to drive out to capture it. The balloon, however, dropped several sandbags and bombs and took off again. Above waited a P-63 which opened fire and shot it down.[45]

Yet, even as the balloons continued to come across in high numbers, the Japanese offensive had been defeated. It had been beaten not in the forests of the Northwest or in the skies above them, but in Japan itself.

Fire Storm

B-29 attacks on Japan began on June 15, 1944. Flying first from bases in central China, then, beginning on November 24, from the Marianas Islands, the bombers attempted to destroy Japanese aircraft plants and other military targets. The results of these early raids were disappointing. Few of the bombs were hitting the targets. The main problem was weather. For the first time, the U.S. realized the power of the jet stream. Flying against it, the B-29s were brought to a near standstill. Flying with it raised the bombers' ground speed to nearly 500 miles per hour—too fast for the Norden bombsight to compensate for. Moreover, clouds often hid the target. Also, the bombs might fall through as many as five different wind currents, scattering them wildly. All this made high-altitude precision bombing impossible.

Maj. Gen. Curtis E. LeMay, chief of the 21st Bomber Command, decided to send the bombers in at night, at low altitude, carrying a full load of incendiaries. Gambling that Japanese night fighter capability was limited, LeMay ordered the guns and ammunition removed from the planes, except for the tail guns. Without the guns, the gunners, and the fuel needed to climb to high altitude, the bomb load could be doubled to six tons. This switch to area bombing was a complete reversal of U.S. doctrine, and many predicted failure.

On March 9, 334 B-29s took off for Tokyo. Just before midnight, the pathfinders began dropping napalm-filled cannisters. Flying on crossing courses, they formed a burning X across the three-by-five-mile target area. Within it were factories, workshops, and a densely packed residential district. The main force of B-29s guided in on the X. Flying at 4,900 to 9,200 feet in groups of three about one minute apart, the planes dropped their bombs.[46]

The flames were whipped by a 28-mph ground wind. Firefighting efforts, built around the "tonarigumi" or neighborhood associations, immediately failed. Amateur firefighters with hand pumps, straw mats soaked in water, and buckets of sand could not cope with the rain of fire bombs. The flames leaped from house to house. People tried to flee but collapsing debris, walls of flame, and downed power lines blocked their way. The smoke and heat seared lungs and people began to drop. Charred bodies piled up in streets and alleys.[47] Then the fire storm began. In its center, temperatures rose to 1,800°F. Water in canals began to boil. A 40-mph wind generated by the flames spread the embers to everything in reach—factories, homes and people. For three hours, the bombers kept coming. Soot blackened their fuselages, turbulence bounced them around, and smoke filled the cockpits with the smell of burning flesh.

Sunrise the next morning saw utter devastation. In ashes were 15.8 square miles: 18 percent of the industrial area and 63 percent of the commercial district. In all, 267,171 buildings were destroyed. The official death toll was 83,793. Over the next ten days, LeMay sent his bombers against Osaka, Kobe and Nagoya. Thirty-two square miles of four cities were burned out and with it, dozens of major industrial targets and hundreds of small feeder plants. Morale began to decline, people fled the cities, and absenteeism in war plants was at a high rate. Japan was beginning to die. On April 13 and 15, the B-29s returned to Tokyo, burning out another seventeen square miles.[48]

The fire raids affected the FUGO program in several ways. The Showa Denko Company and other hydrogen sources were disrupted.

Damage to railroads interrupted the shipment of hydrogen tanks for prolonged periods. The factories that supplied parts were also destroyed (among them, the Fujikura Rubber Company, where the remaining B-type balloons were being prepared for the summer offensive). Finally, the Japanese remained in the dark about the balloons' success or even whether they were reaching the U.S. They checked U.S., Chinese and Russian press reports and U.S. radio broadcasts for any word. The campaign of silence was effective in denying them this information. The damage to Japan and the uncertainty over the program's results forced the army to cancel the summer offensive and curtail FUGO launches. All efforts were now devoted to preparing for the planned U.S. invasion of the home islands.[49,50]

Only about 400 FUGOs were launched during the final weeks of operations in April. The first one and a half weeks were relatively quiet, with only about two balloons per day being reported. Then the Japanese began mass launches. The first Allied territory the balloons crossed was the Aleutian Islands. It was here that U.S. air defenses scored their greatest success. The events began on April 12, when a Navy Grumman F6F Hellcat shot down a balloon west of Massacre Bay on Attu Island. This was only the prologue. The next day, nine FUGOs were shot down over Attu Island. The F6Fs intercepted them at altitudes ranging from 30,000 feet up to 37,000 feet. Another balloon was shot down on April 13, near Little Sitkin Island.

There was a less encouraging side to this, however. The nine shot down over Attu were less than half the number detected by radar. Because of the large number of balloons and their high altitude, the rest escaped and continued to head east. (This was apparently the largest number of balloons detected at one time.) A return to the waves of February and March seemed indicated.

On April 15, a balloon was shot down off Adak Island and the next day, another was destroyed near Platinum, Alaska. The massed balloons arrived in two waves, peaking on April 15 (five) and April 20 (six). It was on the latter date that the last FUGO was shot down.[51,52]

The balloon was first spotted not by radar but by two children, Michael and Sheilagh Harris (ages 12 and 9). They were playing outdoors and saw it through broken clouds at about 2,000 feet. The children's father, Tom Harris, was a Canadian Immigration Officer at Huntingdon, British Columbia, and a captain in the Army Reserves. He immediately reported the balloon to the RCAF, using the proper code word. The operator had either never been briefed on the balloons or had forgotten the code word. This was an "open" phone line, so Harris tried to explain using phrases like "a gas-filled airborne object," "from the west," "a great distance." Finally, the operator realized he was talking about a Japanese balloon and relayed the information. Very soon after, a RCAF Mosquito fighter bomber flew over Huntingdon at low altitude in pursuit of the balloon. The Mosquito found it and Harris heard cannon fire in the distance. The balloon, badly tattered, landed in a tree on Vedder Mountain, British Columbia. Harris changed into his army uniform and crossed into the U.S. to join a U.S./Canadian search party. When they reached it, the balloon was being guarded by Royal Canadian Engineers. No bombs were attached or found in the area. Harris later recalled the varnish on the paper balloon "smelled very strong."

Assuming a three- or four-day flight time, the balloon was launched on April 16 or 17. It is, therefore, presumed that these dates mark the end of FUGO launches, as no others were ever spotted in flight.[53]

Death in the Forest

There was, however, one last, tragic act in the FUGO story. On Saturday, May 5, 1945, a Sunday School class set out on a fishing trip. In the car was the Rev. Archie Mitchell of the Christian and Missionary Alliance Church in Bly, Oregon; his wife, Elsye Mitchell, who was five months pregnant; Jay Gifford, 13; Edward Engen, 13; Sherman Shoemaker, 11; Joan Patzke, 13; and Dick Patzke, 14. Mrs. Mitchell had not intended to go, but changed her mind that morning. They drove toward Gearhart Mt. As they neared Leonard Creek, the road was blocked by a road grader that had been stuck in a mud hole. The three-man road crew indicated the road was impassable and the creek might not be clear for fishing. Mrs. Mitchell and the children got out while Reverend Mitchell went to park the car. It was about 10:20 A.M.

From his seat on the road grader, one of the crew could see Mrs. Mitchell and the children clustered around something in the woods about 100 yards away. It was an armed FUGO balloon. Twice, Mrs. Mitchell called, "Look what I found, dear." The Reverend called back, "Just a minute and I'll come and look at it," as he parked the car.

A loud explosion sent twigs and branches flying, pine needles fell from the trees, and dust filled the air. Reverend Mitchell and the three road workers ran down the hill toward where the group had been. They were lying on the ground, torn by fragments from the 15-kg bomb.

Reverend Mitchell found his wife still alive, her dress on fire. He beat the flames out with his bare hands. She was beyond help, however, and quickly died. The children, with the possible exception of Joan Patzke, had died instantly.

The bodies were in a circle around a crater one foot deep, fifteen inches wide, and three feet long. One of the group had apparently dropped or kicked the bomb. The men were stunned and realized they needed help. Several went to notify the rangers, the sheriff, and the coroner. The others (including Reverend Mitchell) remained at the site to secure the area. As the afternoon wore on, the increasing number of people going into the woods generated rumors among the local townspeople. Some of the rumors reached the parents of Shoemaker and Gifford, who drove to Lakeview. Because of the danger, several of the bodies could not be moved until the four 5-kg incendiaries and the self-destruct charges were disarmed. The balloon had apparently been in the woods for some time, as the paper was mildewed and the gondola, rusted. Six to eight inches of snow remained under the balloon, while it had all melted from the surrounding area. By 6 P.M., the bombs were disarmed and the bodies could be removed. Several days later, a story was released, stating that the six had died from an "explosion of unknown origin."

The deaths in the forest led to the systematic release of information about the balloons. The earlier "word of mouth" warnings were not sufficient. Articles in newspapers and magazines revealed the existence of the balloons and their danger. More details were given in private briefings. They were made to groups of less than fifty school children and Boy Scouts. The text began, "You are being informed about these balloons because they are dangerous. Six people have been killed." Although saying the attacks were "minor in nature," it warned, "Do not touch it . . . stay 100 yards away . . . leave a guard . . . report location of balloon or bomb to sheriff or police." It concluded, "You are now in on the secret. Do not write about it in any letters and do not be unduly alarmed. Let us all shoulder this very minor war load in a way such that our fighting soldiers at the front will be proud of us."[54]

FUGOs continued to be found, ranging from fragments of paper and bombs to complete, armed balloons. Every couple of days, a new report would come in. The snow was melting in the mountains. Balloons that had landed months before were only now being discovered. On June 8, fragments of a balloon were found on Mahogany Mt., Oregon. It had an assembly tag date of "31 January 1945, 7 hour 50 minutes." Presumably, it had been there for three or four months. The warnings also paid off. On July 5, two boys found a balloon and shroud lines in trees near Hyatt Lake, Oregon. Near the lake shore was a 5-kg incendiary bomb. Having been told about the Bly tragedy, they left it alone. In a few cases, a single balloon would generate several reports. An example was the incident at Igo, California, on July 6. Highway surveyors found two 5-kg incendiaries, covered with dried mud, in a field adjoining the road, between Igo and Oak. The gondola and bombs of the balloon found on the power line near Grimes, California (March 14) were also covered with mud. The two points are about 100 miles apart. Presumably, the balloon first landed in the field near Igo and was dragged along the ground, coating it with mud and scraping off the two bombs. The balloon, now lightened, took off again, finally ending up in the power line.[55]

After the nature of the balloons was realized, in early 1945, planning began for an advanced air defense system to replace the early haphazard arrangement. One study envisioned 200 radar sites and an equal number of 90mm or 120mm AA guns along each thousand miles of coastline. Cost would be $31 to $88 million, plus $2.5 million for ammunition for each 1,000 balloons detected. This, however, would still fail to detect up to 50 percent of the balloons. A more ambitious plan was to station 200 picket ships for each thousand miles of coastline. The cost estimate was even higher. Because of the cost, these plans were abandoned. As one report put it: "It is clear that the measure of success to the enemy . . . will be the amount of men and equipment which we divert to defensive measures against it."[56]

In early April, as the final wave of mass launchings was beginning, an air defense test area was established under the "Sunset Project." It extended from Cape Flattery to the mouth of the Columbia River. Six radar stations were to be set up. These would detect the balloons, then guide the aircraft to them. Radar tracks would be reported to the Silver Lake Region Control Center. The balloons would be recognized by their speed, altitude, and relation to the wind. Aircraft to be used were P-38 Lightnings and Northrop P-61 Black Widows, based at Paine AAF, Naval Auxiliary Air Field Quillayute and NAAF Shelton. Installation of the radar began in late April. Most of the work was completed in mid-May, with the final radar set installed in early June.

Although the balloons were no longer coming, sightings continued to be made. Nearly all were traced to weather balloons, blimps, or the planet Venus.[57]

One such "sighting" occurred in the summer of 1945 at Los Alamos.

Several nuclear scientists spotted a bright object in the daytime sky. Through binoculars, they could "see" a gondola under it. A nearby air base was notified and two aircraft took off. They radioed they could not reach the object as it was too high. Dr. Enrico Fermi returned to his office and checked an almanac. He then told the others the object was Venus. Because of its brightness, it was visible even in daylight.[58]

In all, sixty-eight interceptions were attempted against such false targets. The lack of confirmed targets caused the Fourth Air Force to request twenty-five balloons be made to allow testing of the network. Once completed, the critical personnel involved with the Sunset Project could be reassigned. This was refused as impractical and steps were taken to close down the project. On July 11, 1945, the Continental Air Force Headquarters granted authority to end it. This was delayed until August 1 because similar approval was needed from the Western Air Defense Command.[59]

A few days later, two atomic bombs were dropped on Japan, and on September 2, six years and a day after Germany invaded Poland, the Japanese surrendered, ending World War II.

FUGO Assessed

In assessing the history of the FUGO program, one problem is the destruction of records in the fire raids and at the time of the surrender. The actual number of balloons launched is not known for certain. The total is usually given as about 9,300. General Kusaba, who commanded the program, has said only 6,000 were launched (if true, the monthly totals in the text would be reduced by one-third). As for the number to reach the U.S., research by Bert Webber indicates a total of 355 FUGO incidents (a very few of these were duplicate reports of single incidents). This would indicate a minimum of 3.8 to 5.9 percent completed the crossing.[60]

FUGO's military results were mixed. Due to the silence about the attacks, there was no panic. The only deaths were the Sunday School class, and no fires were started. On the other hand, the interruption of plutonium production at Hanford was a major success. FUGO did cause the diverting of men and equipment to home defense. It was also a major headache for the FBI and the military in time and effort.

In economic terms, the program was probably successful. It cost the Japanese some $2 million. The cost of the aircraft and radars tied up in the Sunset Project was probably at least this much, not to mention the time and effort spent investigating the incidents.

The question, however, arises whether the time, people and materials used in FUGO would have been better spent in some other area of the Japanese war effort. This question, however, is rendered meaningless by the mismanagement of the Japanese economy due to interservice hatred and a lack of cooperation between the agencies responsible for production and military manpower. Skilled workers were drafted and replaced by school children, women and Koreans. It took three or four times as many unskilled workers to do the same job. The disruption caused by this was especially felt in the hundreds of tiny firms that supplied parts to the major assembly plants. Here the drafting of a single employee could close down production.

A few examples of the results: in the summer of 1943, before B-29 attacks began, Japanese industry was capable of producing 53,000 aircraft per year. In fact, less than 10,000 were built. Aluminum was in very short supply, yet only 55 percent of the aircraft industry's allotment was actually used. The rest ended up as black market scrap. Sometimes the demands were petty in the extreme—the army would specify a left-handed screw, while the navy wanted a right-handed screw in the same equipment.[61] Clearly, any damage done to the Japanese economy by FUGO's production was lost amid the self-inflicted wounds.

The fundamental problem in Japanese efforts to carry the war to America was the sheer size of the U.S. economy and war effort. During the war, the index of industrial production went from 100 to 196, while the gross national product increased from $91 billion to $166 billion. Put another way, the U.S. was able to shake off the last effects of the depression, build an army from scratch, supply its allies, raise the country's standard of living, and build the bomb. Any damage FUGO did was lost without a trace.[62]

The similarities between the South in the Civil War and Japan are striking. Both faced an enemy that outnumbered and outproduced them. Both needed an early, stunning victory to break U.S. will. Both won early victories but ultimately failed to break U.S. will. Both lost.

The real importance of FUGO was technical: it was the first balloon able to travel vast distances at a controlled altitude. These were two of the technical accomplishments necessary for the U.S. reconnaissance balloon program that was to follow a decade later.

There were still some loose ends. Two years after the tragedy, Reverend Mitchell married Betty Patzke, an older sister of Joan and

Dick Patzke, who had been killed. The newlyweds joined the foreign missionary service of the Christian and Missionary Alliance Church. They were sent to French Indochina, to a leprosarium at Banmethuot in the central highlands. On June 1, 1962, Rev. Archie Mitchell's name was again in the news when it was reported that he and two other Americans had been kidnapped by Viet Cong guerrillas. They have not been seen since.[63]

Since the end of the war, FUGOs have continued to be found. There were eight incidents during the rest of the 1940s. In one, a ballast ring was found in the top of a tree cut down by loggers. At the base of the tree were three six-foot diameter burned spots. In another case, two clam diggers found three 5-kg incendiaries on the beach near Eureka, California. Three FUGOs were found in the mid-1950s, and two more in the 1960s. The most recent incident occurred in the summer of 1978. A ballast ring, fuses, and barometers were found near Agness, Oregon. They are now on display at the Coos County Historical Museum.[64]

It must be presumed there are other FUGOs, lying undiscovered in remote forest areas, still waiting.

3

Skyhook

At the end of World War II, the power to control events had passed from a battered Europe west to America and east to Russia. The stage was set for the beginning of the Cold War. Like the coming of winter, it was a slow process, good days alternating with bad ones. Over time, the good days were fewer and the bad days, colder. The Cold War's roots can be traced to the events of World War II. On the eve of the war, Russia signed a nonaggression pact with Germany. A secret annex of the treaty gave Russia the eastern half of Poland and a sphere of influence in Eastern Europe. The agreement cleared the way for Germany's attack on Poland by eliminating the risk of a two-front war.

For the next year and a half, Communist Russia and Nazi Germany were uneasy allies. Then, in June, 1941, Germany turned on Russia, and the U.S. and England found themselves with a new ally. From the start, Russia sought to hold the gains of the nonaggression pact. The West was reluctant and the press of events pushed the subject into the background. The underlying differences came to the surface in the first half of 1944, when the Russian Army entered Poland and other Eastern European countries. The Soviets moved quickly to install coalition governments (with Communists in key positions) and to freeze out Western influences. The U.S. and England objected to the Russians' actions, and at the Yalta conference in February, 1945, the three powers agreed to the Declaration on Liberated Europe. It called for "free elections of governments responsive to the will of the people." The Soviets, however, continued to tighten their control, and resentment over violations of the Yalta agreements festered. The always shaky wartime alliance did not last much beyond the end of the fighting. In March,

1946, less than a year after Germany's surrender, Winston Churchill spoke of an "Iron Curtain" across Europe.[1]

Outside Eastern Europe, Russia was also trying to expand its power. In the two years following the war, Russia tried to force Turkey to give it control of the Dardenelles and continued to station troops in northern Iran in defiance of an agreement to remove them at the end of the war. In Greece, Communist guerrillas were fighting a civil war that threatened to overthrow the pro-Western government. If successful, these efforts would give Russia access to the Mediterranean and domination of the Near East.

In response, on March 12, 1947, the Truman Doctrine was announced. Although specifically covering only aid to Greece and Turkey, it served notice the U.S. would use the means at its disposal, even force, to halt the spread of communism. This was followed in June by Secretary of State George C. Marshall's sweeping proposal for an aid plan to rebuild Europe—both east and west.

After several Eastern European countries expressed an interest in the Marshall Plan, Stalin began a crackdown. Starting in the summer of 1947, the remaining noncommunist parties in Eastern Europe were abolished and their leaders imprisoned or executed. In February 1948, a coup overthrew the coalition government in Czechoslovakia and installed a communist one. This extinguished the last hold-out to Stalinist control in Eastern Europe. It also convinced many in the West that Stalin's demands were insatiable.

During this same time, differences between the West and Russia over economic and occupation policy in Germany were splitting the country in two. On March 20, 1948, the Russians walked out of the Allied Control Commission, ending the pretext of four-power control. This sparked a war scare that the walkout was a harbinger of the Soviets marching west. Increasingly, Russia was seen in terms of Hitler's aggression of 1938 and 1939. Then, on June 24, 1948, the Soviets closed all rail and road links between the Western occupation zones and Berlin. President Truman decided to resupply Berlin by air. The Berlin blockade was seen as an attempt to force both the West out of Berlin and a settlement of the German question on Soviet terms. World War III loomed.

Others disagreed, arguing the threat from Russia was political—extending its influence into Western Europe through the local communist parties, rather than invasion. With the view of Stalin as Hitler, there was a parallel view that accommodation was still possible.

Moreover, for a nation facing a war with Russia, the U.S. seemed disinterested in the state of its military power. Postwar demobilization had reduced the U.S. military to a pale shadow of its World War II strength. The defense budget for 1947 was $10.5 billion. This was reduced to $10 billion the next year. Intent on balancing the budget, Truman put a ceiling on defense spending in 1949 of $15 billion.[2] The atomic monopoly the U.S. counted on to deter a Soviet attack was an equally hollow threat. The U.S. had two atomic bombs in 1945, nine in 1946, thirteen in 1947, and fifty in 1948—insufficient to knock out Soviet war-making potential.[3]

The Berlin blockade was a turning point in the Cold War, as it galvanized the West into taking actions it had long discussed. The tentative steps toward a formal Western alliance were completed on April 4, 1949, with the signing of the NATO treaty. The formal division of Germany came four days later with agreement of the Western powers to set up the Federal Republic of Germany. By this time, the Russians realized their efforts had failed and in May, they ended the blockade. Then, in September, fallout from the first Soviet atomic bomb test was detected. At the same time, the Chinese Nationalists were forced from the mainland and the Peoples Republic of China was established.

This first tentative phase of the Cold War ended at 4 A.M., June 25, 1950, when the North Korean Army invaded South Korea.

Skyhook

Against the background of the emerging Cold War, there was a breakthrough in balloon technology that was the final link in the U.S. reconnaissance balloon program.

From the start, balloons had been used for scientific research. In the 1920s and 1930s, a series of manned balloon flights had set new altitude records. Yet these flights also indicated conventional balloons were limited to a ceiling of just over 70,000 feet. The problem was the weight of the rubberized fabric envelope. The *Explorer II* balloon, which set an altitude record of 72,395 feet in 1935, had a volume of 3.7 million cubic feet and weighed 6,500 pounds. Simply making the balloon bigger increased the weight without significantly enlarging the volume of lifting gas.[4]

The key to higher altitudes was to use new materials. In 1936, Jean Piccard and John D. Akerman of the University of Minnesota test-flew the first plastic balloon. It was made of cellophane and scotch tape with its lower end open. The balloon could reach high altitudes and float at a constant altitude. Although the balloon became brittle and tended to crumble in the cold of high altitude, it was a start. Piccard also looked at clusters of balloons hooked to a common payload.

After World War II, the importance of high-altitude research increased. Development of jet aircraft meant men would soon be flying at unprecedented altitudes. It was essential to understand air currents, temperature, pressure and other weather phenomena. There was also long-standing interest in studies of cosmic rays, the radiation streaming in from deep space. The earth's atmosphere absorbed most of them but above 100,000 feet, less than 1 percent of the atmosphere remained. Balloons had another advantage; although rockets like the V-2 could reach higher altitudes, their flight times were only a few minutes. A balloon could remain aloft for hours or even days.[5]

With the end of the war, Piccard was eager to resume stratospheric research, and in late 1945, he proposed Project Helios. This would use a cluster of 80 to 100 cellophane balloons to carry a sealed gondola to 100,000 feet. The crew would be Piccard and his wife, Jeannette.

During his search for funding, Piccard, purely by accident, met Otto W. Winzen, chief engineer at Minnesota Tool and Manufacturing Corporation, who was visiting the University of Minnesota aeronautical laboratory on other business. Winzen was intrigued by Project Helios and agreed to work on the gondola and life-support system.

Piccard and Winzen went to Cmdr. George W. Hoover of the Office of Naval Research. Hoover had a reputation for supporting research projects that others would have rejected. Winzen began his briefing by saying, "I hear you'll buy anything!" Despite such levity, Hoover was interested in use of plastic balloons for high-altitude research. He gave Piccard and Winzen a small classified contract to develop Helios.[6]

Piccard went to General Mills and asked its mechanical division to build the spherical aluminum gondola. (General Mills was selected primarily because it was close by.) He ran into more difficulty finding a manufacturer for the plastic balloon. Piccard first went to plastic manufacturers but they refused, saying they lacked the technical knowledge to make a bag that large. Next, balloon makers were approached. They turned it down, saying they had no knowledge of plastic. Finally, he went back to General Mills. Although lacking knowledge about both building balloons and handling thin plastic, General Mills accepted the challenge.[7]

The first question was what plastic to use. Cellophane was tested but was found to have low tear resistance and a tendency to shatter in low temperatures. Nylon had relatively low tear resistances and the additional problem that it was only available in 12-inch-wide strips. The lifting gas leaked through ethyl cellulose. Saran became brittle at low temperature and had poor tear resistance at all temperatures. One promising candidate was pliofilm, which had been used in a few early balloons, but was found to be brittle at low temperatures and was broken down by the strong ultraviolet in unfiltered sunlight.[8]

Polyethylene was the plastic finally selected. It was first developed by Imperial Chemical Industries, Ltd. in England just before World War II. During the war, it was produced by Union Carbide and E. I. DuPont de Nemours for use as insulating material in radar construction.

Polyethylene seemed to have been made for use in balloons. It was strong at temperatures ranging from 120°F to -40°F, had adequate tear resistance, was not affected by ultraviolet or ozone, and was chemically stable. It held gas well and produced little superheating of the gas through the absorption of sunlight. More importantly, the Visking Corporation was able to produce wide sheets of polyethylene in thicknesses of one-thousandths of an inch. The melted plastic was forced through a die and then air pressure expanded the tube into a very thin film as it cooled. The tube was then slit lengthwise into sheets 100 inches wide in a continuous length. The material was clear with a metallic sheen.[9]

The sheets were cut into long, petal-shaped gores, which were carefully laid out on long tables. Through long trial and error, a procedure was developed to heat-seal the gores together, using hot gas or heated electric elements. The seams were immediately cooled with nitrogen. The seams were reinforced with adhesive tape. This both sealed them and carried the weight of the payload, which was suspended from a long nylon line attached to an open ring at the lower end of the baloon.[10]

Despite the difficulties, polyethylene caused a revolution in balloon technology. It weighed only 0.7 to 1 ounce per square yard. Rubberized fabric, in contrast, weighed 4 ounces per square yard. Costs were also lowered: 3.5 cents per square yard for polyethylene versus $2 per square yard for rubberized balloon fabric. The plastic could be sealed using semiautomatic equipment, while rubberized fabric had to be hand-cemented. Thus, higher altitudes were possible while the cost for very large balloons could be kept within reach.[11] There still remained the final test in the unforgiving sky.

The first test balloon was ready in the late summer of 1947. It was launched on September 25, 1947, from St. Cloud, Minnesota. The balloon had a volume of 30,000 cubic feet and carried a 63-lb payload. Despite, as Winzen later wrote, "millions of tiny pinholes in the film, leaky seams covered with adhesive tapes, and makeshift launch method," the balloon reached 100,000 feet, landing at Eau Claire, Wisconsin.[12,13]

The next two attempts were failures, and meetings were held to sort out the problems. An important development came when flights resumed. George Hoover authorized two scientists, J. Hornbostel and E. O. Salant of the Brookhaven National Laboratory, to fly a pair of cosmic ray plates on one of the balloons. The flight did not go smoothly; the balloon refused to come down for three days. The problems indicated additional work was needed on radio and control systems, as well as on insulated containers able to stand the cold and low pressure for prolonged periods. All this was forgotten when Hornbostel and Salant examined the plates, which showed a wealth of cosmic ray data. As Winzen later noted, "cosmic ray research and plastic balloons became inseparable."[14]

The success of the Brookhaven experiment spelled the end of the Helios Project. Although the gondola shell was finished, there remained many technical unknowns. Studies indicated Helios would require 70 balloons of 200,000 cubic feet each. The total volume of 14 million cubic feet was too unwieldy to be practical.[15] Accordingly, Helios was shelved for the time being and work was shifted to use of single plastic balloons for high-altitude research. Capt. H. B. Hutchinson of the Office of Naval Research named them "Skyhook."[16]

Independent of the General Mills effort, a second group at New York University was also working on plastic balloons. The NYU meteorologists and physicists, under the leadership of Athelston Spilhaus, were developing acoustical sensors and the balloons to carry them. Although described as meteorological devices, it is suspected they were actually for detecting the shock waves generated by Soviet nuclear explosions. The balloon, for the equipment to be successful, had to fly at a specific altitude for a very long period of time. This meant an automatic altitude control system. The NYU group studied the ballast system used on the FUGO. The balloons were assembled from "carrot bag grade polyethylene." By 1947, the NYU group was enjoying considerable success—one balloon launched from White Sands, New Mexico, landed in Norway. When they became aware of the much larger General

Mills program, the NYU group abandoned balloon construction and simply bought the envelopes from General Mills. Over the next few years, several of the people involved in the NYU program would be hired by General Mills to work on Skyhook.[17]

It was at this same time that Skyhook balloons became involved with a modern legend. On the afternoon of June 24, 1947, Kenneth Arnold was flying above the Cascade Mountains of Washington state. He spotted nine disk-shaped objects flying in formation toward Mt. Rainier. Describing them to a reporter later, Arnold said they "flew like a saucer would if you skipped it across the water." Thus was born the phrase "flying saucer." The sighting made the front pages across the country. Soon people everywhere were "seeing" flying saucers. (It was subsequently suggested Arnold saw reflections from aircraft, a mirage which distorted mountain peaks, or disk-shaped wave clouds.)[18,19]

The sightings were interpreted as being extraterrestrial spacecraft. This reflected the new technological age—jet aircraft, the V-2 rocket, and the atomic bomb. Another factor was the influence of *Amazing Stories*, a science fiction magazine edited by Raymond Palmer. For several years before the Arnold sighting, it had been running stories about alien invaders. In editorials, Palmer strongly implied alien spacecraft really were visiting earth. Through *Amazing Stories*, millions of people were subconsciously preconditioned to believe in alien visitors, to watch the sky, and told what to look for.[20,21]

Three months after the Arnold sighting, the first Skyhook balloon was launched. Their huge size, high altitude, and metallic appearance sparked many flying saucer reports. It also led to a tragedy.

Between 1:15 and 1:30 P.M. CST on January 7, 1948, a flying saucer was reported to the Kentucky State Highway Patrol from Maysville, Owensboro, and Irvington. At about 1:20 P.M., the tower crew at Godman Field near Ft. Knox sighted the object, which was variously described as round, a parachute, ice-cream-cone-shaped or a teardrop. At 2:30 to 2:40 P.M., four North American F-51 Mustangs of the Kentucky Air National Guard approached the field.[22] They were on a low-level cross-country flight from Marietta, Georgia, to Standiford Field. The flight leader was Capt. Thomas F. Mantell, Jr. Godman tower asked the fighters to investigate the "unidentified balloon-like object" hovering to the southwest of the field. Mantell replied his mission was ferrying aircraft but would try. One of the flight, 1st Lt. R. K. Hendricks was low on fuel and continued on to Standiford Field. The other three aircraft turned toward the object and began a left spiral climb. Reaching 14,000 feet, they began a maximum-rate straight climb.[23] Mantell was out ahead of his two wingmen, 2nd Lt. B. A. Hammond and 1st Lt. A. W. Clements, and was barely visible. At about 2:45, Mantell radioed the Godman tower and said, "I have an object in sight above and ahead of me, and it appears to be moving at about half my speed or approximately 180 miles an hour." One of his wingmen asked, "What the hell are we looking for?" Godman tower asked Mantell to describe the object and he responded, "It appears to be a metallic object, or possibly a reflection of sun from a metallic object and it is of tremendous size. I'm going to 20,000 feet." By the time Mantell reached 22,500 feet, his two wingmen broke off pursuit owing to lack of oxygen (before takeoff, none of the aircraft had been serviced with oxygen as none was available at the base). Mantell told them he would continue to 25,000 feet and remain there for about ten minutes. At about 3:15 P.M., he radioed that the object was "directly ahead of me and slightly above, and is now moving at about my speed or better. I am trying to close in for a better look." A few moments later, as his plane reached about 25,000 feet, Mantell passed out from lack of oxygen. The F-51 continued to climb to about 30,000 feet and began a gradual turn to the left caused by engine torque, then went into a steep spiraling dive. As the plane neared the ground, its structural limit was exceeded and the left wing and tail broke off. The wreckage landed on the Phillips farm near Franklin, Kentucky, narrowly missing a house and barn. The main fuselage hit the ground on its left side. Mantell's body was still in the plane. His watch was stopped at 3:18 P.M. CST.[24,25,26]

The *Louisville Courier* had the headline, "F-51 and Capt. Mantell Destroyed Chasing Flying Saucer." Wild rumors spread: it was a Russian missile; the saucer had, deliberately or accidently, shot down the aircraft when it got too close; Mantell's body was riddled with bullets; the plane had been disintegrated in midair; the debris was magnetic or radioactive. None was true. To the Air Force investigators, the how was clear: a person can remain conscious for only three to six minutes at 25,000 feet without oxygen. The emergency canopy release was still locked; Mantell had apparently not tried to bail out. The throttle was set at one-fourth open, mixture control was at "Idle Cutoff" and the prop control at "Full increases R.P.M." This indicated Mantell regained consciousness as the aircraft descended into denser air, realized the danger, throttled back and tried to slow the aircraft. Instead, the aircraft was overstressed.[27]

What was unclear was the why and what. Why had Mantell continued to climb until he could not breathe? A friend who had flown with Mantell for years and considered him a cautious pilot said, "The only thing I can think was that he was after something that he believed to be more important than his life or his family."[28] (Another reason could have been inexperience—Mantell had 1,608 hours flight time but only 67 hours in F-51s. Of this, 41 hours were in the ninety days before the accident.)[29]

The Air Force saucer investigation unit, Project Sign, tried to determine what Mantell had been chasing. A few weeks before, another F-51 had tried to intercept Venus and there were similarities in the two incidents. Additionally, Venus was south-southwest of Godman at an elevation of 33° at the time of the incident. The tower crew reported the object was to the southwest at an elevation of 45°. This was within the limits of human error. Venus had a brightness of magnitude -3.4 and so could be visible in the afternoon sky. This explanation was given to the press. It was reasonable but nobody yet knew it was wrong.[30]

The first public announcement of the Skyhook project was made on March 3, 1948, two months after the Mantell crash. It is important to stress that in the months and years to follow, Skyhook balloons received a fair amount of publicity. *Look* magazine photographed a Skyhook launch at Camp Ripley, north of St. Cloud, on March 20, 1948. During early 1949, the *Saturday Evening Post, National Geographic,* and *Popular Science* did stories on Skyhook.[31] *Aviation Week* also published a digest of a scientific paper which said some fifty-two flights had been made with altitudes exceeding 98,400 feet.[32]

Neither was the link between Skyhooks and flying saucer reports hidden. The first oblique mention was in a 1948 article by Winzen, who noted "thousands of people" had seen the balloons and reacted "with mixed emotions, ranging from mild interest to terror."[33] An article in *Science News Letter* in July 1949 mentioned, "Some of the flying saucers that have been reported were undoubtedly these high-flying balloons shimmering in the sky."[34] On September 7, 1950, the *Chicago Tribune* published photos of a Skyhook launched from Stagg Field at the University of Chicago with the caption, "That 'Saucer' You Saw Was a Skyhook."[35] None of these reports seems to have made an impression with the public.

This changed with the publication of the February 27, 1951, issue of *Look* magazine. The story began when General Mills personnel advised Dr. Urner Liddel, chief of the nuclear physics branch of the Office of Naval Research, they could locate "lost" balloons by reports of flying saucers. (These were balloons that high winds had carried out of tracking range.) Dr. Liddel and his associates studied about 2,000 reports. After eliminating hoaxes and hallucinations, they were left with accounts by pilots, scientific observers, and reliable laymen. After investigation, Dr. Liddel concluded, "There is not a single reliable report of an observation which is not attributable to the [Skyhook]."[36] (Air Force data for 1947 through 1952 indicated 18.51 percent of reports were due to balloons. This was the largest single reason.) Then, in November 1950, a telescopic photo was taken of a Skyhook. When seen from below the balloon appeared disk-shaped. The photo and outline was submitted to *Life* (which rejected it), then to *Look*.[37] In the *Look* article, Dr. Liddel explored how a balloon could be mistaken for a saucer: "The lateral rays of the sun at dusk illuminate the base of the balloon. . . . If your imagination soars, the light reflection . . . may impress you as the glow of an atomic engine. The wisp of the balloon's instrument-filled tail may impress you as the exhaust. The sun's rays may suffuse the plastic bag with a fiery glow."

The article also revealed that Mantell had not been chasing Venus, but a Skyhook.[38] A year later, the Air Force reopened the Mantell case. Capt. Edward J. Ruppelt, director of Project Blue Book (the new name for the study), and Dr. J. Allen Hynek (the astronomical consultant) reviewed the old file and concluded the object was not Venus. It was not bright enough and the witnesses were describing a large object, not a point source of light. Ruppelt looked at the possibility that it was the sun reflecting off a layer of clouds or a cockpit reflection but eliminated both. Finally, he checked the possibility that it had been a Skyhook. (In his book, Ruppelt never mentioned the *Look* article's solution to the Mantell incident.) In the file were two mentions of balloons. At about 4:00 P.M., a witness at Madisonville, Kentucky, had observed the object through a telescope and said it was a balloon. An astronomer near Nashville called at 4:45 P.M., saying he had seen it through a telescope and it was a balloon. Ruppelt also discovered this had not been thoroughly investigated in 1948. One reason was that many of the Air Force investigators were convinced the saucers really were alien spacecraft. As time passed and no proof was found, the sceptics came to the fore and the Venus theory became an easy out. Also, they had only checked for conventional weather balloons, not Skyhooks. Ruppelt also found Skyhooks were being launched from Clinton County AFB in southern Ohio during early 1948. The wind currents on January 7, 1948, were in a southerly direction. Unfortunately, he could not locate records of the launches.[39] Years later, it would be stated the records had been found. These showed no Skyhook launches were made from Clinton County on January 7 or for two days after. A Skyhook *had* been launched from Camp Ripley early on the morning Mantell died.[40]

Although the *Look* article provided the true solution of the Mantell incident, there was a negative aspect. Dr. Liddel said, "When this project first began it was kept secret. Now, there is no longer any need for secrecy on a scientific basis. And certainly, there is no longer any need to keep the public in the dark about what flying saucers are."[41] This sparked a number of angry editorial responses. The *Philadelphia Inquirer* and the *Washington Star* both asked, "Why haven't we been told this before?"[42] *Aviation Week* was particularly outspoken, calling it a "scandal" the explanation was kept "secret for so long." An editorial asked, "Why there was ever any need for secrecy . . . on the simple fact that larger balloons were being used" and "What secrets does a balloon's configuration betray?" Such phrases as "unnecessary secrecy," "classify everything as secret," "hush-hush project" were used.[43]

The *Look* article and the reaction it caused created a myth about the early history of the Skyhook: that the project had been top secret until unveiled in the *Look* article. The actual situation is more complex. After the March 1948 press release, several articles on Skyhook appeared, but no one noticed. It was not until Skyhook appeared in a mass circulation magazine *and* was linked with flying saucers that it was impressed on the public's mind. Because this "first impression" described it as a secret project it "became" a secret project.

Skyhook Flight Profile

The Skyhook balloon had a distinct flight profile that posed many challenges. The balloon was handled with care to prevent any holes being ripped in the thin plastic. It was found that a balloon with a 250,000-square-foot surface area could have no more than 0.2 square inch of holes. Even strong flexing during fabrication, shipping and launch would increase the rate at which the gas leaked through the plastic, even though no visible holes appeared.[44]

The early flights were made from Camp Ripley, Clinton County AFB, and University Airport, Minneapolis. In 1948, the first shipboard Skyhook launch was made from the USS *Norton Sound.* Aircraft carriers were also used as launch platforms. During April and May, 1949, launches began from Holloman AFB, New Mexico.[45,46] By early 1951, some 270 flights had been made.[47]

The launch process itself was difficult. To protect the plastic, the balloon was laid out on a ground cloth. The launch crew sometimes wore gloves but not shoes as a further measure. Weather conditions also had to be right: ground winds had to be less than 10 mph. The balloon acted like a giant sail, whipping and oscillating in the breeze, which can puncture or even tear it apart. For this reason, launches were often made in the calm predawn hours.

Once inflating began, the crew was committed—the balloon must be flown or thrown away. The gas used was helium which has a number of disadvantages. Available only from natural gas wells in Texas and Kansas, it was more expensive than hydrogen. Also, helium had only 92.6 percent as much lift per equal volume. There was one supreme advantage with helium—it did not burn.[48] The envelope was filled to only 1.3 to 5 percent of its total volume. This formed a "bubble" at the top of the balloon.[49,50]

As with an airplane, takeoff was critical. The speed of ascent could not be too slow—a gust would scrape the payload against the ground. Yet the rate could not be greater than 500 to 1,000 feet per minute. As the balloon climbed, its "tail" (the lower part of the balloon) whipped back and forth, which put stress on the balloon. This became critical as the balloon passed through the tropopause (the base of the stratosphere) at 40,000 to 50,000 feet. Here the temperature was at its minimum of -75 to -94°F and the plastic was very brittle. Moreover, high-velocity winds can blow in opposite directions, bending the balloon into an "S" shape. The stresses from a too-fast climb, the cold, and the wind sheer could tear the balloon apart.[51,52] Once through the tropopause, the rate of ascent was cut in half.[53] The balloon reached its maximum altitude in about ninety minutes.[54]

During the climb, the gas expanded as the air pressure dropped. This changed the shape of the balloon. At low altitudes, the Skyhook was pear-shaped. By the time it reached maximum altitude, it was spherical. The lower end of the balloon, called the appendix, was open. This allowed the Skyhook to maintain a relatively constant altitude. As the sun warmed the helium, it expanded out the appendix, rather than causing the balloon to go higher. By 1951, constant altitudes had been maintained for twenty-four hours without a ballasting system. Because the internal pressure of the balloon and the outside air pressure were the same, Skyhooks were known as "zero-pressure" balloons.[55,56] (In contrast, a rubber weather balloon was sealed. As it climbed, the gas expanded, stretching the balloon until it burst.)

The balloons drifted on the wind. They might travel only sixty miles in three days or be carried on a 200-mph jet stream. The Skyhooks were chased by aircraft. On one flight, a Boeing B-17 Flying Fortress was tracking a balloon launched from Holloman AFB. After watching the balloon in the evening sky, the pilots had a cup of coffee. In the meantime, the balloon drifted off, but Jupiter rose at about the same spot. The crew watched Jupiter for an hour until they realized the "balloon" was not moving. The Skyhook was long gone. Skyhooks were visible in the daytime sky, looking like a shiny dime. They were most spectacular at dawn and sunset. Because of the balloon's high altitude, it was in sunlight when the ground was in darkness. The light filtered through dust and clouds could color the balloon white, red, purple, or green and cause it to twinkle. (It was this which generated the flying saucer reports.)[57]

Another time, a Skyhook was "lost" over east-central Texas when it was caught in a wind current. The crew of the pursuing B-17 looked for it in vain until the crew radioed Barksdale AFB and asked them to phone the newspapers in nearby Shreveport, Louisiana, for any flying saucer reports within 500 miles. The newspapers had been inundated with reports around sunset from Waco, Texas, through upper Louisiana and the edge of Mississippi, traveling north-northeast. The B-17 headed after it. Several hours later, over Mississippi, the balloon's radio beacon was picked up.[58]

After nightfall, the gas cooled and contracted by about 5 percent. This loss in volume caused the balloon to descend several thousand feet. Upon reaching 60,000 to 70,000 feet, the balloon's equilibrium was restored and it remained at this altitude through the night. The next morning, the rising sun warmed the balloon and it climbed back to its maximum altitude.[59]

Above more than 99 percent of the atmosphere, the Skyhook was a unique research platform and carried a variety of payloads. Most were related to cosmic ray studies. One type of cargo was dozens of film plates. When a cosmic ray struck the plate, it passed through at nearly the speed of light. As the cosmic ray consists of positively charged nuclei of atoms, it stripped off the negatively charged electrons from the atoms in the plate. Some were carried along with the cosmic ray; other electrons were sent zinging through the plate as secondary particles, in turn knocking others out of their orbits. In their wake, the cosmic rays left tracks of silver particles in tree-shaped patterns. These allowed scientists to determine their numbers, composition, and energies. By 1949, data from early Skyhook flights indicated primary cosmic rays were nuclei of heavy atoms such as carbon, sodium, iron, cobalt and nickel.[60,61]

Another important payload was biological specimens: radish seeds, fruit flies, mice, hamsters, and monkeys. They tested the effects of prolonged exposure to cosmic rays. Keeping them alive at 100,000 feet was a difficult task. The gondola had to be pressurized, of course, but this was not the only problem. The carbon dioxide and water vapor exhaled by the animals had to be absorbed. Temperature extremes had to be controlled. The subzero cold would quickly kill any organism. Yet the insulation could not trap the heat given off by the animals. A number of ingenious solutions were developed. To cool the gondola, several gallons of water were carried in a soup pot. At the low pressure of 100,000 feet, water boils at 50 to 60°F. The heat from the gondola warmed the water and it boiled off, carrying away the excess heat as the steam escaped through a vent. Aluminum foil and Styrofoam prevented the sunlight from overheating the gondola by day and losing heat by night. Soda lime and silica gel absorbed carbon dioxide and water vapor. It was the first life-support system for space.

By the early 1950s, the first mixed results were in. On the positive side, hamsters exposed to a heavy dose of cosmic rays on one balloon flight showed no ill effects whatever.[62] Although most flights indicated cosmic rays were harmless, there were disquieting exceptions. Oat seeds sent up and then planted showed mutations from radiation through three generations.[63]

Payload weights had increased from about 70 pounds on the first flights up to 300 pounds in the early 1950s. Because each extra pound reduced the altitude the balloon could reach, the Skyhooks also encouraged the development of some of the first very crude printed circuitry. One altitude reporting device used an epoxy cylinder cast in a Minute Maid frozen orange juice can.[64] Flight times had also increased from 4 hours to 74 hours by 1954.[65-67].

Once the mission was over, the payload was cut free from the balloon by a radio signal. As it fell, a cord tore the balloon into thousands of fragments. The payload would descend by parachute to a landing. The recovery was made by a ground crew. This sometimes proved difficult. In a few cases, the radio system failed. On one flight, the payload was cut down when a radio station played the "Tiger Rag," which coincidentally matched the coded signal. Once on the ground, the gondola had to be quickly recovered as the animals could die from heat, cold or starvation.[68]

The Skyhook was the beginning of space science. It was the first to explore the borders of space. The experiments carried on the Skyhooks would later go into orbit on satellites. But these were the years of the Cold War and the balloons could also carry reconnaissance cameras high above the reach of fighters and across the heartland of Russia.

4

Moby Dick

The Korean War changed everything. What had been a rivalry was now a real war that carried the potential of spreading worldwide. In this new situation, there was a desperate need for information on Soviet military strength. U.S. knowledge was both inadequate and out of date. A major source was the German photo reconnaissance library captured at the end of World War II—the "Turban" material. The photos were limited to western Russia, however—a major shortcoming. After the Germans attacked, the Soviets packed up complete factories and moved them east of the Ural mountains. These great industrial complexes, which made up a large part of Soviet war-making potential, had never been seen by Westerners.[1] Soviet Central Asia and Siberia were without photographic coverage. The best information on these areas came from World War II maps produced by Mil-Geo, the geographic section of the German Wehrmacht.[2] Needless to say, this captured material could shed no light on reports of postwar reconstruction, new industrial construction or, most importantly, atomic production facilities.

Postwar photography was largely limited to coverage of the Siberian coast by U.S. aircraft flying outside Russian territorial waters. RB-29s were fitted with a 100-inch focal length K-30 camera mounted at an oblique angle. Targets were limited to those a few miles inland. When cloud cover was too heavy for photography, the aircraft's radar would be used to spot targets on the ground. The echoes showed coastlines and built-up areas. The radar scope would then be photographed.[3]

Another procedure was to fit aircraft with receivers to pick up Soviet radar and radio signals. This was called "Electronic Intelligence" or ELINT. Flying off the coast, the aircraft could plot the locations of

Soviet radars. However, because radar signals travel in a straight line, ELINT coverage was limited to fifty miles of the border. The interior of Russia was an unknown area.

Early Overflights of Russia

The aircraft conducting photographic or ELINT missions were to stay at least twelve miles off the Russian coast. On a very few occasions in the late 1940s, Western aircraft crossed the line and overflew the Soviet Union on probing missions. The Royal Air Force used de Havilland Mosquito PR.34s to cover such targets as Murmansk and Arkhangelsk through the 1940s. Stripped of armor, the Mosquitos were able to reach over 43,000 feet which placed them above Soviet fighters.[4]

According to one account, the U.S. conducted a brief series of overflights of Siberia during the late summer of 1948 (about six weeks after the start of the Berlin blockade). The aircraft was a stripped-down B-29 fitted with ELINT consoles for five to eight operators. The crew was all-volunteer. The first flight was made on August 5, 1948. The B-29 took off from Ladd Field near Fairbanks, Alaska, and exited U.S. airspace near Point Barrow. It then entered Soviet airspace and flew deep into Siberia, finally leaving over the Sea of Japan and landing at Yokota Air Base outside Tokyo after 19 hours 45 minutes. The second flight was made on August 8 from Yokota to Ladd; two more followed on September 1 and 6.[5]

Soon after the North Korean attack, President Harry S Truman authorized reconnaissance flights along the Chinese coast opposite Formosa to spot any preparations for an invasion. The bulk was to be done by aircraft flying outside Chinese airspace. When a penetration was necessary, it would be done by a single fast aircraft. Although authorized to defend themselves, the pilots would attempt to evade attack. Deep penetrations and formation flights were not to be made "to avoid giving . . . any impression that the United States is making a serious attempt to penetrate the mainland."[6]

In the fall of 1950, the Joint Chiefs of Staff prepared a plan for systematic probing flights over Russia. Air Force Vice Chief of Staff Gen. Nathan Twining took the plans and maps to the White House. Truman asked, "Chiefs all buy this?" Twining responded, "Yes sir. We're very anxious to start on this program right away. We realize the seriousness of it, but we feel this is the only way we're going to get this information." Truman agreed.[7] Soon, U.S. aircraft were darting across the borders of the Soviet Union, China, and Eastern Europe on a fairly regular basis. These overflights covered port facilities, coastal areas, and islands. To escape detection, the aircraft relied on gaps in Soviet defenses, altitude/speed, and the short duration of the overflight. The overflights provided much valuable information, but most of Russia was still out of reach. To fill this blind spot, something new was needed, and something old.

Gopher

On September 11 to 15, 1950, the Air Force Scientific Advisory Board held a meeting to examine ways to extend photographic coverage to the interior of Russia. There were major diplomatic and technical problems, however. Use of manned aircraft to overfly the Soviet Union in peacetime could be viewed as an act of aggression. Use of the Snark cruise missile with inertial guidance for photo reconnaissance was a possibility, but it would not be ready until 1953. A reconnaissance satellite was looked at but it would take several years. It was therefore concluded the only feasible means was reconnaissance balloons. There was believed to be no technical problems, and although some meteorological unknowns existed, these seemed manageable. It was estimated a balloon reconnaissance system could be operational in 1951.[8]

The idea of using balloon reconnaissance over Russia had been germinating for some time. It was first proposed in a 1946 study by the RAND corporation.[9] Some years later, it was independently suggested by Gen. George W. Goddard, a pioneer in the development of reconnaissance cameras and systems since the 1920s. He was watching a Skyhook ascend when it was suddenly caught by the jet stream and headed east at high speed. General Goddard realized that a balloon riding the jet stream could travel great distances and, as he wrote later, "take some mighty pretty pictures on the way." Back at Wright Field, he talked with several intelligence personnel about the idea.[10] Then, in the fall of 1949, it was proposed a balloon be fitted with ELINT equipment. The project was abandoned due to a lack of funding and questions about its feasibility.[11] Finally, in July 1950, General Mills had test flown a camera package to over 90,000 feet which took excellent pictures of the ground.

Following the recommendation of the Scientific Advisory Board, there was a flurry of activity. The balloon reconnaissance project formally began on October 9, 1950. It was given the code name Gopher and received a 1-A priority with initial funding of $100,000 for fabrication of the first test vehicles. The general characteristics were also set:

Camera systems: scale of 1:100,000; time of day, altitude and direction recorded if possible. Cameras shut off at night.

Flight profile: altitude between 60,000 and 80,000 feet; flight time would be several days at a constant altitude.

Recovery: The balloon and equipment had to be recovered. Air, land, and sea pickup would be examined. A timed beacon would be used to locate the balloon, then another timer would vent gas from the balloon to lower it for air pickup. Development of the recovery system was not to delay the initial test program. This would use existing components.

Camouflage: The equipment would be designed to minimize detection from the ground or air.[12,13]

The program was under the control of the Equipment Division, Directorate of Research and Development. Maj. J. J. Pellegrini was named Gopher project officer.

In mid-October 1950, the role of Gopher was expanded with the suggestion that it be used for additional missions such as ELINT. The balloons would be released to drift over Soviet radar sites. The intercepted signals could either be retransmitted to friendly ground stations and aircraft or be recorded on board by a camera (this would require payload recovery). The equipment should also show a balloon's location and the direction from it to the radar site.[14] Other missions the balloons could undertake, once the basic system was proven, included Electronic Counter Measures (radar jamming), weather studies, psychological warfare, and guided missiles.

On January 8, 1951, a briefing was held on the Gopher project in the office of Gen. Donald N. Yates, Director of Research and Development. At the meeting, a five-phase schedule was established:[15,16]

Jan 18,	1951	Balloon vehicle development
Feb	1951	Upper air trajectory test
Mar	1951	Gondola design
Apr	1951	Test flight across U.S.
Jul	1951	Balloon recovery tests

The reconnaissance balloon was to be ready for operational flights over

Russia during the winter of 1951–52. Yet, even as Gopher was getting underway, it was running into problems.

In light of the successful July 1950 camera test, General Mills was awarded the first Gopher contract for $97,000 to develop the balloon system and gondola.

In January and February 1951, General Mills launched four 70-foot Gopher test balloons. Each carried a total load of 1,300 pounds. All four balloons failed at various altitudes. General Mills engineers suspected the failures were due to a poorer grade of polyethylene film and began tests. Unfortunately, existing tests of plastic brittleness could not meet their needs so a new one was devised. A sample of polyethylene was stretched on an embroidery hoop and chilled to a low temperature. A metal ball was then dropped through the plastic. As long as the plastic remained flexible, the ball tore a single slit in it. Below a certain temperature, the polyethylene became brittle and shattered, looking like a glass window hit by a baseball.

This brittleness temperature was constant for each grade of film. It turned out that for some films, this temperature was the same as that encountered by the balloon at 40,000 feet. Samples of the plastic used in successful balloons had a brittleness temperature of -85°F. In the failed balloons, it was -67°F. As a general rule the higher the molecular weight of the film, the lower (i.e., better) the brittleness temperature. The engineers also found that changes in the extrusion conditions could vary the brittleness temperature by 18°F. Additionally, fine scratches in the film's surface caused abnormally high brittleness temperatures. Clearly, the plastic film would have to be produced under carefully controlled conditions.

After studying the test results, Bakelite's DE-2500 was picked as the standard for balloons. Although DE-2500 had not been produced in thin films at that time, the Visking and Plax Corporations were soon producing high-quality sheets of the material. General Mills used it to fabricate balloons up to 115 feet in diameter, which made twenty-four successful flights out of twenty-five tries.

Although this solved the problem of faulty plastic, there were other areas that needed research before larger Skyhooks could be built to carry the heavy payloads required by Gopher. Bakelite's DYNK plastic was tentatively selected for use on future large balloons. (This was akin to an aircraft designer selecting a particular aluminum alloy.) New manufacturing techniques were developed that eliminated lumps in the plastic which were a leading cause of holes. The bursting strength of the plastic was increased 25 percent. This meant a heavier payload could be carried by the same thickness of plastic. Both Plax and Visking also made improvements that resulted in films of more uniform thickness. (The strength of a balloon was set by the thinnest spot; thicker areas were just dead weight.) Finally, the stresses of the balloon's ascent were studied. It was found that rapid flexing and twisting of the cold plastic caused a large increase in gas leakage.

One series of tests involved putting 40-foot model balloons into a climatic hangar at Eglin AFB, Florida. They were inflated, then the temperature was lowered and a wind machine was turned on. Examining how the "balloons" failed under these simulated flight conditions would indicate weak points.[17]

The tests would pay dividends in the construction of larger balloons. For the short term, however, the problems upset the ambitious Gopher schedule. There were two other factors as well. The Navy's Office of Naval Research objected that Gopher was interfering with Skyhook and refused use of Navy-owned equipment at General Mills (balloon tables, heat-sealing machines, and vehicles). A meeting was held between the Under Secretaries of the Air Force and Navy to settle the problem. They agreed that all Skyhook-related development work would be under the Office of Naval Research. The Wright Air Development Center transferred funds to the ONR for Gopher development. Additionally, the Air Research and Development Command had failed to push the project and coordinate the work. In early April 1951, Major Pellegrini reported neither phase 1 nor 2 had been completed.

At the same time, doubts surfaced on the ELINT payload for Gopher. A study indicated a number of shortcomings. Capture of a payload would compromise the latest U.S. analysis techniques, the frequency range was too small, no direction-finding information would be provided, and it would take three years to develop—a long time, given what was called "the present emergency." The payload would weigh at least 1,000 pounds and need 1,500 to 2,000 pounds of ballast. This was beyond the balloon technology then available. It was felt it would be better to wait until the reconnaissance balloon had proved itself before making any additional effort.[18]

On November 23, 1951, a conference was held on Gopher. It dealt with two questions: was there continued interest in Gopher and what were the future requirements? The answer to the first was a firm "Yes." The second was dependent on the status of other projects and world conditions, but it was felt Gopher should proceed on a "crash" basis.[19]

Despite this vote of confidence, Gopher was clearly in trouble—by this time operational flights were to have started. In fact, a year had passed with little progress.

Moby Dick

Another project was also getting underway at this time, one that would play a major role in reversing the misfortunes of the U.S. reconnaissance balloon program. It was a study of high-altitude wind currents. Before World War II, 10,000 feet was considered high altitude. Development of the B-29 raised this to 25,000 feet and jet aircraft doubled this in the early postwar years. In 1950, there was little data about conditions above 50,000 feet.[20] A few things were known: at 50,000 feet, the temperature was around -70°F, but at 100,000 feet, the air became hot again. Although the winter jet stream flows west to east, winds are from the east at 50 to 60 mph at 70,000 feet during the summer.[21] The problem was there had been no systematic study of these air currents. Very soon, aircraft and missiles would be flying at these altitudes. The time was ripe for study and the Skyhooks would provide the means.

In May 1951, Paul Worthman, at Air Force Headquarters at the Pentagon, wrote a directive to the Cambridge Research Center to undertake the high-altitude study. The balloons would be flown at staggered levels between 50,000 and 100,000 feet, and have an automatic ballasting system to maintain a constant altitude. They would carry a transmitter for tracking. Flight time would be three days.[22] Because 1951 was the 100th anniversary of the publication of Herman Melville's most famous work, the weather balloon program was called "Moby Dick."[23]

A friend of Worthman's, in the Geophysics Branch around the corner, was working on Gopher. Comparing notes, they agreed the projects complemented each other.[24] Plastic balloon technology was still relatively primitive, and the advances Moby Dick would produce would help Gopher. Also, Moby Dick was a nearly perfect cover for Gopher. Gopher would be just another "weather study," a continuation of Moby Dick.

On June 1, 1951, a contract was issued to New York University to design a suitable vehicle, and Tufts College was selected to develop the gondola (transmitter, power supply, and ballast system). Dr. Alvin H. Howell designed the gondola.[25] He used the Japanese FUGO as his starting point. Instead of sand, Dr. Howell first tried compass fluid as ballast. This was a kerosenelike liquid that was supposed to withstand very low temperatures. It was found that at temperatures of -94°F, the compass fluid froze. The work was stopped and ground tests were made with dry ice. These finally proved the fluid was not suitable. Finally, it was decided to use very fine steel shot (as fine as dust). It did not freeze, had a low volume for a given weight, and poured like a liquid.[26] To release a controlled amount of ballast, a "magnetic valve" was developed. A permanent magnet was mounted at the opening and held the ballast in place. When an aneroid switch detected a drop in altitude, it turned on an electromagnet which neutralized the permanent magnet's field, allowing the steel shot to fall.[27]

Development of the gondola, transmitter, and insulation took two months. It was a metal box 22 ;x 19 ;x 22 inches in size. Inside the box was a layer of Styrofoam, then a layer of aluminum foil, another of Styrofoam and so on until a 3-inch thick insulated wall was formed. As a second defense against the cold, several cans were filled with fifteen pounds of water. This retained heat through the night to keep the power source, a 6-volt car battery, above 32°F. Below this temperature, its electrical output was too low.[28]

The gondola had an empty weight of 150 pounds and carried another 250 pounds of steel shot in two hoppers on its sides. The package was built by Ultrasonics Inc. The gondola's payload was a small transmitter. It broadcast a direction-finding signal, balloon identification number, altitude, and amount of ballast used. To conserve battery power, the transmitter used a 30-second-on/90-second-off cycle. The balloon's location was plotted by ground direction-finding stations. Signals could be picked up 250 miles away. This would show the speed of the wind currents carrying the balloon.

Considerable effort was made to reduce the risk of a midair collision with a Moby Dick balloon. Some 60 percent of the payload weight was for safety devices. A timer allowed the balloon 100 minutes to reach 28,000 feet. If it was still below that altitude at the end of this time, the balloon would automatically be cut down. This was to prevent a leaking balloon from drifting into airlanes. The gondola also carried flashing lights for visibility at night. Two independent systems were used to terminate the balloon's flight. One was a three-day timer, the other was a barometer which cut the gondola free if it descended below 28,000 feet. The gondola was attached to a 24-foot parachute. Any remaining ballast was also dumped when the gondola was released.[29,30]

To prove the various systems, test flights were made. By mid-1952, quality production could begin.[31]

Because of the scale of launches (some 1,000), additional personnel were needed. These came from the three squadrons of the Air Force's Air Resupply and Communications Service. Their Boeing B-29 Superfortresses and Grumman SA-16 Albatross amphibians were used to parachute agents and supplies into Communist China.[32] Given its secret mission, ARCS was the logical group to use any operational balloon weapons system that might be developed. Working on Moby Dick would provide experience. They were designated the 1300th Air Resupply and Communications Squadron.

Gopher Flies

Meanwhile, with the problems with defective polyethylene solved, General Mills could begin flight tests of various Gopher components. Balloons were launched from Minneapolis, Minnesota; Holloman AFB, New Mexico; Pyote AFB, Texas; and Tillamook, Oregon. A major problem was designing a balloon able to carry a very heavy payload for a very long-duration flight (raised by the Air Force to fourteen days in May 1951). The balloon for these long-duration test flights was 116 feet in diameter with a volume of 711,000 cubic feet. The shape was a modified sphere-on-cone which reduced stress. The plastic was .0025 inch thick. Total weight of the balloon was 620 pounds. Its payload was 500 pounds plus 1,000 pounds of ballast. This was sufficient for up to fourteen days aloft. A number of these balloons were launched. The best performance was 8.75 days. This balloon had a gross load of 2,366 pounds of which 955 pounds was payload. After launch, it reached a maximum altitude of 74,000 feet. Altitude was controlled by a "solar engine" control system. This allowed the balloon to descend at a controlled rate during nighttime hours. The minimum nighttime altitude ranged from 54,000 to 40,000 feet. Each day, the balloon's maximum altitude dropped about 3,000 feet due to air entering the balloon. The flight ended when the ballast system power supply failed. It was estimated only 215 pounds of ballast, or 18 percent, had been used up to this point. A much longer flight would have been possible had the malfunction not occurred. These test flights indicated the basic feasibility of very long duration balloon flights.

Throughout 1951, even as the test flights were underway, the Wright

Air Development Center and General Mills came increasingly into conflict. WADC felt the company was showing poor management and inadequate technical supervision. This resulted in money and effort being expended in areas that did not advance the project. General Mills seemed also to be very reluctant to follow Air Force wishes. In particular, the Gopher project needed a balloon system which could be launched on a preset schedule regardless of weather. The General Mills test balloons were inflated and allowed to stand in a vertical position before launch. This meant they could not be used in winds above 1–3 knots. General Mills ignored the contract obligation and argued repeatedly that development of a reliable launch system required the balloon first be developed. The Air Force countered that this forced the launch team to wait for perfect weather, upsetting the schedules and keeping the personnel idle. General Mills's only action was to set up a balloon launching site at Tillamook, Oregon, an area known for a high percentage of calm periods.

The problems with General Mills were reflected in contract negotiations. The increased flight duration of fourteen days and early technical problems with the defective plastic meant the program's scope would be much greater than first thought. Accordingly, the original contract was dropped, the gondola development was split off, and new agreements worked out. General Mills, in July 1951, submitted a 14-month development program costing just under $1.7 million. The Air Force, in turn, rejected this as too slow (a completion date of July 1, 1952 had been set) and too costly. General Mills resubmitted a 12-month/$1.14 million proposal. This was also unacceptable and the WADC and ONR began looking for a second contractor. Goodyear, Milprint, and Winzen Research were all approached but they lacked the background and capabilities needed for Gopher. This also resulted in disagreement between WADC and ONR over use of Gopher funding. This, in turn, caused delays that could not be tolerated, given the urgency of the project. WADC ultimately received a waiver from ONR to contract directly with General Mills. Finally, on October 19, 1951, a 9-month/$1 million contract was signed with General Mills. (The Air Force, in order to test gondola systems independently of General Mills, did order thirty 70-foot balloons from Winzen Research.)

The contract for development of the gondola was issued in November 1951. The winner was Stanley Aviation Corporation. The work, with a price tag of $387,498, was also to be completed by July 1, 1952. The complete prototype system was to be designed and nine production gondolas delivered. The gondola was in two parts: the outer shell or hood, and the inner rack. The outer shell carried the load-bearing structures and the hydrogen peroxide heater. This was fed from two tanks holding 150 pounds of hydrogen peroxide. The heater was operated by a thermostat and kept the systems warm. The inner rack held the gondola systems: batteries, the controller which turned the camera and tracking beacons on and off, the aneroid switch, timer and cut-down system. The inner rack fitted inside the outer shell. This allowed easy access. The complete package was surrounded by a 5-inch layer of insulation. This both protected the systems from cold and allowed it to float. The ballast container was fitted on the underside of the gondola. Like Moby Dick, steel shot and a magnetic valve were used.

The camera used on the test flights was a K-17, modified to reduce its weight and power requirements. It was fitted with a 6- or 12-inch focal length lens and various filters and film combinations. In order to get full 360° coverage, the camera was mounted at an angle and the gondola was slowly rotated. The result was a complete circle with coverage from directly below the balloon to the horizon. With a 6-inch lens, the photos could show landmarks such as racetracks, airports, hangars, bridges, and dams, and allow limited analysis of industrial complexes such as steel or shipping. The camera could be preset to take one photo every five minutes or a group of five photos every half hour. At night, the camera would be shut off by a light-sensitive switch. The location of the photos was determined by a "Navigator"—a device which recorded the angle of the sun. This, along with a clock, allowed an accuracy of 30 nautical miles. The complete gondola weighed 446 pounds and was 33 ;x 44 ;x 48 inches. Due to the speed of development, it was not possible to test the gondola's systems under the extreme cold and low pressure in an altitude chamber. This would be done as part of the actual test flights.

The Gopher gondola carried safety and tracking devices similar to those on Moby Dick. The gondola carried a flashing warning light and would be automatically cut down if the balloon descended below 30,000 feet. Ground stations tracked the balloon by a high-frequency radio beacon which could be received up to 1,000 miles away. Aircraft tracking the balloon homed in on a VHF beacon. Two systems could be used to end the balloon's flight. A tracking aircraft could transmit a coded signal to a VHF receiver and decoder which would cut the gondola free. A preset timer could also be used. (Because the beacons and receiver used over 50 percent of the gondola's electrical power, they were turned on and off on a 20-minute cycle.)

Once the flight ended, the gondola would jettison its remaining ballast and hydrogen peroxide and descend to earth under a drogue chute and four 28-foot main parachutes.

Ground recovery represented a security problem. Gopher was a top secret project, yet the gondola could fall (literally) into anybody's hands. Moby Dick was used as cover. All complete gondolas were labeled "Moby Dick" and lacked any security classifications. They also carried a sign warning the finder of a fire hazard and requested the Air Force be notified. A reward would also be paid. This would satisfy the curious and reduce speculation it was anything more than a weather study. It was felt that unless a finder tried to disassemble the gondola (which required special tools), the chance of a security breach was low.

Also in November 1951, the Equipment Laboratory at WADC was requested to begin tests of the midair recovery system at El Centro, California, a major Navy parachute test center in the desert east of San Diego. A grappling hook and winch were fitted in a Fairchild C-119 Flying Boxcar. Fifteen parachutes were dropped and the C-119 was able to contact twelve of them. It was found that, weather permitting, at least three passes could be made at each parachute from an altitude of 10,000 feet. On the negative side, not all the parachutes contacted were recovered, owing to equipment failure. More importantly, during one attempt, the recovery failed and the C-119 nearly crashed. Although it was believed improvements in technique and equipment would allow nearly a 100 percent recovery rate, further work could not be done owing to WADC's inability to get the necessary test aircraft.

By mid-April 1952, the gondola and balloon systems were deemed ready for full-scale test flights. The first was made on April 14, 1952, from Minneapolis, Minnesota. Although it reached 69,200 feet and remained aloft 22.8 hours, a bad launching caused the gondola to strike the ground, damaging the battery. No data or photos were obtained. The next flight (April 30) was a slight improvement—the camera failed after twenty exposures. The third flight, on June 4, was all the Gopher personnel could hope for. The balloon reached 69,990 feet and remained aloft five hours. Over 200 photos were taken with many groups of four shots having complete 360° coverage. A number of the photos went to Air Force intelligence for an assessment.

That Gopher was still in an early stage of development was shown by the disappointing performance of the next five flights. The June 12 mission returned only about forty photos, their quality reduced by clouds and haze. The first launch of July 10 produced approximately thirty photos. Again they were of low quality, apparently because the camera had not been sharply focused.

The second flight of July 10 was a wild adventure. The balloon, carrying a complete gondola and ballast weighing 914 pounds, ascended through a thunderstorm. As it did, the balloon made a large unexplained oscillation, then climbed to its maximum altitude of 60,700 feet. The balloon then drifted east, tracked by General Mills ground crews and Stanley Aviation aircraft. When the call-down signal was transmitted, there was no response and the balloon was soon lost. It was believed the gondola had come down in central Pennsylvania and the Civil Air Patrol began an extensive area search. Later, the plastic balloon was found in the Atlantic Ocean by a passing tanker. The gondola had apparently been released after an estimated 120-hour flight and was lost at sea.

Nor were the next two Gopher flights any better: (July 15) camera failed at or before reaching maximum altitude; (July 26) twenty photos of poor quality taken.

The situation on the ground was no better. Even as the gondola test flights were starting, General Mills indicated more money would be needed. WADC was opposed to this because of General Mills's poor performance. On April 17, 1952, it was agreed General Mills would continue with remaining funds. To continue test flights after the July 1 cutoff date, more than $60,000 was added to the contract, but General Mills's role in launch operations was nearing an end. In August 1952, the contract was terminated—the balloons would now be made by Winzen Research and launched from Holloman AFB.

The first Holloman launch on August 29 fared little better than its predecessors. After reaching 75,000 feet, the camera took four pictures before the rotary head on the gondola failed. This triggered the camera so no more photos could be taken. The cut-down signal also failed. This was not a hardware failure, however. It was subsequently traced to the VHF antenna's position on the underside of the tracking aircraft. The antenna was shielded and the signals were too weak to be received.

The next attempt was made on September 4 and was a success with 202 good-quality photos being returned. This was followed by another successful flight on September 10. The rotating head was modified with an additional bearing to cancel the effects of the balloon on the gondola's rotator motor. The rotation was timed at one revolution per five minutes. Four shots were taken during each rotation (i.e., every 90°). After recovery, it was found 236 photos had been taken; each frame covered 90° on the ground and each series of four covered at least 300° on the ground and a total area of 300 square miles. The scale was 1/60,000—better than the 1/100,000 called for in the development plan. This was accomplished at the expense of coverage, as only major geographic features were visible beyond forty miles. It was felt, however, this would aid in finding the location of objects in the photos. Increasing the number of photos taken during each rotation would ensure 360° coverage. The high frequency beacon was also tracked by NAS Dallas at a range of 550 nautical miles. The only disappointment on these two flights was the failure of the cut-down signal to release the gondola (again due to the antenna's location).

A random hardware failure prevented three successes in a row. Launched on September 15, the balloon floated at 60,000 feet for four hours. At the end of this time, the tracking aircraft transmitted the cut-down signal. The antenna had been repositioned on the top and the gondola released. However, when the parachute opened, the shock broke the lines connecting it to the gondola, which fell to the ground and was destroyed on impact. The infrared film was exposed to sunlight.

This setback was the start of another bad streak. The next flight was made on October 2. It was to be a long-duration flight—the on-board timer was set for 53 and 54 hours. This mission also used a new launch system: a truck crane anchored the balloon and transferred the load to the load ring, the load was then anchored to a movable platform, and the balloon was released by firing explosive squibs.

The balloon rose to 67,000 feet and remained within 25 miles of the Holloman launch site, owing to very light winds, until sunset. On the second day, a B-26 was used for aerial tracking. Two visual sightings were made at 12:45 and 4:15 P.M. MST. This was the last time anyone saw the balloon. The B-26 landed at NAS Dallas to rendezvous with a second tracking aircraft. This aircraft suffered engine problems and could not track the balloon during sunset. This was critical as the balloon was now lost. On the third day, the Air Force tried to find it using an estimated position. This failed, first owing to interference from a ground station, then engine trouble on the tracking aircraft. It was believed the gondola landed in the Beaumont, Texas, area but nothing was found.

The next long-duration flight (October 14) was also unsuccessful. For the first day and a half, the balloon was tracked by a B-17. The winds were higher than expected. (It had traveled 1,200 nautical miles in 34 hours.) Because there were still 32 hours remaining on the timer, it was decided to end the flight. The cut-down signal was transmitted but there was no response. The B-17 returned to Wright-Patterson AFB and was not available the next day. The Air Force attempted to locate the balloon through ground stations but the last signals were picked up 44 hours after takeoff. It was estimated the balloon came down during the night of October 16 owing to leakage (the ballast system had failed earlier). Owing to winds of jet-stream velocity, the balloon was lost.

This was the third time a gondola had been lost because of shortcomings in tracking. There were several problems. It was impossible to accurately predict the balloon's launch time or trajectory. The long duration also caused difficulties. There were more important reasons. The full ground-tracking network could not be used due to manpower and funding shortages. As substitutes, WADC requested assessment of six long-range tracking aircraft. This was refused and WADC had to make do with several test aircraft available on a "standby" status. This was not effective owing to poor maintenance and disinterest by the flight crews. The loss of the three gondolas represented a possible security breach. Accordingly, on October 27, a halt was ordered in long-duration test flights until adequate tracking support could be provided. As a partial step, an SA-16 amphibian was assigned to Gopher for tracking.

There remained two more gondola flights. The first was made on November 14. Because of the ban on long-duration flights, the timer was set for only 36 hours. Soon after the balloon reached its maximum altitude of 62,000 feet, the tracking beacons failed. The Air Force tried to track it visually but this was unsuccessful. On November 22, the gondola was found in a field near Roadstown, New Jersey. The film spool had jammed, breaking the film, after only fifteen exposures. The recording barograph indicated the balloon had been aloft three and a half days. The flight had been ended when the balloon descended below 30,000 feet and the safety switch cut the gondola free.

The final flight was made on November 21, 1952. Again the timer was set for 36 hours. Throughout the flight, the balloon was tracked by the SA-16 aircraft. When the timer ended the flight, however, the balloon could not be sighted owing to weather. The gondola was found on November 28. Postflight analysis indicated the hydrogen peroxide heater had kept the temperature inside the gondola between 80 and 120°F. During the first day, 176 photos had been taken. These covered a strip about 90 nautical miles wide and 600 nautical miles long. The only problem was possible fogging of the filter. During the night, the rotation motor failed, preventing the camera from taking any more photos. On this note, the Gopher test flights ended.

Although the two November flights met with only limited success, analysis of the recovered gondolas, along with tests of a complete gondola in a WADC altitude chamber, did much to explain the hardware failures which had occurred during the test flights. They were, for the most part, due to failures of minor components which could easily be corrected.[33]

Soviet Balloon Reconnaissance?

As Gopher was making its test flights, some believed the Russians had beaten the U.S. to the punch. This concern was generated by a sudden increase in flying saucer reports during the spring and summer of 1952. From the first sightings in 1947 through the early 1950s, the Air Force had received around 150 to 200 reports per year. The 1952 flap saw as many as 50 reports per *day*.[34] The flap climaxed with "the invasion of Washington." At 11:40 P.M. on July 19, 1952, controllers at Washington National Airport spotted seven unidentified "blips" on their radar. They seemed to be flying above the White House and the Capitol. Several airline pilots also reported strange echoes on their aircraft weather radar or unexplained lights in the night sky. Just before dawn, a jet interceptor searched the area but found nothing. One week later, almost to the hour, the blips returned.

At 10:30 P.M. on July 26, the same team of radar operators who spotted the earlier "invasion" picked up another group of blips. They were arranged in an arc around Washington. Air Force intelligence personnel were called to the radar room, commercial aircraft were diverted, and interceptors took off to defend the capital. The jets were guided to the targets by ground controllers, but each time they got close, the radar echoes would fade out. The interceptor's own radar was unable to "lock on" for more than a few seconds. The rest of the night was spent in fruitless chases. None of the pilots was able to get a good look at the "objects." By sunrise, the radar targets were gone.[35,36]

The Air Force had concluded by August 1949 that flying saucers were only misinterpretations of known objects—balloons, aircraft, astronomical bodies such as planets and meteors, ducks over a drive-in, or searchlights on clouds. The reports continued to be investigated, however. The reason was that if the Russians should begin overflying the U.S. with some exotic aircraft, it might be reported as a flying saucer. An example of this possibility was the Japanese FUGO balloon.[37]

After the 1952 flap, some believed this was not just a possibility, but reality—the reports had been generated by waves of Russian reconnaissance balloons. They were believed to be high-altitude developments of the FUGO, which carried preset flares. The resulting press reports were used to check the flight tracks.[38] Presumably, the Soviets had developed their own plastic balloons independently, or copied the idea from published accounts of Skyhook. Their use for reconnaissance followed in due course. Despite the open nature of American society, the Soviets would need coverage of atomic weapons development and production facilities. Liaison teams, during the war, would have provided information on U.S. industry. In contrast, the Hanford Works and Oak Ridge had not been and were not accessible to the Soviets.[39]

Flaws in the theory were readily apparent, however. No hardware of unknown origin (either Russian or Martian) had been recovered after a sighting.[40] This was in contrast to FUGO. Within six weeks of the first incident, U.S. intelligence had a very complete picture of its design and mode of operation. Also, the FUGO had been specifically designed to self-destruct, yet numerous intact balloons were recovered. If the flying saucers really were Russian balloons, the same thing should have happened.

In retrospect, it was clear the 1952 flap had its roots in a number of factors. One was an increased amount of publicity, specifically, an article in the April 7 issue of *Life* magazine which contained exaggerated and inaccurate accounts of several sightings, and the issuing of an Air Force directive two days before on the procedures to report a sighting (and which seemed to indicate greater official interest). This was combined with public anxiety over the Korean War and upcoming presidential elections, hot weather during June and July which drove people outdoors, and two major meteor showers which provided stimuli for reports. The sightings received press attention, which fed the process. The Washington "invasion" was nothing more than temperature inversions that caused false echoes.[41,42]

Moby Dick Flies

The operational plan for Moby Dick envisioned year-round flights to map the upper air currents. During the winter, three west coast sites would each launch one balloon per day. In the summer, when the jet stream reversed direction, activities would shift to two east coast bases.[43]

The first Moby Dick launch was made on February 19, 1953, from NAS Vernalis, California. A total of six were flown by the end of the first week. The gondolas also carried fruit flies for cosmic ray studies.[44] Flights soon began from NAS Tillamook, Oregon, and the dry lake bed at Edwards AFB, California.

A unique launch system was developed which allowed operations during conditions that normally would have been too windy. The standard method was to lay the balloon out on a ground cloth. When inflation began, the bubble formed at the top of the balloon and it rose off the ground. At this point, the balloon was extremely vulnerable to gusts. Moby Dick used a "covered wagon." The balloon was inflated inside a trailer 42 feet long with sides almost 40 feet high. A canvas cover, stretched across the top, held the balloon in place and protected it from the wind.[45] The gondola was then brought up on a three-wheeled cart and attached to the load line. At the proper moment, the cover was released and the top of the balloon came billowing out of the covered wagon, swung upright, jerked the payload off the ground, and headed into the sky. Within minutes, it was a silver teardrop on an endless field of blue.[46] The covered wagon allowed launches in winds up to 25 knots. This was 2.5 times higher than standard methods would permit. Thus, Moby Dick could fly when other balloon projects were grounded.[47]

Moby Dick used a bewildering variety of Skyhook balloons. They came in three diameters: 49 feet, 69 feet, and 83 feet; four volumes: 28,885 cubic feet, 49,100 cubic feet, 150,000 cubic feet, and 223,000 cubic feet; and three shapes: a sphere with a cone base, a cylindrical shape, and a "natural"-shaped balloon.[48,49] The latter is based on the shape the bubble of gas will take when enclosed in a nonrestrictive envelope. It is almost flat on top with cone-shaped sides, like an inverted pear. This equalized stresses on the balloon and increased the load it could carry.[50,51] For all Moby Dick sizes, the plastic was only .002 to .0025 inch thick.

The balloons floated at preset altitudes between 50,000, 67,000 and 75,000 feet. A few operated at altitudes of 35,000 to 45,000 feet. Initial tracking was by the VHF direction finding networks of the Air Force Airways and Air Communications Service and the U.S. Navy. The position reports were sent to the plotting center at Lowry AFB, Colorado. Later flights carried high frequency direction finding equipment, which allowed use of FCC receiving stations.[52]

A typical Moby Dick flight was that of balloon C-65. It was launched at 10:42 A.M. PST on April 17, 1953, from Edwards AFB. After a rapid climb, it peaked at nearly 60,000 feet. Over the next few hours, the balloon slowly descended until about sundown, when it finally leveled out at 55,000 feet. The automatic ballasting system kept the balloon at this altitude for the next three days and nights. The wind currents carried C-65 in an easterly direction. The balloon crossed into Arizona and passed directly over the Grand Canyon. It continued on to New Mexico (overflying Albuquerque), then across the northern panhandle of Texas and over Oklahoma, Arkansas, and Tennessee. The wind then shifted direction to the northeast and the balloon's course roughly paralleled the east coast. The flight path took it over West Virginia, Pennsylvania (overflying Pittsburgh), New York, then across the border into Canada and over the city of Montreal. The balloon finally came down after 75 hours 33 minutes, some 135 miles northeast of Quebec, near the St. Lawrence River.[53]

In August 1953, the two eastern bases, Sedalia AFB, Missouri, and Moody AFB, Georgia, were being prepared for launches.[54] Although comparatively few flights were made from these bases, they allowed year-round operations. (Due to the east-to-west summer jet stream, balloons from the three west coast bases would be carried out over the Pacific and could not be tracked.) The fall saw another development, one with long-term importance. On November 13, 1953, the 1110th Air Support Group was formally established, replacing the temporary 1300th Air Resupply and Communications Squadron. The 1110th Air Support Group would have responsibility for all Air Force balloon launches, both scientific and military. Its headquarters was at Lowry AFB with detachments at the launch sites.[55]

In 1953, 482 Moby Dick flights were made. As the balloons floated so high above the world, they attracted the attention of the multitudes below. One Moby Dick balloon floated over San Francisco during the parade welcoming Gen. James Van Fleet home from Korea, looking like a brilliant white sphere. As thousands watched, jet fighters vainly tried to reach it. A San Francisco newspaper, in reporting the true explanation, said the saucer had been "reduced literally into a lot of hot air." In another case, aircraft from Strategic Air Command bases in Texas were sent after a Moby Dick shining in the twilight sky. B-36 crews flying at 45,000 feet were unable to reach it, while jet interceptors stalled out at their maximum altitude with the "object" still high above them. The failure of these would-be Captain Ahabs no doubt encouraged the developers of the reconnaissance balloons.[56,57]

The three-day flight time was intended to prevent the balloons from drifting outside the continental U.S. Sometimes a Moby Dick balloon would be caught by the jet stream and travel long distances in a surprisingly short time. Among the 1953 flights, the record holder was a balloon launched from Edwards AFB which landed in the Atlantic Ocean 630 miles east of Miami, Florida, a total distance of 3,800 miles. This was surpassed in early 1954, when a balloon from NAS Vernalis came down 52.5 hours later in Badajoz, Spain—a distance of 5,700 miles. Another gondola was recovered from the Shetland Islands, Scotland. The longest duration flight was 92 hours.

At the end of its flight, the gondola was cut free from the balloon and parachuted to earth. This was not the end of Moby Dick's odyssey. It was important, both for the success of the project and to keep costs down, that the gondolas be found and returned. They could often be repaired for a fraction of the cost of a new one.[58] (A Moby Dick flight cost $1,500 of which $800 was for the balloon envelope.)[59]

To encourage their return, a $25 reward was offered and a label was attached to the gondola which instructed the finder to send it railway express collect. In the event the gondola came down in Mexico or eastern Canada, another label repeated the message in Spanish and French. Finally, to reassure anybody who remembered FUGO and was reluctant to handle a strange object in the woods, it stated in large letters: THIS EQUIPMENT IS *NOT* DANGEROUS.[60]

The homeward journeys of the Moby Dick gondolas were, in their own way, as remarkable as the balloons' flights in the stratosphere. One landed on the Hollywood Freeway in Los Angeles and drew a large crowd of spectators. As a general rule, however, they tended to land in the woods or other rugged areas. The recovery rate was about 40 to 50 percent (15 percent fell into the ocean and were lost). The number jumped during hunting season when sportsmen would come across the gondolas. One was found on the shore of James Bay, Canada. It was taken by canoe to Moosonee, Ontario. The finder later made a special trip to drop the gondola off at a railroad station. Another finder in Texas traveled 200 miles to an Air Force base to hand-deliver it. Another gondola was carried out of the Umatilla Forest in Oregon by pack horse. At the other end of the transport spectrum, a Coast Guard helicopter was used to make a recovery from a North Carolina swamp.

For self-sacrifice in returning a gondola, recognition must go to an Indian in Mexico. He found the gondola in a remote area, loaded it on his burro, and traveled 100 miles to Ciudad Juarez. Then, using a hired truck, he delivered the package to the U.S. Consulate. In the words of the Consul, "He arrived here penniless and it will be necessary for the Consulate to advance him funds for his return unless payment of the reward is received promptly." In the end, Moby Dick gondolas were found in forty of the forty-eight states, Canada, Mexico, and overseas.

By the spring of 1954, the Moby Dick program was winding down. The Tillamook, Edwards, and Moody bases were closed down. The remaining launches were conducted from Sedalia AFB and NAS Vernalis.[61,62] The formal end of the Moby Dick program came on June 30, 1954, with a final total of 640 balloons having been launched. The program provided a unique opportunity for research into the upper atmosphere and resulted in the best information to that date about wind currents. During the next two years, the raw data was used by the Air Force and scientists. In July 1956, ten volumes of Moby Dick weather data were published. In the area of technology, different types of balloons were tested for reliability and suitability. Methods of balloon fabrication and instrumentation were both improved. New inflation and launching procedures were developed. The administrative techniques of large-scale balloon operations had also been refined.

The picture also had a negative side: the data were not as complete as had originally been hoped. In some locations, such as the Rocky Mountains, it was very difficult to track the balloons. Thus, data for these areas were either fragmentary or nonexistent. As a general rule, data from later flights were better than from the earlier ones. Another shortcoming was the limited duration of the flights. Over 33 percent of the flights ended in less than ten hours. Only 14 percent lasted more than sixty hours. (Average duration was twenty hours.) Despite these problems, which are, perhaps, inevitable in a pioneering effort, Moby Dick was judged a success and served as the basis for subsequent high-altitude balloon research, including reconnaissance.[63]

The Overflight Program Continues

As the Gopher and Moby Dick balloons were being developed and flown, the overflight program approved by President Truman in the fall of 1950 was underway. One type of aircraft used was the Convair RB-36D Peacemaker. Driven by six pusher prop engines and four jets, it was slow, huge, and seemed an easy target for Soviet air defenses. Appearances were deceiving. The aircraft's 230-foot wings generated tremendous lift, which translated into altitude. To further improve their altitude capabilities, any unnecessary equipment, including all the guns except the tail turret's twin 20mm cannons, was removed. These modified aircraft, called "Featherweight" RB-36s, could reach altitudes in excess of 58,000 feet. This was above the ceiling of jet fighters. They could only reach these altitudes after a long slow climb which used up most of the jet's fuel supply. If the fighter should get close to the RB-36, the pilot got a rude surprise. The "lumbering" RB-36 could *outmaneuver* the jet fighter. This was because, for all its size, the RB-36 had a low wing loading (weight of aircraft per square feet of wing area). The fighter, in contrast, with its heavier wing loading was flying on the edge of controllability. Any sharp maneuvers would cause it to lose altitude or flame out. This meant the RB-36 had virtual immunity from interception. On overflights of China, for instance, MiGs were frequently seen or picked up on radar but were never able to engage. The RB-36 was well equipped for overflights of Russia and China. The forward bomb bay carried fourteen cameras, including one with a 48-inch focal length. Also fitted into the bomb bays were a 3,000-gallon fuel tank and ECM equipment. The aircraft, in addition to photographic intelligence, could gather ELINT data. Four operators monitored incoming radar and radio signals while over hostile territory. These capabilities made it a mainstay of the early years of the overflight program.[64,65]

Another type of aircraft used for early overflights was the North American RB-45C Tornado. A light jet bomber, it relied on speed rather than altitude. One RB-45 overflight took place on October 9, 1951. An RB-45 of the 91st Strategic Recon Wing took off at 10:30 A.M. from Yokota Air Base, Japan. The flight, designated Project 51, covered the southern end of Sakhalin Island. Flying at 18,000 feet, the crew photographed both the ground and the radar image of the targets. All the targets were covered and no flak or fighters challenged the penetration of Soviet airspace. The RB-45 landed back at Yokota at 2:40 P.M. after 4 hours 10 minutes in the air.[66]

RB-45s were also flying missions over Eastern Europe and western Russia. These aircraft were from the 19th Recon Squadron at Seulthorpe, Norfolk, in England. Originally, they were in normal U.S. Air Force markings. Soon after January 1952, they underwent a change. At least four were repainted with RAF markings and bogus serial numbers. The aircraft were reportedly flown by mixed crews (pilot and navigator, RAF; copilot and tail gunner, USAF).

The RB-45s would be refueled by a KB-29P tanker over Germany or Greece shortly before entering hostile airspace. A full fuel load allowed the aircraft to accelerate to maximum speed well before reaching the target area, thus minimizing the risk of interception. These "RAF" RB-45s were considered sensitive. Their existence was officially denied and two young aircraft spotters who photographed one had their film seized.[67]

Use of the RB-45s was apparently brief. Despite an all-jet design, it was less suited to the high-risk overflights than the RB-36s. The RB-45 was handicapped by outdated aerodynamics, specifically, straight wings. It was slower than the MiG-15 and fared badly over Korea. One shot-up RB-45 made it back to Japan on one engine. The RB-45s were subsequently restricted to flights over the relatively quiet eastern section of the peninsula.[68]

At about the time Moby Dick flights were underway, these aircraft were being replaced in the overflight program by the Boeing RB-47 Stratojet.[69] This was a six-jet medium bomber. Although a near contemporary of the RB-36 and RB-45, it used the advanced aerodynamics, particularly sweep wings, developed in Germany during the war. This made it a fundamentally new generation of aircraft design. The first reconnaissance version, the RB-47B, was delivered to the Strategic Air Command in 1953. It carried eight cameras in a heated capsule fitted into the bomb bay. The production reconnaissance version, the RB-47E, followed about a year later.[70,71] The RB-47 had nearly twice the speed of the RB-36, combined with a relatively good altitude capability.

The overflights were being directed at coastal areas and islands. A May 1954 memo summarized the activities during the early part of the year:

> Murmansk-Kola Inlet area—two missions completed with radar scope photography being obtained on the first mission and visual photography obtained on the second mission;

> Siberian area—four flights over Siberia including coverage of Wrangel Island and Vol; three of these flights obtained radar scope photography and the fourth obtained partial photographic coverage.[72]

The short-range overflights helped to clear up some of the unknowns about the state of the Soviet military. The Kola Inlet and Siberian coast, for instance, were the areas the Soviets would use should they launch long-range air attacks on the continental U.S.[73]

There were shortcomings, however. One was the overflights' dependence on the world political situation. During January 1951, shortly after the Chinese intervention in Korea, photographs of China's coastal areas and Manchuria were restricted.[74] In March 1952, the Air Force refused to overfly Franz Josef Land (an island north of the Soviet mainland) "due to international complications."[75] The fundamental problem was of coverage: the aircraft could only photograph coastal areas, port facilities, and islands. The sprawling interior of Russia and its many areas of interest were out of reach.

The risks of deep overflights were shown by an incident which occurred in July 1953. Western intelligence had known since the late 1940s about a Soviet missile test site at Kapustin Yar in the Ukraine near Stalingrad. The area was some 600 miles from the border, too far for one of the shallow overflights. Robert Amory, the CIA's deputy director of intelligence, felt it was important the site be covered. Philip Strong, one of Amory's aides and a retired Marine general, was able to persuade the British to try. They had a suitable aircraft, the English Electric Canberra. It was a twin engine light jet bomber with much better speed and altitude capability than the RB-45. The Canberra PR 3, the photo reconnaissance version, had become operational with the No. 541 Squadron in early 1953. On May 4, 1953, a modified Canberra B2 bomber with more powerful Bristol Olympus engines set a world altitude record of 63,668 feet.

The Canberra used for the overflight was stripped of unnecessary equipment and fitted with cameras and extra fuel tanks. The aircraft took off from West Germany and headed over southwest Russia at maximum altitude to Kapustin Yar. Over the site, it took "some fair pictures." The flight was in great danger—as Amory recalled later, "The whole of Russia had been alerted." Soviet air defenses made several hits on the Canberra, but it was able to reach the landing field in Iran. The British told the CIA: "Never, never, never again."

Despite the near failure of the mission, Amory and Strong were convinced the future of intelligence was extremely high-altitude aircraft.

Despite an Air Force belief such an aircraft would not be ready before the end of the decade, Strong flew out to California to see a friend, Clarence L. "Kelly" Johnson of Lockheed. Kelly suggested fitting an XF-104 with very long wings. A small seed had been planted.[76,77]

Gopher Development Continues

With completion of the gondola test flights in November 1952, it was time to take stock of Gopher's accomplishments and shortcomings. On the positive side, the Gopher test flights had met the program's basic objective: to develop and demonstrate a balloon able to carry a useful reconnaissance payload for a prolonged period.[78]

Yet Gopher was not yet ready for Russian skies. There were still major development efforts needed on the balloon, the gondola, and the launch and recovery systems. More importantly, the frustrations of the project, the failed flights, problems with General Mills, lost gondolas and the near-crash of the C-119 had reduced morale among the development personnel. As Paul Worthman would later say, "[WADC] technicians considered the project a disaster. . . . No one had much stomach for carrying the work any farther."[79]

In January 1953, responsibility for both Moby Dick (then beginning operational flights) and Gopher was transferred to the newly organized Atmospheric Devices Laboratory. With the transfer came a number of assessments of Gopher. So far, $1.8 million had been spent and it was time to decide whether to press on to production. Gopher remained the only means of deep reconnaissance, both photo and ELINT, of the Soviet Union that was available within the immediate time period and would be politically acceptable. In its assessment, the RAND Corporation stated:

> It should be emphasized that although no complete balloon reconnaissance system has ever functioned in its entirety, every component of the system has now been investigated to some extent by actual field tests. The conclusions arrived at in this report may be somewhat in error due to lack of quantitative data on which to base them, but it can now be said with certainty that *no single component is unproven*. . . . It is generally felt that the operation could be conducted using present equipment, but a major program would have to be undertaken to coordinate and combine the various components of the research and development phase into a complete system. Such a program, if undertaken energetically, should result in an operational capability in about a year.

This later step would involve finding the most desirable camera and instrumentation systems and incorporating them into the production prototype models. The launch, tracking, and recovery techniques would be finalized and production could then begin. This step would cost more than the early feasibility tests. Up to February 28, 1953, $1.8 million had been spent on Gopher. Based on this, a rough estimate of $2.5 to $3 million would be needed for final development.[80]

At this point, two major factors entered the picture. One was the "campaign" costs. In early 1953, the Air Force envisioned a relatively modest effort, once Gopher was ready. About 100 to 150 balloons would be launched over a 45-day period. Operations would then halt. The assumption behind this was that once the balloons began overflying Russia, the secret would be out. A short period would limit the Soviet's ability to make propaganda over the balloons.[81] RAND suggested a different plan: large-scale launches able to photograph between 85 and 90 percent of the Soviet land mass. This degree of coverage, however, carried a large price tag: 85 percent coverage would cost $31 million while 90 percent coverage would run $51 million. (As the number of balloons and the degree of coverage was increased, so too was the probability that later launches would duplicate the ground tracks of earlier flights.) Given the budgetary limitations the Air Force faced, it was not clear that sufficient money and resources would be made available to conduct the "campaign."

A more significant problem was political: would the Joint Chiefs of Staff, the State Department, and most importantly, the new president, Dwight Eisenhower, agree to conduct such an operation? It was entirely possible that Gopher could be successfully developed and the money provided for the campaign, yet never be allowed to overfly Russia. The reason for this belief was the easing of Cold War tensions following the death of Stalin in March 1953.[82] The new Soviet leadership—Georgy Malenkov, Klim Voroshilov, and Nikita Khrushchev—began slowly to remove the psychological and cultural chains Stalin had held Russia in for almost thirty years. In time, this period would be known as "The Thaw." Internationally, Russia began to move away from the rigid frozen hostility of the postwar years. The chances for accommodation had not seemed so bright since the end of World War II.[83,84]

Yet, amid this brightening landscape, there were dark clouds. The Soviet Union remained a dictatorship, ideologically hostile to the West. Its military power was growing. The Soviets had made two more atomic bomb tests in 1951, and were preparing to explode their first hydrogen bomb. To carry their slowly expanding stockpile of atomic bombs, the Soviets had several hundred TU-4s (copies of the B-29). On the horizon were more ominous threats. The Mya-4 jet bomber, equivalent to the U.S. B-52, would soon begin flight testing. The TU-95 propjet bomber was also under development. Work was continuing on ballistic missiles. In the end, the urgent need for coverage of the Russian interior outweighed the questions of cost and political approval.

On June 11, 1953, Brig. Gen. John B. Ackerman of the USAF Directorate of Intelligence requested the Air Force seek Joint Chiefs of Staff approval for the project and that the Secretaries of Defense and State be requested to approve a Gopher campaign. This would allow development to go forward. He also requested a realistic date be set for flight testing of the complete Gopher system. It was believed Hawaii or Japan would be used as the launch site.[85]

Reflecting the shift to full-scale development, the project's code name was changed in late June. The reconnaissance balloon program was now called Grandson.

On July 3, 1953, a meeting was held to decide the future of the project. It was felt that no monetary value could be placed on the photos that Grandson could provide. Further, the RAND estimate of $31 to $51 million would be a small price since there was virtually no risk and manpower requirements were low.[86] It was therefore decided to go full speed for development and to begin planning for a four-month-long campaign, to begin on November 1, 1955. (The timing was set by the winter jet stream.) The campaign was along the lines of the RAND study with some 3,000 balloons to be launched. It was also decided that the approval of the Secretaries of State and Defense be sought at an early date.

As a first step, the Directorate of Plans prepared an outline of the Grandson plans for Air Force Chief of Staff Gen. Nathan Twining. On September 11, he informally submitted it to the other Joint Chiefs of Staff. Grandson was approved in principal by the Joint Chiefs, but was returned to the Air Force with the recommendation that it did not require formal JCS approval. Rather, it should be submitted through the normal channels for political approval. On September 23, General Twining sent an Air Staff Summary Sheet to the Secretary of the Air Force, along with a memo to Secretary of Defense Charles Wilson, requesting he seek approval from the other government departments. As late as December 1953, no response had been given to General Twining.[87,88]

Despite this lack of high-level response, the effort continued. In mid-September 1953, the Cambridge Research Laboratory had prepared a development plan for the Air Force. It had a completion date of July 1955, for all development phases. After this, the move to the Western Europe launch sites could begin. By the start of January 1954, the effort was well underway. Operations were being conducted by the Directorate of Operations and Headquarters Command, with good progress being made. It is worth remembering that the launch crews, tracking stations, and recovery aircraft were scattered halfway around the world and would require hundreds of tons of equipment (3,000 balloons and gondolas, film, forty tank cars of steel shot, fuel, spare parts, and the other components of a technological project). One problem that appeared was in flight testing. Originally planned for March–May 1954, by January this had slipped by perhaps two months. Despite this, the target date of July 1955 for the completion of development work was still felt to be valid.[89]

The Grandson test flights were completed by August 1954, and production of the hardware could begin.[90] By October, Air Force Headquarters had set the basic military characteristics of the balloons. The campaign was intended to provide almost complete pioneer photographic coverage of the Soviet "target system." The highest priority was for information on the Soviet Union's ability to attack the continental U.S. and its allies. The secondary goal was for data on Soviet air defenses. The breakdown of targets was as follows: (1) bomber bases, fighter airfields and missile launching sites, especially those with stockpiles of nuclear weapons; (2) military installations indicating Soviet intentions; (3) industry, transport, and economic development with specific detail to show both current status and potential growth; (4) antiaircraft artillery and radar sites.[91]

Although the balloons would float on random wind currents and so could not be directed at specific targets, it was felt the extended duration and coverage of the campaign would provide the needed information.[92] One indication of how badly this information was needed: the reconnaissance balloon had the highest national priority of 1-A. The only other project to share this priority was the hydrogen bomb. Knowledge is power.

The primary mission was and remained photo reconnaissance. A separate ELINT was also being developed. Interest in a "Ferret Gopher" revived in March 1953, during the review of the balloon reconnaissance project. It was noted the U.S. had adequate knowledge of Soviet radars only within fifty miles of the border. Beyond this, little was known about types and development of radars.[93] One possible reason for this interest was the high loss rate of ELINT aircraft: from April 1950 to the end of March 1953, one Air Force, two Navy, one RAF, and one Swedish AF ELINT aircraft had been shot down. Three more were destroyed by November 1954. The aircraft were converted transports or bombers, frequently unarmed, flying slowly off the coast, which made easy targets. By July 1953, the situation had become so dangerous that ELINT aircraft were restricted to night missions. The only exception was an RB-29 used to monitor Soviet radio communications (such messages were more frequent in daytime). It, however, was restricted to no closer than fifty miles from the coast.[94]

The balloon itself would have the following characteristics:

1. Total load of between 1,500 and 2,000 pounds; of this, 450 pounds would be payload.

2. Capable of being launched in moderate weather conditions: light rain, haze, snow, freezing temperatures, and winds up to 15 knots, both day and night.

3. Gondola systems able to operate for a minimum of ten days at a temperature of -94°F. The balloon was to be strong enough to withstand wind gusts up to 100 knots at this temperature.

4. The camera system would have a navigation system to show both the orientation of the photos and their location.

5. The balloon would float at a minimum altitude of 57,000 feet during daylight hours and no lower than 45,000 feet at night.

6. Once the balloon was clear of Communist airspace, on-board radio would signal its location to ground stations up to 1,500 miles away upon demand. The C-119 recovery aircraft could pick up the signals 100 miles away, also on demand. Once the aircraft closed to 20 miles, it could transmit a cut-down signal.

Considerable study was made of the balloon's vulnerability to Soviet air defenses. Detecting the balloons was the first problem. Winter cloud cover would prevent visual sightings 50 to 85 percent of the time, even if a large number of ground observers were mobilized. (Of course, if the balloon was hidden from the ground, the ground was also hidden from the balloon's cameras.) On clear days, the balloon could be spotted and tracked visually. Radar could "see" through clouds, but U.S. experience indicated the balloons were difficult targets. During the test balloon flights, tracking attempts met with limited success only, at short ranges after the balloons had been located. The reason was the balloon's altitude carried them above the radar's antenna pattern. To reduce the chances of being picked up, the system was to be designed for minimum radar return and be electronically silent in hostile airspace. (The term "stealth" was still a quarter century in the future.)

Should the Soviets detect and start tracking a balloon, its only defense was altitude—it would have to ride above trouble. To maximize this, hydrogen was used, rather than nonburning helium.[95] This meant, however, if hit by an incendiary round, the reconnaissance balloon would burn like its forbears of the Western Front. In the final analysis, this did not matter. The smallest puncture would allow the lifting gas to leak out and bring down the balloon. A hit was as good as a kill.

U.S. Balloon Bomber

Paralleling the Grandson reconnaissance project was the effort to build a balloon weapons system. The idea was that the equipment developed for Grandson would be interchangeable, or at least compatible, with the weapons system balloons. A number of payloads were envisioned, such as leaflets, counterfeit money, or ration coupons for psychological warfare. The goal was to undermine morale, the economy, or food distribution to impede the Soviet war effort. For thirty target cities, forty-five tons of leaflets aboard 300 balloons would be needed. Another payload was ECM jammers to protect U.S. bombing raids. To blank out the Soviet radar network, a large number of balloons would be needed.[96]

One payload was out of the past. Incendiary bombs could be carried to set fire to enemy forests. The circle that began with Outward and FUGO had come around.

Another possibility was far more lethal: chemical or biological weapons.[97] The first included poisons like nerve gas or herbicides. Biological weapons included anthrax spores, bacteria such as undulant fever, or viruses like smallpox and yellow fever. Biological attacks on crops and livestock would use wheat and potato blight, foot and mouth disease, or hog cholera.

Both chemical and biological weapons were carried in cluster bombs. The cluster bomb releases a mass of small bomblets at a preset altitude. On impact, the bomblets explode, releasing a cloud which drifts on the wind. An area comparable in size to that affected by a low-yield nuclear weapon can be contaminated. The alternate method of dispersing biological weapons was use of insects or small animals (yellow fever is spread by mosquitoes, for instance).[98]

The Grandson reconnaissance balloon was meant for use in a cold-war environment. In contrast, the balloon weapons system would be used only in the event of a general war between the U.S. and Russia.

Initial testing of the balloon weapons system began in early 1953. (A December 1952 memo refers to a planned starting date of January 15, 1953.) These early flights were to test the feasibility of several innovations, specifically, a balloon of a radically new design and use of ammonia as a lifting gas.[99] (The latter did not work out.) In March 1953, the Air Research and Development Command began full-scale development which was to be completed in two years or less. The project was given the designation WS-124A and the code name Flying Cloud.

The WS-124A system was designed for a flight duration of 60 hours and a range of 1500 nautical miles. It could maintain a constant altitude and used hydrogen as a lifting gas. Because it was a combat system, the balloons were designed to be launched in much worse weather conditions than Grandson (winds of 30 knots with gusts up to 45 knots).[100] A target might have to be attacked within a narrow time period; a weather delay could upset this.

A WS-124A attack would involve launches from one or more sites. Because of the nature of the payloads, these would be relatively close to the front lines to prevent a malfunctioning balloon from landing on friendly troops. The timing and location of the launchings would be based on forecasts of upper air currents. The balloons would float at 38,600 feet for one or two days. The payload would be released, apparently by a timer, when the forecast indicated the balloon would be over the target area. Free of the weight of the payload, the balloon would rise, burst, and fall to the ground. Clearly, the accuracy of the weather forecast was critical. It had to be reliable enough so that a sufficient number of the balloons, unguided except by the wind, would reach the target area at the predicted time in order to do significant military damage. WS-124A also had the seasonal restriction that flights would be made in the spring (presumably, because growing crops would be most vulnerable to biological attack at this time).

By the fall of 1954, work had reached the point that testing of the complete WS-124A system could begin. The test plan was an ambitious one, meant to both prove out the system and simulate its use in combat.

The launches would be made from NAS Vernalis, California. The trajectory of the balloons was calculated using limited weather data. It was presumed that under wartime conditions, no weather information would be available from inside Russia or Soviet-occupied territory. To simulate this "silent area," weather information was used only from western California, southern Nevada and Texas, western Canada, Alaska, Mexico, and ships at sea. From this, the balloon's trajectory would be estimated. The target line was 90° W longitude (a line from Michigan through Mississippi). Where the balloon's estimated flight path crossed 90° W was the center of the target area. This was a rectangle 360 by 480 nautical miles. After launch, the WS-124A balloons would be tracked through an on-board radio beacon. The balloon's actual location, at the time it was predicted to be at the center of the target area, indicated the accuracy of the system. (The accuracy of the system and the accuracy of the forecast were synonymous.) The average distance between NAS Vernalis and the target area was 1,566 nautical miles. In the tests, nothing was dropped from the balloons.

The first flight, F-1, was made on October 8, 1954. F-2, launched the next day, had a projected impact point only 228 nautical miles west and 260 nautical miles south of the aim point (i.e., 80 nautical miles from the southwest corner of the target area). The next flight, F-3, was less encouraging. Launched on October 11, its projected impact point was 900 nautical miles from the aim point. Predicting the trajectory was made difficult by frequent periods of "stagnation" in the upper air wind currents. F-7, F-26, and F-27, in particular, went wide of the mark owing to this.

As the launches continued into the fall, not all were accuracy tests; some involved special equipment, launching tests, or short duration flights. Several of the balloons also failed.

By the end of November, the upper air currents stabilized. The first "hit" was F-28, launched on November 30; it had a projected impact point on the target area's eastern edge. Five more hits were made in the next two weeks. These were F-31, F-32, F-33, F-37, and XF-41, the program's final flight, on December 13, 1954. Of the forty-one flights, twenty-five were usable to determine system/forecast accuracy. (The other sixteen were equipment tests or failures.) In addition to the six hits, five more balloons: F-2, F-9, F-22, F-30, and F-34, had projected impact points within 150 nautical miles of the target area's boundaries. F-35 was within 200 nautical miles. Although, strictly speaking, these were misses, it was argued their proximity to the target would contribute to the success of the attack. The final estimate was that the WS-124A system had a minimum 24 percent probability of hitting the target area. It was also believed that this figure could be raised to about 40 percent with operational experience and slight improvements in weather forecasting.

The final report on the project was sent to the Air Force's Air Weather Service, which objected to several of its conclusions. The Weather Service questioned the belief that the October–December period was representative of spring conditions. This period was the transition from summer to winter weather patterns. The improved accuracy in the late fall was due to the improved, more predictable, weather patterns, not their operational experience. It also suggested the same would occur in reverse during spring (better accuracy during the early spring which would then deteriorate as the winter wind currents broke up). Another reason was the close spacing of the latter flights: twelve launches in two weeks. There were many flights on consecutive days. The fixes from these balloons would be of great help in preparing forecasts for those to follow. (In contrast, the first thirteen balloons were launched over two months.)

The final objection was statistical. The use of a select portion (twelve flights) of a limited sample (twenty-five flights) was not seen as valid. They also objected to including flight XF-41 in the sample. It was launched to test a special piece of equipment. Accordingly, all available weather data was used, rather than the "silent area" forecast which would have placed it 2° east of the target area.

The Air Weather Service refused to endorse WS-124A's feasibility and asked that consideration be given to a reevaluation of the test results. The report on its objections was completed in August 1955. With this, WS-124A faded from the scene and with it, a history going back through FUGO and Outward to the siege of Venice.[101]

The failure of WS-124A should also be seen against the changing background of U.S. nuclear strategy. In the early postwar years, the atomic bomb did not play a big role in planning. There were simply too few of them. Moscow and Leningrad could be destroyed, but it was impossible to, say, knock out Soviet oil production capability. By 1952, when Gopher and the balloon weapons program were underway, the Soviets had broken the U.S. atomic monopoly. With a Soviet stockpile only a matter of time, the strategy changed. It was now felt World War III would start with a nuclear exchange, lasting a relatively brief period but causing great damage. After this, hostilities would continue at a reduced level as both sides attempted to recover and carry on the struggle as best they could.[102]

In either of these two scenarios, a repeat of World War II or the "broken back" phase after the initial exchange, WS-124A could have played a valuable role.

By the time the Flying Cloud test flights were underway, this changed. Both the U.S. and Russia had tested hydrogen bombs. These weapons had yields of ten of millions of tons of TNT. This was a thousand times greater than the early atomic bombs. With this increase in explosive power came the belief these weapons would not only destroy an enemy's military power, but even its ability to function as a society. In a matter of days, military operations would stop, both the U.S. and Russia having been destroyed.

In this vision of a thermonuclear spasm, WS-124A was meaningless. No message its leaflets could carry would equal the effect on the Soviet will to fight of having every major city obliterated. The area its chemical and biological weapons could contaminate was small compared to that affected by the fallout from over 1,000 U.S. nuclear weapons.

Open Skies

Just as the start of the Korean War marked a major shift in U.S./U.S.S.R. relations, the death of Stalin heralded another. The new Soviet leadership was quick to make a number of conciliatory gestures. At the end of March 1953, an exchange of sick and wounded POWs was arranged, and in July, a truce was signed, ending the Korean War. Other gestures included talks with the British on air safety in the Berlin flight corridors and a visit by U.S. newspaper editors to the Soviet Union which signaled an expansion of cultural and political contacts. By late 1954, there was increased public support in Western Europe for a summit meeting. Opinion in the U.S. was also becoming favorable to such a meeting—Senator Joe McCarthy had faded from the political landscape and bitterness over the "betrayal at Yalta" was easing.

In the spring of 1955, these gestures took concrete form when the Soviets agreed to the Austrian peace treaty which required the Soviets to remove their occupying forces. It also made a summit meeting inevitable. President Dwight D. Eisenhower instructed Secretary of State John Foster Dulles to let it be known the U.S. would consider such a meeting. At a NATO meeting in Paris on May 6, Britain, France and

Germany agreed to extend an invitation to the Soviets. This was sent to Moscow on May 10 and discussed with Molotov a few days later at the signing of the Austrian State Treaty. By June 13, a formal agreement was reached. Dulles proposed a five-day meeting at Geneva, Switzerland, where the leaders would only define the critical world problems and then order their foreign ministers to conduct negotiations. One of President Eisenhower's aides disagreed. Nelson Rockefeller felt this was too limited and had something much more ambitious in mind.

In May, when it became clear a summit was likely, Rockefeller and his staff organized a group of eleven men. They would take stock of the U.S. position in the world and recommend courses of action for the president at the summit. They met at the Quantico Marine Corps base between June 5 and 10, 1955. Quickly, several points emerged. One was based on a detailed intelligence briefing on the relative technical and military capabilities of the U.S. and Russia. It showed the U.S. lead was narrowing. In particular, it noted a remarkable growth in the number of Soviet scientists and engineers in the postwar years. From this came the belief that the summit should be used to test Soviet intentions. This would be done by giving the Soviets a range of proposals, from cultural exchanges, through disarmament, and the unification of Germany. If they showed a willingness to tackle the "hard" proposals, then the Soviets intent to ease the Cold War was genuine. But if agreement was reached only on the "easy" ones, then it was just talk. In this case, the U.S. would have to face up to the need for an increased defense budget and a more energetic foreign policy.

On June 7, Max Millikan, of the MIT Center for International Studies, proposed a plan for mutual aerial inspection. It was quickly included in the list of proposals. One member, Hans Speier of RAND, was distressed by the idea and took Stefan Possony, an air intelligence specialist with the Air Force, and the Group chairman, W. W. Rostow of MIT, aside. He warned them the idea was dangerous, implying the U.S. might be making plans for unilateral reconnaissance of Russia. (It will be remembered RAND did several studies on Gopher/Grandson.) Possony and Rostow disagreed but included a footnote to the effect the Department of Defense would want to examine this idea.

After the report was completed, it became a pawn in the relationship between Rockefeller and Dulles. "Special assistants" like Rockefeller brought back painful memories of how Dulles's uncle, Secretary of State Robert Lansing, had been bypassed by President Woodrow Wilson. There were also deep fears of what could go wrong at Geneva. Dulles noted in a private conversation that despite Eisenhower's knowledge of foreign affairs, his inclination "to be humanly generous, to accept a superficial tactical smile as evidence of inner warmth" might cause him to accept some Soviet proposals without thinking out the consequences. This could lead to Dulles's having either to go along with a foreign policy akin to appeasement, or to be forced to act in a way that would end his usefulness as Secretary of State: thus, Dulles's insistence the president's role be limited to generating a spirit where later negotiation could make progress.

Rockefeller disagreed, noting the Soviets, French, and British would all be making proposals. To have Eisenhower come all the way to Geneva just to identify the problems and give them to the foreign ministers to solve, would be a disaster; the world was looking to him for leadership.

Athough Eisenhower formally agreed with Dulles, he hedged his bets by having Rockefeller and several others go to Paris during the summit to be ready if needed. At the least, he wanted the proposal as a contingency. It is possible he had already decided to put the idea forward.

The Geneva summit began on July 18, 1955. British Prime Minister Anthony Eden, French Premier Edgar Faure, and Soviet Premier Nikolai A. Bulganin made up the rest of the "Big Four." In his opening statement, Eisenhower gave a veiled preview of what was to follow:

> Surprise attack has a capacity for destruction far beyond anything which man had yet known. . . . Perhaps therefore, we should consider whether the problem of limitation of armament may not best be approached by seeking—as a first step—dependable ways to supervise and inspect military establishments, so that there can be no frightful surprises, whether by sudden attack or by secret violation of agreed restrictions.

In Paris, Rockefeller was briefing the others in his party on the inspection proposal. He was able to convince Chief of Staff Adm. Arthur W. Radford. Admiral Radford then briefed Alfred Gruenther, the commanding general of allied forces of NATO.

On the afternoon of July 19, Rockefeller and Harold Stassen were ordered to fly to Geneva to brief the president the next day. When they met on the morning of July 20, President Eisenhower told them he had discussed the initial aerial inspection plan with Anthony Eden at breakfast that morning. Eden was enthusiastic and wanted to discuss the idea. Accordingly, Radford and Gruenther flew to Geneva.

At 6:00 P.M. that evening, Eisenhower, Dulles, and the others met in the library of the Chateau de Creux de Genthod where they had been staying. The scheduled topic for the next day's discussion was disarmament. The question before them was whether Eisenhower would simply stress the central role of inspection and then refer the issue for later negotiation or place the aerial inspection proposal before the other leaders. Dulles and Stassen were reluctant but the president's support, along with the senior military officials' support, carried the day, Dulles noting it would be "drama and substance" and have "very great effect." He also stressed the need for surprise to have maximum impact. The meeting closed with an agreement on tactics: there would be an opening statement followed by the mutual overflight proposal put forward as a more or less spontaneous suggestion.

The next afternoon, Eisenhower began reading the prepared text. About two-thirds of the way through, he sprang his little surprise:

> Gentlemen, since I have been working on this memorandum to present to this conference, I have been searching my heart and mind for something that I could say here that could convince everyone of the great sincerity of the United States in approaching this problem of disarmament.
>
> I should address myself for a moment principally to the delegates from the Soviet Union, because our two great countries admittedly possess new and terrible weapons in quantities which do give rise in other parts of the world, or reciprocally, to the fears and dangers of surprise attack.
>
> I propose, therefore, that we take a practical step, that we begin an arrangement, very quickly, as between ourselves—immediately. These steps would include:
>
> To give to each other a complete blueprint of our military establishments, from beginning to end, from one end of our countries to the other; lay out the establishments and provide the blueprints to each other.
>
> Next, to provide within our countries facilities for aerial photography to the other country—we to provide you the facilities within our country, ample facilities for aerial reconnaissance, where you can make all the pictures you choose and take them to your own country to study; you to provide exactly the same facilities for us and we to make these examinations, and by this step to convince the world that we are providing as between ourselves against the possibility of great surprise attack, thus lessening danger and relaxing tensions.
>
> Likewise we will make more easily attainable a comprehensive and effective system of inspection and disarmament, because what I propose, I assure you, would be but a beginning.

As he finished speaking, there was a crash of thunder outside and all the lights went out. It was a stunning counterpoint to the drama that had just taken place. Once the lights came back on, the British and French leaders both approved the plan. Bulganin spoke last; his tone seemed agreeable. He said it seemed to have real merit and the Soviets would give it complete and sympathetic study.

With this, the session adjourned and the delegations headed for the cocktail lounge. Eisenhower was walking with Nikita Khrushchev when he said, "I don't agree with the chairman." Khrushchev was smiling when he said it, but there was no smile in his voice. Eisenhower realized at that moment who the real leader of Russia was. From that moment, Eisenhower forgot about Bulganin and, instead, concentrated on convincing Khrushchev of its merits. The effort was in vain. Khrushchev called it an espionage plot against Russia. Eisenhower argued that, in view of Russia's professed peaceful intent and its accusations that NATO was planning an attack, it would be in their interest to agree. Russia could keep watch on NATO's every move. All the West asked was reciprocal rights. Khrushchev's refusal was made laughingly, but was unbending. In his memoirs, Eisenhower remarked, "His protests were, of course, spurious. Khrushchev's own purpose was evident—at all costs to keep the USSR a closed society."

U.S. and Western European reaction to the "Open Skies" proposal was uniformly favorable. Senate majority leader Lyndon B. Johnson (D-Tex) spoke for many when he called it "the daring, imaginative stroke for which a war-weary world has been waiting."

Eisenhower knew the only reaction that mattered was that of the Soviet leadership. On August 4, Bulganin addressed the Supreme Soviet, rejecting Open Skies. This was followed on August 18 by a letter. It brought up three points: The U.S. and U.S.S.R. were too vast for aerial inspection to be effective, the plan did not provide for aerial inspection of troops and bases outside the two countries, and it did not include provisions for arms reductions. In effect, Bulganin rejected the central basis of Eisenhower's proposal: for arms control to be effective, there first would have to be proven verification procedures to back it up.

The U.S. kept trying. At the U.N. Disarmament Commission, which met from August 29 to October 7, 1955, Stassen presented a detailed version of Open Skies. The subject was also brought up at the foreign ministers meeting in Geneva, which was held from October 27 to November 16. Molotov bluntly rejected it.

The correct but sterile exchanges continued into the new year. On one occasion, Bulganin made the following statement:

> It seems to us that in the present international situation and, moreover, under conditions of a completely unrestricted armaments race, the carrying out of such flights would not only fail to free the peoples from the fear of a new war, but on the contrary would intensify that fear and mutual suspicion. Judge for yourself, Mr. President: what would the military leaders of your country do if it were reported to them that the aerophotography showed that your neighbor had more airfields? To be sure, they would order an immediate increase in the number of their own airfields. Naturally, our military leaders would do the same in a similar case. It is not difficult to understand that the result would be a further intensification of the armaments race.

In effect, "ignorance is bliss." At the same time, the Soviets had a complete understanding of Western military strength through reading the public press. To accept Open Skies meant giving away this relative advantage. It meant also losing the power to intimidate through fear of the unknown.[103]

The Soviets' unwillingness to deal seriously with Open Skies must have been very frustrating for Eisenhower. He really believed Open Skies was a potential stabilizing device for the nuclear age and one which might open the way for arms control.

What cannot be done the easy way can still be done the hard way. In Western Europe, Japan, Alaska and the Pacific, the hosts were gathering. High above, the winter jet stream once more followed its regular path. The great white whale was ready.

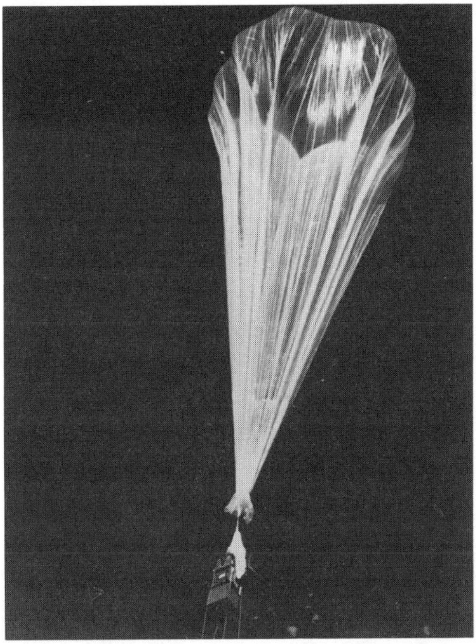

An Air Force Skyhook balloon launched from Holloman AFB, 5 February 1954. Photo shows the translucent nature of the plastic balloon. Although clear, it could reflect light like a mirror. This particular launch was a parachute test. *U.S. Air Force photo.*

Launch of a Skyhook balloon from a "covered wagon." This device, originally developed for the Moby Dick weather balloon program, allowed launches at higher wind speeds than possible for an open-air inflation. (The thin plastic of the Skyhook balloon was extremely vulnerable to damage from wind gusts.) The balloon was inflated inside the covered wagon. At the proper moment, the canvas cover was released and the balloon billowed out. *U.S. Air Force photo.*

A Skyhook balloon soon after launch, 3 September 1952. It used a configuration similar to a Gopher test balloon, specifically, a small tow balloon *(at left)* to help support the load. As the balloon climbed, the gas bubble expanded, filling the lower part of the balloon, forming a sphere. *U.S. Navy photo.*

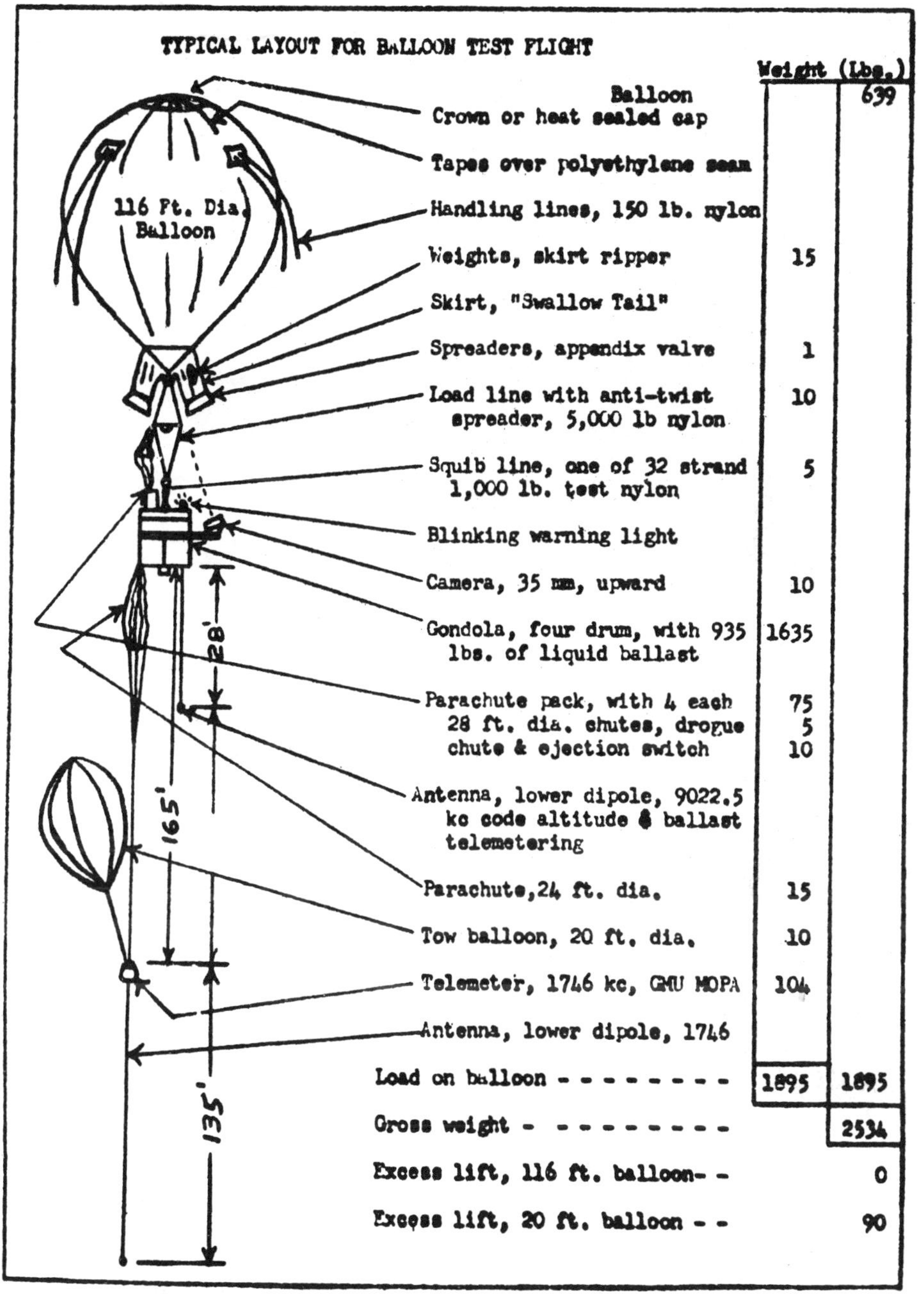

Drawing of a Gopher test balloon. The Gopher flights tested the basic technology for the reconnaissance balloons: improved balloons, a rotating gondola, and midair cutdown by an aircraft. Although there were problems, specifically camera failures and lost gondolas, the test flights indicated the basic feasibility of reconnaissance balloons. *U.S. Air Force drawing.*

The B/U section of the instrumentation section, 1110th ASG, Incirlik AB, Turkey. *Back row, left to right,* M/Sgt. Elvin Geigum, A/1C William Thorne, A/1C David Douglas, S/Sgt. Ben Dillahay, A/2C James Pulliam, and 2d Lt. Lloyd Mitchell. *Front row,* A/1C Richard Candy, T/Sgt. Robert Burch, M/Sgt. Preston Culpepper, Marty Staub (Kodak Technical Representative), and A/2C Joseph Godlewski. *Photo courtesy of Robert Burch.*

George Mathews in the Navy exposure suit. This was called a "poopie suit," because as Mathews noted, "After you had worn it for a 12-hour flight you smelled like 'poopie'." Despite the discomfort, the suit was essential to stay alive in the cold Arctic water should the C-119 go down. *Photo courtesy of George Mathews.*

In quarters at Kodiak. *Left,* Jim Kittock (pilot), *right,* Ron Pinette (navigator). Pinette is wearing the thermal underwear worn under the "poopie suit." *Photo courtesy of George Mathews.*

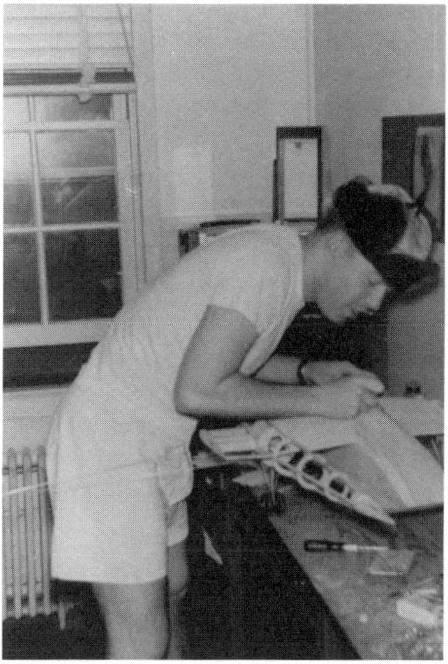

Larry Lant working on a control line C-119 flying model. It has been fitted with a "beaver tail." *Photo courtesy of George Mathews.*

Preparations for the first flight of Larry Lant's model C-119. *Photo courtesy of George Mathews.*

WS-119L balloon being inflated before launch. Rather than using the covered wagon as on Moby Dick, the WS-119L balloon was held in place by a roller, allowing only the inflated portion to lift off the ground. At the moment of launch, a truck (the Fisher Launcher) holding the WS-119L payload was driven toward the ascending balloon so as to be directly below it when the payload was released, the roller was released, and the balloon swung vertically and lifted off. In the background can be seen the hydrogen gas supply. *Photo courtesy of Robert Burch.*

View of the launch preparations. In the center is the Fisher Launcher with a balloon extending to the left. At the right is a fire truck (hydrogen is highly flammable) and behind it is an ambulance. Visible behind the hood of the fire truck is the crane holding an assembled WS-119L payload. *Photo courtersy of Robert Burch.*

Soviet drawing of the WS-119L payload. *Left to right,* ballast box, control box, camera gondola, and ballast box. The two ballast boxes held the fine steel shot. This was released under automatic control to compensate for cooling or loss of hydrogen gas. The control box carried the radio that transmitted the homing signal which allowed the balloon's position to be determined. The camera gondola was a large polystyrene-covered box. This material protected it from the cold of high altitude and kept it afloat if the gondola came down at sea. The camera had two 6-inch lenses and was turned on and off by a photo cell. To allow panoramic coverage, the payload was slowly rotated. The long rodlike object on the gondola is the ocean/ground recovery pole. It was planned that once the gondola was cut free and landed, the pole would extend and allow a pickup by the C-119 recovery aircraft. Owing to failures and the injury of a "Friendly National," the pole was disarmed. *Photo courtesy of R. W. Koch.*

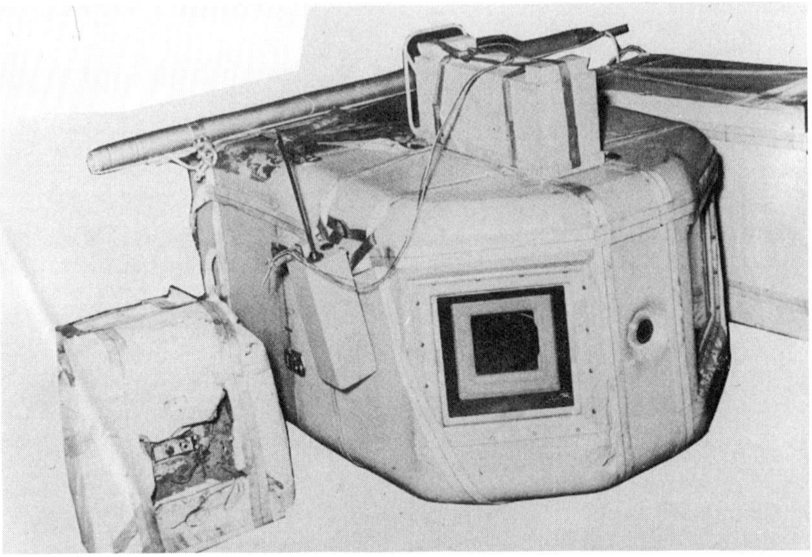

One that did not get through: a Genetrix payload brought down over Czechoslovakia. This view shows a ballast box with magnetic valve, and the camera gondola with ocean/ground recovery pole *(back)*, radio beacon *(side)*, and battery pack *(top)*. The two camera windows and photo cell which turned the camera on and off can be seen in the front of the camera gondola. In the backgound is the control box. The recovery pole greatly increased the radar echo of the balloon. The Genetrix pioneered much of the technology later used on the Discoverer photo reconnaissance satellite. *Photo courtesy of R. W. Koch.*

A MiG-15 in Communist Chinese markings. The MiG-15, along with the similar MiG-17, constituted the day fighter forces of Russia, the Warsaw Pact countries, and Communist China. At 55,000 feet, the Genetrix balloons were just above the MiG maximum ceiling. Owing to a number of factors, however, the balloons spent only a relatively brief time at this altitude. During the afternoon, they descended to lower altitudes, which put them in easy reach of the MiGs. *Photo courtesy of Corwin Crowell.*

A recovered gondola is returned to Johnson AB, Japan, by helicopter. *Top left,* the Sikorsky H-19 helicopter coming in for a landing, the gondola suspended on a cable. *Bottom left,* the helicopter has landed with the gondola lying on its side. *Top right,* round object on top of gondola is parachute attachment point. *Bottom right,* side view of gondola. As can be seen, the gondola is in two parts: the lower section holds the camera and the gondola's inner framework; the upper shell slides over the framework and is attached with latches. The object sticking upright is the ocean/ground recovery pole. The helicopter crewman is holding the hook the C-119 would try to snag. *Photos courtesy of Paul Lovrencic.*

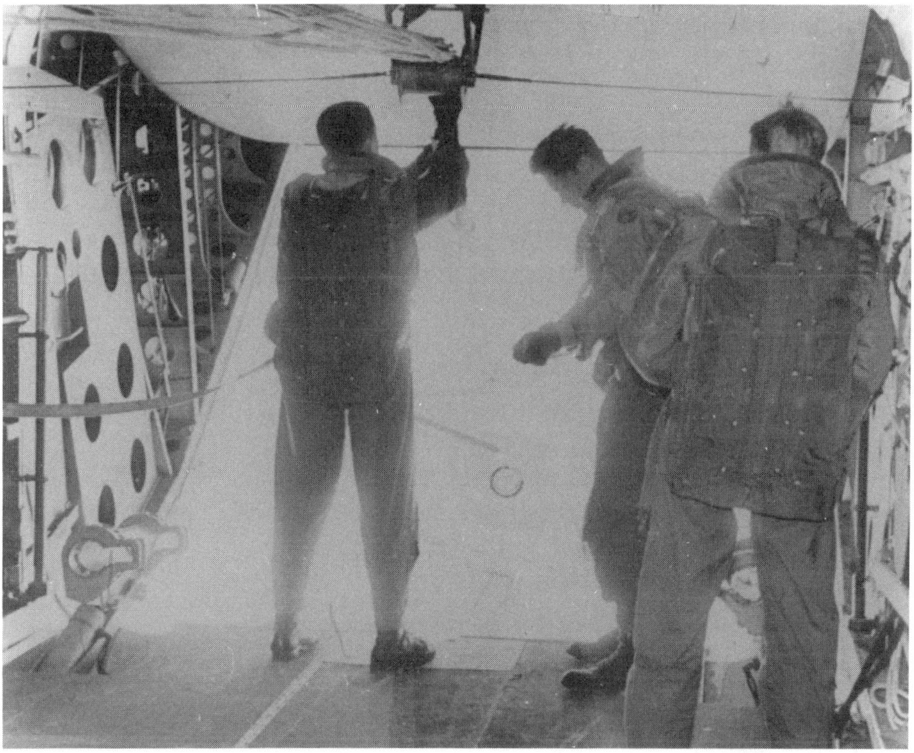

Photos taken in flight during the third midair recovery of a gondola by Capt. Slaughter Mimms's crew on 23 January 1956. This was the most successful C-119 crew with three midair recoveries and a ground and ocean assist. *Photos courtesy of Paul Lovrencic.*

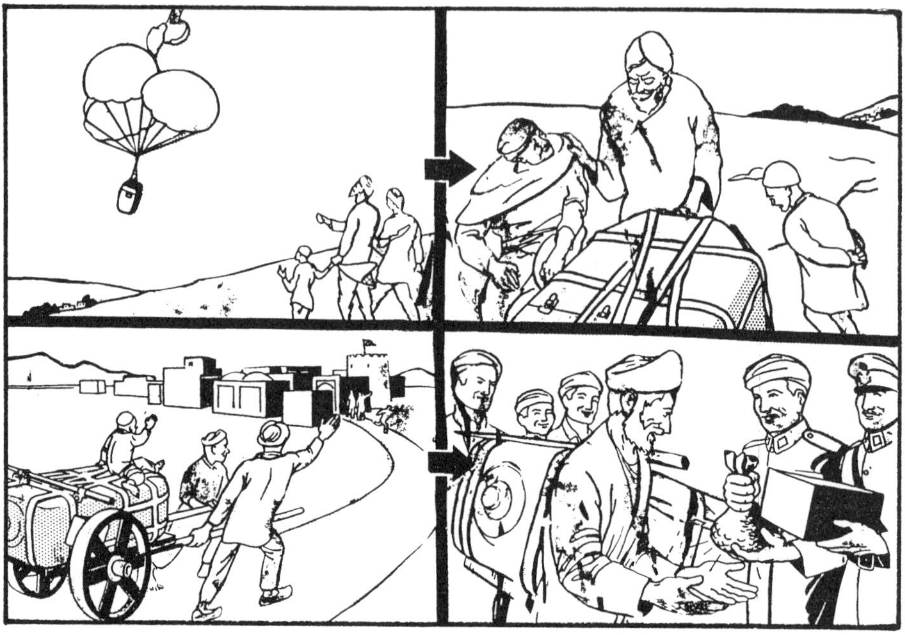

One of the placards carried on the Genetrix gondolas. This was aimed at illiterate finders, as there was no telling where the winds would carry the balloons. A press report from Pakistan said a $200 reward would be paid to anybody finding a gondola. Leaflets in English and Japanese were dropped by C-119 aircraft to help in recovery. *Courtesy of Paul Lovrencic.*

A WS-461L reconnaissance balloon from the flight deck of the USS *Windham Bay* in July 1958. *Photo courtesy of Leroy C. Stables.*

5

Grayback

With the completion of system development (Project Grandson) in August 1954, production could begin. Preparation of the Air Force units that would undertake the operational flights was also started. Existing units would be used; their involvement with reconnaissance balloons caused changes to a greater or lesser degree. The 1110th Air Support Group would handle launches as they had for other Air Force balloon projects. Tracking of the balloons would be the responsibility of the 6926th Radio Squadron (Mobile) of the U.S. Air Force Security Service. This would be a simple add-on to its normal function of monitoring Soviet radio signals (for intelligence) and U.S. communications (to ensure security regulations were observed).

The biggest change was made by the unit given the task of midair recovery—the 456th Troop Carrier Group. Up to this point, it had undertaken the normal troop transport and cargo missions. Now it was to modify fifty C-119 cargo planes for midair recovery on a "crash" basis. Once operational, it would send small detachments to isolated locations where they would have to be self-sufficient in regards to maintenance, security, and medical services. Responsibility for this task was given to its commander, Col. James L. Daniel, Jr., in September 1954.

Preparations were to be completed by the spring of 1955. Training was to begin May 1 and be completed by September 1. The units would then move overseas. The transfer was to take a month while another month was planned for the overseas shakedown (setting up equipment and working out problems).

If all went well, the first reconnaissance balloon would take off on November 1, 1955, and operations would end on May 1, 1956. To signify the shift from development to training status, the project's code name was changed. It was now called Grayback.[1,2]

Grayback

With the new mission came new people. One of these was A/3C Paul M. Lovrencic. After completing basic training in November 1954, he was assigned to the 456th TCG at Charleston AFB, South Carolina, as a helicopter mechanic. After arrival, he and several others were told they were there for a special project and would be told the details later. In the meantime, they were put out on the flight line to assist the mechanics working on the C-119s. These were "F" models, that is, "C" models fitted with Wright R 3350 engines rather than the R 4360s.

The first experiences of the group on the flight line were typical of those of young naive airmen fresh out of basic. Lovrencic was sent from the tool crib to the maintenance hangar and finally to base supply looking for a bucket of prop wash. "Made sense to me," he would say thirty-one years later. "They were changing a prop and it was covered with oil and I thought they had to have something to wash it with." (The mechanics later asked for twenty yards of flight line but by this time all the young recruits had wised up.)[3]

With the new year, training got underway in earnest. The first five aircraft commanders had begun training for air, ground and sea recovery in November 1954 at Langley AFB. By January 18, 1955, three were fully qualified with the other two trained in ground and air pick-up. The winch operators and pole handlers also began training in the recovery systems at All American Engineering in Georgetown, Delaware, in January.[4] This was the first introduction of the crews to what they were actually to do. It was a ground school where the personnel learned how to splice ropes, make the loops, and operate the equipment. The personnel came from a wide variety of backgrounds. Some, like Lovrencic, were just out of basic. Most were ex-B-50 gunners who wanted to remain on flight status. With no other openings, they were assigned to the project. The course lasted about two weeks. Because there was no base in the area, the Air Force made arrangements for the trainees to have room and board in private homes. Lovrencic, on his first TDY, remembered it as "quite nice to almost be part of a family." Once the school was completed they returned to Charleston AFB.[5] By the end of February, some fifteen winch operators and thirty pole handlers were qualified.

During February the Air Force was also conducting a review of the project and whether to delay it. A delay was not considered acceptable. At the same time, it was suggested a low-altitude balloon be developed to allow more operational flexibility. The balloon could be used year-round as it would not be dependent on the jet stream.

At the same time, the pilots were beginning their initial training. This included flight refresher courses on emergency procedures and instrument training. This involved both standard procedures and emergency situations such as a single engine instrument landing.[6]

The training of the navigators involved four long over-water flights. 2nd Lt. George Mathews, who joined the unit in late March after completing Aviation Cadet training, recalled many flights from Charleston to Tampa, then across the Gulf to Harlingen, Texas, and back to Charleston. Other flights were made to Puerto Rico and Bermuda.[7] This navigation training was necessary, as once the reconnaissance flights began, the C-119s would fly long patrols waiting for the balloons to return to friendly airspace.

On March 1, 1955, the first of a series of organizational changes was made. The 456th Troop Carrier Group was formally deactivated. It shed a number of support units and was reactivated as the 456th Troop Carrier Wing. This was composed of three units—the 744th, 745th and 746th Troop Carrier Squadrons.

March 1, 1955, was also the date midair recovery training was to have begun. To this end, the first four sets of experimental recovery equipment along with three prototype sets had been delivered to Charleston AFB. Arrangements were made to use Warning Area 177 just offshore from Charleston for air and ocean recoveries. Ground pickup training was to take place at Georgetown County Airport. The five qualified aircraft commanders were to be joined by the qualified winch operators and pole handlers to produce seven additional instructor crews. The remaining thirty-six crews would then be trained.

The plan was delayed owing to a lack of supplies and equipment. Several hundred small items were needed to rig the recovery equipment and the simulated gondolas. Only 10 percent were listed in supply catalogs. The needed equipment arrived slowly owing to budget restrictions, the limited capability of suppliers (many were small marine hardware stores), and cumbersome Air Force purchase regulations for local supplies. The net result was to push back the start of recovery training.[8]

As the recovery crews waited, the second organizational change was made. The three units assigned to Grayback belonged to different commands (456th TCW—Tactical Air Command, 1110th ASG—Headquarters USAF, and 6926th RS(M)—USAF Security Service). A single command was needed to coordinate the project. The Strategic Air Command was selected. SAC had responsibility for strategic reconnaissance and would be the primary "user" of the information the balloons would provide. On April 1, 1955, it activated the Headquarters Strategic Air Command Task Force Moby Dick (Provisional). Its commander was Brig. Gen. William P. Fisher; the headquarter's staff was composed of forty-four officers and fifty-eight airmen at Offutt AFB, Nebraska.

On April 22 its name was changed to the 1st Air Division (Meteorological Survey). Its cover mission was high-altitude weather studies. General Fisher and his staff immediately began orientation briefings, meetings with the other commands to develop a good working relationship and to survey the problems and needs of the units involved. The 1st Air Division had three tasks that had to be done nearly simultaneously—train the crews, conduct an Operational Suitability Test of the balloon, and then be ready to launch the operational missions over Russia.[9]

Drag Net

Not until mid-April were enough supplies on hand for recovery training to begin. The recovery effort was given the appropriate, if transparent, code name "Drag Net" (a police term for the systematic rounding up of "the usual suspects").

The trainees made their own kits—loops, hooks, and crimpers. The loops were strung out to the correct length in a large hangar. One of the skills the trainees had to learn was how to splice rope with a marlin spike. Everything was on-the-job training—one learned by doing and there were no checklists.

The "gondolas" used for the recovery training simulated the weight and parachute configuration of the real packages. They were concrete blocks weighing 250 to 300 pounds. Sand-filled 55-gallon oil drums were also used. They descended under the four main parachutes and the drogue chute. For the practice gondolas, the parachute shop rigged four old 28-foot white personnel chutes to the top of the block. The 15-foot drogue chute was attached to the block by a 100-foot drogue line. It was also fitted with nylon reinforcements so it would not be torn apart when caught by the hooks. A half dozen of the blocks would be loaded on a C-119 for a practice mission.

The aircraft used for the early training flights were nearly "stock." The only major change was the removal of the rear camshell doors. The fuselage now ended in a "big open hole." This permitted the recovery gear to be deployed in flight. It also gave the trainees a lot of fun.

Each crewman wore a safety strap called a "dog leash." One end was attached to a cable that ran the full length of the aircraft. The other end snapped on a D ring on the parachute harness where the life raft would normally go. Each crewman had his individual dog leash with his name on it. The length was adjusted by tying knots in it so a crewman could work hanging out of the aircraft and still feel secure. The crewmen soon found it "was quite a bit of fun" to sit on the cargo floor with their feet dangling out the back and see if they could touch the concrete runway as the plane took off. Another amusement was to roll an orange down the floor and out the back of the aircraft. It would be caught by the slipstream of the C-119 and actually follow the aircraft without falling. The crew would time it to see how long the spinning orange would remain in this position before finally leaving the slipstream and plunging toward the ocean.

Once over the training area, the recovery gear would be rigged. Two metal poles were extended below and behind the aircraft. Between them were several loops of rope with hooks to catch the drogue chute. There were three hooks spliced into each loop. At one point early on, they had tried using five hooks (three on the loops and two on the poles) but it was too difficult to get it out into the slipstream, as it would get tangled. The loops were attached to the poles by spring clips safetied with "5-cord" (a kind of heavy string). These were clipped to hooks attached to the poles with masking tape. The crews would frequently have to keep the masking tape by the heaters to keep it pliable and sticky in the high-altitude cold. Spliced onto the loops was another rope which led to the winch in the forward end of the cargo compartment. It was officially called the Model 80 winch and equipment but was sometimes referred to as the "Cadillac" gear.

Once it was rigged, the recovery practice could begin. A half dozen of the concrete blocks were carried on each flight. A block would be pushed out of the aircraft at an altitude of from 15,000 to 20,000 feet.

The C-119 would then fly a figure eight pattern. Three or four attempts could be made before the training package hit the water. If the recovery attempt was successful, the crew would drag it back into the aircraft. A typical training mission would last four hours. There was a great deal of trial and error in the early training flights. For instance, during the recovery, a transfer cable had to be attached to a loop spliced into the drogue line. The placement of the loop was critical because the nylon line stretched. If the splice was even a little too far down the line, it would be difficult to reach out and attach the transfer cable. Lovrencic said later, "I can recall lying on my stomach, inching out of the aircraft along the cable with the other crewmembers holding on to my legs, to be able to reach out far enough to put the transfer cable on that transfer loop." In time, the correct position was determined.

Once midair recovery was mastered, training was begun on ground pickup. The concrete block would sit on the ground with a 20-foot-high bamboo pole sticking up some twenty to thirty feet away. A hook was taped to the top of the pole and about 100 feet of accordion-folded line connected the bamboo pole and training package. The crew would rig a loop without hooks between the aircraft's two poles. The aircraft would sweep across the field at minimum altitude with the ends of the twin recovery poles just above the ground. As the aircraft reached the bamboo pole, the aircraft commander called for full power, then began a maximum performance climb. The bare loop would, if they were lucky, catch the hook. If the capture was successful, the crew would then bring it aboard.

Next was ocean pickup training. A metal "can" was used. This was a cube about 4 feet square, painted yellow and weighing about 300 to 350 pounds.[10,11] It would float in the water with the pole (called the water station) sticking up. The procedure was much the same as a ground pickup. The C-119 would fly toward the training package at a speed of 110 or 115 knots and gradually descend until the tips of the recovery poles were only eight feet above the water. Just before reaching the water station, the pull-up would be made (the exact timing depended on wind speed and direction and the ocean swells). The aircraft would pull between 1.8 and 2.4 G. It would climb at a 30° angle for the first 500 feet, then level out. As it went over the top, the crew was momentarily weightless.

The difficulties and dangers of ground and ocean recovery were many. If the aircraft came in too low, the poles could be broken, the loops knocked off or the water station destroyed by hitting it too low. If the pull-up was delayed, the training package would not be lifted up but be dragged through the water. Finally, if the contact speed was below 110 knots or the pull-up too abrupt, the aircraft could go into a high-speed stall. If this happened, the aircraft would be too low to recover. As a pilot acquaintance colorfully put it, "To go up pull back, to go down pull back more." Correct speed at the top of the climb was 95–100 knots.[12]

The supply shortages continued to be a problem during April and May. There were only seven sets of recovery gear on hand. Of these, three sets were committed to launch site support at NAS Vernalis. Maintenance of the equipment was also difficult owing to the wear and tear of training. Because of this, the training schedule became very flexible and even fluid, depending on what equipment was on hand. Another factor was the shortage of instructors. Some were qualified in one recovery phase but not in another.

Finally, throughout May, June, and most of July, there was a shortage of aircraft. Although pilot familiarization was not completed until May and navigator training was not finished until June, the major reason was aircraft modification.[13] The C-119 Fs were fitted with a new, longer, and more pointed rear door called a beaver tail. It was hinged on the top edge (rather than on either side as with the camshell doors) and the underside folded upward. This allowed the beaver tail to be opened in flight. The aircraft were also fitted with a raised floor under which ran the recovery cable. (Before, it had been exposed.) The recovery cable now sat in a trough which the crew could close with a cover. This protected the crewmen, should the cable whip around or break. Two long-range "Benson" fuel tanks were added which held 500 gallons each. This would give the aircraft a very long range for the patrols along the balloon's estimated flight path. It also raised the aircraft's gross weight to 72,800 pounds or more. This was above the maximum single engine take off weight of 68,000 pounds. It was known and accepted that if an engine was lost during certain phases of flight, the aircraft would crash.[14] Three aircraft were modified in March, fifteen in April, seventeen in May, and fifteen in June.[15]

The lack of aircraft, supplies and instructors caused a great deal of uncertainty in the training schedule. One thing that remained a constant on these flights was lunch. The trainees were given ham and cheese sandwiches. As Lovrencic remembered, "that's all we had for days, day in day out . . . it was terrible. To this day I cannot eat a ham and cheese sandwich."[16]

Moby Dick Hi

While the 456th TCW was beginning recovery training, the 1110th Air Support Group was being readied to start training launches. Code named Moby Dick Hi, these flights were to have several purposes: to test the reconnaissance balloon's operational suitability, develop procedures and tactics, spot deficiencies, determine capabilities, and provide launch crew training. This experience was badly needed, as little information was available and much of this was only theoretical. Additionally, none of the launch crews was considered fully trained.

The training flights were to be made between May 10 and September 1, 1955. Twenty-five launches were initially planned. As the start date grew closer, it was clear both the equipment and personnel would require a much larger-scale test. The 1st Air Division estimated a minimum of 150 balloons would be needed to accomplish all the test and training requirements. Initial guidance was provided by the Air Force Cambridge Research Center and General Mills. The 1110th ASG's activities then shifted to launch operations at Lowry AFB outside Denver.[17,18]

The reconnaissance balloon payload was a complicated device with several separate elements. A spreader bar carried the equipment. Hanging at each end was a box of steel shot ballast. Between them were two containers, the large control box containing the electronics, and the reconnaissance payload—either photo or ELINT.

The camera gondola was designated DMQ-1. It was a fiberglass box, 36 x 30 x 57 inches, insulated with polystyrene foam against the cold. The camera, made by Kodak, had two 6-inch lenses on opposite sides at a 34.5° angle to the horizon. (Four other companies also made the cameras: Bill Jack Instrument, Chicago Aerial, Fairchild Camera, and Hycon Corporation.) The camera held enough film for 500 photos. The film frame was 9 inches square. It could cover an area 50 miles on either side of the balloon. On the bottom of the box was a photo cell which turned the camera on when the light level rose above 70 footcandles. The camera gondola weight was 380 pounds. The payload was mounted on a rotator unit which slowly spun to allow panoramic coverage. The gondola also carried a 16-mm gun camera. Its small-scale photos indicated the balloon's altitude, azimuth, and a wide-angle view of the ground which showed the general geographic location.

The ELINT package, designated DMQ-2, was about the same size: 37

x 37 x 52.5 inches, 380 pounds. Unlike the DMQ-1, it was still being developed when the test flights began.

Above the gondola on the spreader bar was a container holding the five recovery chutes. The gondola would be separated either by a radio signal or when the balloon descended below a preset altitude of 30,000 feet. To assist in recovery, four packages of chaff were attached to the spreader bar. They would scatter when the gondola was released to allow radar to pinpoint its location. The complete payload weighed about 1,430 pounds. The payload was attached to the balloon by several load straps. Between the balloon and the payload was a 24-foot emergency parachute. If the balloon burst, this would prevent the payload from free-falling to earth.[19,20,21]

The complete system was given the unclassified designation Weapons System-119L (WS-119L). In most cases the number is assigned at random. In this case this might not be true. In many documents from the 456th TCW, it was referred to as "Project C-119L." The designation may have been an attempt to make the project appear to be simply a new model C-119.[22]

The first WS-119L balloon was launched on May 11, 1955. Although it lifted off properly, the balloon did not complete a successful flight. This was a harbinger of troubles to come, as none of the nine balloons launched in May was successful. Although the pace of flights picked up in June, there was not a corresponding improvement in performance—of twenty-six attempts, there were only six flights considered fully successful. July was no better. Due to a lack of hydrogen gas, homing beacons, and supplies, there was a virtual stand-down in operations. Only twelve launches were attempted, four of which were successful.

It was clear WS-119L was not as ready as the 1st Air Division had been led to believe. In June a group of specialists called in to examine the situation identified a number of problem areas. Although inexperienced personnel contributed to the 70 percent failure rate, the primary reasons were: increased payload weight which increased vertical strain, summer operations, daytime launches, the use of hydrogen, and the operating altitude which caused a maximum rate of change of free lift with respect to altitude. The lift of the balloon changed as it rose. If this was too great, the internal pressure would increase faster than the balloon could compensate for and it would burst.

In July, General Mills made an analysis. It blamed faulty equipment and improper practices by the launch crews, along with defects in the duct valves of the balloons. Representatives of the 1110th ASG, 1st Air Division, and General Mills met to work out solutions. General Mills made several changes in its production and inspection procedures.

The situation was complicated by the fact that nobody really knew what was causing the balloons to burst. Any improvement would be due as much to trial and error as to careful analysis.

The high failure rate caused a reassessment of Grayback. Maj. Gen. John P. McConnell, Division of Plans, told the 1st Air Division there was a possibility SAC would recommend a one-year delay. After a briefing on the project, the SAC staff met with SAC Commander Gen. Curtis LeMay. Afterward, General LeMay decided to request a one-year postponement. General Fisher, 1st Air Division commander, was told of the decision on July 10 while on an inspection tour of Europe. He responded by suggesting a less radical solution: push the date of the first operational launch back two months to January 1, 1956. He believed the technical problems could be solved and crews trained, given this added time. He also suggested again the development of a lower-altitude balloon able to be used in the spring and summer. Generals LeMay and Fisher discussed the matter and decided on a December 1, 1955 start date. This was informally suggested to the Air Force and approved on August 3.

August brought both good and bad news. Many of the problems of launching the balloon were solved with development of the "Fisher" launcher. This was a 6 x 6 truck with a rack mounted on the bed. The rack held the payload until launch. The Fisher launcher provided greater mobility and safety. Previously, a forklift had been used to release the payload but this had proven both unwieldy and dangerous. Another problem cleared up in August involved the supply of hydrogen gas from Francis E. Warren AFB. Changes in procedures and use of mechanical aids had resulted in hydrogen of both the quality and quantity needed. This allowed the number of balloon flights to pick up in August.

But all of these improvements meant little because the balloons continued to burst. The failure rate was around 50 percent through August.[23,24]

One spectacular failure occurred on August 17. At 10:15 A.M., Mrs. Charles Argo saw a balloon descending toward her house on South Glencoe Street in University Hills near Denver. She told the *Denver*

Post later, "I looked out the front door and saw all this equipment dangling in the air and moving toward the house. My three children and a neighbor's child were playing in the front bedroom and I called to them to get out of that part of the house. About that time it hit the corner where they had been playing, bounced off and broke a power pole just across the street." Damage (a shattered large bedroom window and the power pole) was estimated to be $4,000. Electrical power to several homes was temporarily knocked out. Within minutes of the balloon's landing, some 2,000 people had gathered. Local children soon tore up the thin plastic balloon and took home the pieces as souvenirs.[25]

It was now clear the root cause of the problems was the balloon itself. The balloon used was the 128TT. It was about 176 feet tall and had a diameter of 128 feet when fully inflated to its 800,000 cubic-foot volume. It could reach an altitude of 75,000 to 85,000 feet. This was 20,000 to 30,000 feet above the maximum altitude of Soviet fighters. The high failure rate, however, made it only marginally serviceable. Accordingly, the contract was terminated at its midpoint and the 66CT balloon was substituted. Its cylindrical shape was thought to be stronger and less likely to fail during ascent. The 66CT had a theoretical life expectancy of seven days (versus eight days for the larger 128TT). The two types would be used in a 50/50 split. There were two shortcomings with the 66CT. Although it had been developed specifically for the reconnaissance balloon project, it was not yet fully tested. It was, however, the only balloon available.

A more significant problem was that the 66CT could reach only 45,000 to 60,000 feet. The lower end of this range was less than the maximum altitude of Soviet jet fighters. Balancing this, the lower altitude of the balloon meant it would pick up stronger winds which would double the expected rate of arrivals in the recovery zone. To determine the balloons' vulnerability, the Air Defense Command ran a test. The ADC was told the launch times, estimated flight paths, and locations of the balloons. It would then attempt to locate and shoot them down. The results were mixed—jet fighters could reach the balloons and destroy them. However, tracking the balloons by either radar or ground observers proved to be difficult. The lower-flying 66CT balloons appeared only slightly more vulnerable than the 128TT. This, however, was based on a sample of only fifteen to twenty flights. It was clear the balloon's vulnerability was directly proportional to Russia's radar capabilities. It was estimated that the risk was acceptable.[26]

The Bomber Gap

While the launch and recovery crews struggled with their various problems, the need for intelligence on Russian military power was growing. The pace of Soviet nuclear testing was picking up. After the first test in 1949, there were two explosions in 1951 and another two in 1953. The first of these, in August, was the Soviet's prototype H-bomb. During 1954 there were one or two more. In 1955 there were four tests, including a megaton-yield H-bomb.[27] The increased pace indicated the Soviets had built the large-scale facilities to produce fissionable material in the volume needed for a stockpile of bombs.

The Soviets were also narrowing the U.S. advantage in bombers. On May 1, 1954, a single Mya-4 Bison jet bomber made a flyover of the May Day parade. At the time, the U.S. had two Boeing B-52 Stratofortress prototypes and the first production model flying. The Air Force believed the Mya-4 would not enter full-scale production until 1956. This estimate was undermined on May Day, 1955. During the flyover, ten Mya-4s appeared. Clearly, production had already begun. The Soviets also had a formation of nine TU-95 Bear prop-jet bombers. At the time, the U.S. had about thirty B-52s. At the same time, a new estimate of Soviet capabilities was being made. It was approved on May 16, 1955. The report gave current Soviet heavy bomber forces as 20 Bisons and 20 Bears. This would rise to 80 of each in mid-1956, 200 Bisons and 150 Bears in mid-1957, and 350 Bisons and 250 Bears in mid-1958. The final total for 1959 was 400 Mya-4s and 300 TU-95s. When compared to SAC's plans for B-52 production, this estimate would give the edge to the Soviet Air Force.

This estimate was revised in August. During the Air Force Day ceremonies, first ten, then eighteen Mya-4 bombers made flybys of the western air attaches. Taken at face value, the numbers of bombers had already exceeded the May estimates. The estimates were revised upward to between 600 and 800 Mya-4s by 1959 or 1960. The "Bomber Gap" controversy had begun.[28,29]

These estimates were particularly disquieting when seen against the current state of U.S. air defenses. The F-89s, F-86s, and F-94s were adequate against the TU-4 but lacked the speed and altitude to intercept the Bison. Worse, the pilots lacked training and the complex radar system (huge, crude, and using unreliable vacuum tubes) meant service rates were low. Within a year, the ADC would study ramming as a last resort.[30]

The Soviets were also making strides in development of ballistic missiles. At the Kapustin Yar test range near Stalingrad, the Soviets began an ambitious missile test program in mid-1953. Flights with ranges of 150, 300 and 650 nautical miles were made.[31] To learn more about Soviet missile activities, the U.S. built a giant radar at the Turkish resort of Samsum on the Black Sea. It went into operation in mid-1955. With a range of about 1,000 miles, it could track ballistic missiles from Kapustin Yar once they rose above the horizon and determine data such as speed, altitude, direction and approximate range. The irregular launches indicated the missiles were still in the research and development phase.[32]

Training Continues

Also during the summer of 1955, as the launch crews were coping with the bursting balloons, the 456th Troop Carrier Wing was overcoming its earlier problems. Starting on June 1, the personnel were organized into combat crews. Each consisted of an aircraft commander, two pilots, a navigator, a flight engineer, one radio operator, a winch operator, and four pole handlers: eleven in all. (A normal C-119 crew consisted of two pilots, navigator, radio operator, and flight engineer.) 2nd Lt. George Mathews was assigned as navigator to a 746th TCS crew commanded by Capt. Harold E. Mitchell. A/3C Paul M. Lovrencic was a pole handler on Capt. Slaughter D. Mimms's crew in the 744th TCS.

Once the crews were organized, they would train as a unit. With the last of the fifty modified C-119Fs back from the factory and deliveries of the production recovery gear, training could be stepped up.[33,34] The crews had to become familiar with the beaver tail doors—opening them in flight, rigging the poles, and making midair ground and ocean recoveries.

Mimms's crew became very proficient in recovery and was named lead crew and standardization crew (although, given the nature of their mission, there was little that could be called standard). They taught the other crew members. Mimms, as aircraft commander, would fly with the other pilots, and the four pole handlers, Lovrencic included, would fly with other crews or have an individual join their crew temporarily. Mimms's crew soon acquired the nickname "El Tigre"—the tiger crew.[35]

The step-up in training also made clear the risks of the mission. The C-119 would fly just above the drogue chute. If it was too low, the aircraft would hit the drogue. In most cases this was no problem, unless the chute went into an engine. This happened three times. On two occasions the chute became tangled in the propeller. The heat of the prop dome melted the nylon, fusing it around the dome and preventing the prop from being feathered. On the other occasion, the propeller cut through the chute, damaging the blades (ironically, all three times it was the left engine).[36]

A far more serious incident befell a crew commanded by Noel Wien, son of the founder of Wien Alaska Airlines. They were making practice passes on a training package. Instead of the loops and hooks catching and collapsing the drogue chute, it passed over them and behind the aircraft like a drag chute. Remaining inflated, the drogue passed under the horizontal stabilizer, then went upward. The line that attached it to the package struck the elevator, forcing it up. The C-119 went into a violent nose-up condition. It lost speed, stalled, and fell through into a dive. As this happened, the chute collapsed and the C-119 was able to recover. As it did, the normal slip stream was restored, the drogue reinflated, the line again hit the elevator sending the aircraft into an uncontrollable climb. This cycle repeated several times until a crewman was apparently able to cut the line with a knife or an ax. The co-pilot was newly assigned to the squadron. After landing he walked into squadron operations and told all within earshot he was all through with that operation. He was apparently grounded owing to fear of flying.[37,38] To prevent a recurrence, a cable cutter was developed and fitted to the aft end of the C-119. The cable passed through it. If a drogue problem occurred or it was necessary to get rid of the load, the winch operator would throw a switch which fired a .32-caliber blank cartridge which severed the cable.

Tragedy

At 2:04 A.M. on August 23, 1955, a C-119F began its takeoff roll down runway 15 at Charleston AFB. Flying the aircraft was Capt. Robert L. "Square Deal" McNeal (instructor pilot); beside him, at the controls, was 1st Lt. Francis L. McShane (pilot). The rest of the crew was 1st Lt. Robert B. McGovern (co-pilot), 2nd Lt. James J. Maher (navigator), A2/C John Glahn (flight engineer), A1/C Thomas P. Korshalla (radio operator), M/Sgt. William H. Rich (winch operator), and A3/C's Bobby H.

Bruce, James C. Miller, Lawrence G. Bradley and Keith Halls (all pole handlers). An early morning takeoff was normal owing to the C-119's over-gross-weight in order to get acceptable temperature and air density. Just after takeoff, the left engine failed. The pilot came on the intercom, reported the problem, and said, "I am trying to make it to the dual lane." This was a four-lane highway that ran past the base. About 1,000 feet past the airfield boundary, the aircraft began a left turn. The crew feathered the left propeller, lowered the flaps and landing gear, shut off the magnetos and turned on the landing lights. They were trying to reach the highway and make a crash landing. But the C-119 was losing altitude too rapidly to make it. The aircraft was still in a steep left bank when time and altitude ran out. The right wing struck a hickory tree about 35 feet above the ground. Simultaneously, the left wing smashed into a telephone pole about 6.5 feet off the ground and the main landing gear hit the ground. The aircraft began breaking up as it skidded another 287 feet until it finally came to rest. The wreckage burst into flames. McNeal, McShane, Maher, Glahn, and Halls were killed in the crash and fire. McGovern, Korshalla, Bruce, Rich, and Bradley sustained major injuries, while Miller escaped with only minor injuries.[39,40]

The plane had crashed into a residential district. Flaming debris was scattered amid several houses. Damage was estimated at $10,000.

An accident review board investigated the crash. It found there were several write ups on the left engine during July and early August (primarily for excessive backfiring). Between August 8 and 22, eleven flights had been made with no problems noted. Although it was suggested the engine failed due to faulty carburetion, water injection or ignition system breakdown, no cause could be determined owing to crash and fire damage.

Midair Recoveries

The crash of the C-119 and the deaths of half its crew came at a turning point for the reconnaissance balloon program: the wrapping up of training and the start of the move overseas. Before a crew was deemed combat ready, it had to not only master midair, ground, and ocean recovery, but also fly a series of patrols and intercepts, and, as a final "graduation exercise," successfully cut down and recover a Moby Dick Hi balloon.[41] The intention was that each crew was to recover an actual gondola. The high failure rate of the early balloons prevented this, however. As of the end of July, only two balloons had reached the recovery area. Both were successfully recovered in midair.

In September both the launch and success rates picked up. Of the last thirty-two of the large 128TT balloons, twenty-six were successful (81.2%). All these were from the production series numbered over 1,000. Several factors contributed to the higher success rate: improved manufacture and inspection techniques for the later balloons, better weather, and experience. (A small test was made with a few of the earlier balloons but the later ones still had the better results.)[42]

With the improvement in the launch crews' fortunes, there was also an increase in the number of actual midair recoveries. One of these was by Capt. Harold E. Mitchell's crew. They took off from Charleston and flew to Hamilton AFB, California, and from there out over the Pacific. This was the first time they had worked with an actual balloon. As they headed west from Hamilton, they tuned to the balloon's frequency. Each balloon transmitted an individual three-letter Morse code signal. They picked up the signal, identified it, and then began to home in on it (using a procedure George Mathews, the plane's navigator, remembers as being made up on the spot). The C-119 had a direction finder hooked to a needle instrument which gave a left/right indication. When it was centered, the aircraft was pointed directly at the balloon. The crew did this and Mathews recorded the magnetic heading. They then turned 90° right and flew for 10 minutes. The plane was again turned toward the balloon and a second bearing was taken. When plotted, they showed the balloon was about 200 miles west of the C-119. The crew continued to track it until they picked it up visibly. Mathews remembered it "appeared as a very bright light high in the sky." The aircraft then climbed to its maximum altitude of 20,000 feet and the recovery gear was rigged.

To cut down the balloon, a device resembling a rotary telephone dial was used. The crew was given a set of code numbers which were dialed into the device. The balloon received the signal, decoded it, then cut the gondola free. The balloon, relieved of the weight, rose and burst. The gondola's parachutes deployed and it began to drift lower. The aircraft lined up and the recovery gear snagged it. The gondola was winched in until it was dangling a few feet behind the plane. Mathews then picks up the story:

At this point the line had to be transferred to an upper pulley so the package could be swung in and on to the floor of the plane. We had all kinds of trouble doing this. We were all in the rear leaving the poor co-pilot flying the plane. He kept sending messages back that the engines were overheating, we were running low on fuel and various other kinds of problems all of which we ignored being determined not to lose the package. We got it on board and I remember it as a cream colored plastic box about as tall as I was with several glass covered apertures on it.[43]

The activities related to Grayback attracted a certain amount of public attention. The balloons had started several flying saucer reports in the Colorado Springs area and at Durango, Colorado, for instance. The most serious "leak" began on September 11, when a C-119 "weather plane" (as newspaper reports later called it) caught up over Indiana with a WS-119L balloon launched from Lowry AFB five days before. It was cut down successfully but the midair recovery failed. The gondola and control box landed near Fowler, Indiana. Several enlisted crewmen bailed out to guard the packages. A crowd of bystanders gathered, and one of the crewmen told them the balloon had been brought down by "electrical impulse guns" and that one of the boxes contained "small animals" used to study high-altitude effects. Two trucks from Chanute AFB showed up to haul away the packages. The comments sparked newspaper reports and inquiries. Winzen Research, a balloon manufacturer, suggested "electrical impulse guns" were radio control devices. Officials at Lowry denied animals were carried on the balloon flights and Chanute AFB said the balloon project was classified "and we can't talk about it."[44]

Such attention was dangerous, as it generated speculation and further leaks. To spike the rumors, the Air Force invited the press to watch the launch of a WS-119L balloon from Lowry AFB on September 14. They saw the 176-foot-tall balloon being inflated, then launched. The *Denver Post* carried a photo of Maj. Joe Collins, 1110th ASG operations officer, and Maj. Thomas McBroom, Detachment 1 commander, standing in front of a WS-119L payload—two ballast boxes, the control box, and the reconnaissance gondola.[45] By being forthright about the balloons, the Air Force was able to conceal the true purpose of the program. To prevent any more "speaking out of turn," a commander's call was held to discuss "certain newspaper articles."[46]

The Operational Suitability Tests formally ended on October 16. A total of 141 balloons were launched. These fell into four types: eighty-four high flyers ballasted for 80,000/50,000 feet and a flight time of one to seven days, thirty balloons fitted with water stations but with similar altitude and flight durations, seven special balloons filled with a mixture of hydrogen and impurities to form a larger bubble with less expansion at all altitudes, and, finally, twenty low flyers ballasted for 60,000/50,000 feet.

Flight durations ranged from less than 1 hour (26) to over 144 (14). There were two reasons for the relatively short durations. First was the high failure rate of the early 128TT balloons. The other was that many flights were either shot down by fighters or cut down by the C-119 recovery aircraft. Thus very few of the balloons were allowed to fly their full lifetimes. This was a shortcoming whose importance was not then realized.[47]

The Operational Suitability Test, in addition to crew training and sorting out the hardware problems, marked a number of advances. The techniques for varying the balloon's initial floating altitude were perfected. It was also found that ascent rates and hydrogen purity were not as critical as earlier thought. However, although it was believed the balloon was capable of performing the mission, it was also clear there were major shortcomings. The 1st Air Division requested the Air Force begin development of a more advanced, higher-flying, and more reliable balloon system. This was accepted. The balloons were to be launched during the winter of 1956–57.[48]

For the recovery phase, a total of thirty-three balloons were electronically cut down. Of these, eleven were recovered in midair. The rate of success was lowest for balloons equipped with water stations. Out of nineteen tries, only five gondolas were successfully recovered. The high failure rate was due to the increased weight of the gondola (710 pounds total with the water station versus 650 pounds without). This caused equipment failures (six drogues separated or torn, four loops broken, and four miscellaneous failures).[49]

In addition to the Moby Dick Hi recovery tests, a series of trials of midair and water pickups were made during September and October. One involved dropping 175 training packages of which 54 were successfully picked up. As with the Moby Dick Hi recoveries, drogue and loop failures were to blame for the low recovery rate.

The second series involved tests of the water station equipment. Fifty-one packages were dropped, but only twenty-three of the water stations sucessfully extended. Of the twenty-eight failures, twenty were due to the malfunction of the explosive squib which extended the water station.

The third involved ocean recovery. Attempts were made on thirty-eight training packages with twenty-one successes. Hardware failures of poles, loops, and leaders were at fault, rather than incorrect techniques. The limited number of ocean recovery tests raised doubts about the ability of the 456th TCW to make ocean recoveries.[50]

Besides the training and development of procedures, the exercises highlighted shortcomings in hardware before operations began. In particular, it was found the cast aluminum hooks were not strong enough, and bronze hooks were substituted. An initial supply was acquired from the Navy base in Charleston. The bronze hooks were often in short supply because the hooks were frequently lost when the loops or cables broke.

Another shortage was of tool kits. There were thirteen sets for twenty aircraft on recovery missions. Frequently, aircraft returning from chase missions would be "intercepted" at some distant base in order for the new aircraft to "borrow" a set of tools.

Maintenance problems also interfered with training. The Wing was beset by defective propellers. Up to 30 percent of the blades delivered were defective and 50 percent of the aircraft had defective props fitted. The prop shop worked a 24-hour schedule to rebuild blades. The aircraft of the 456th TCW also required engine changes at a rate higher than normal. These problems both created a heavy work load and affected aircraft availability.[51]

The time of test and training was over. The aircraft, personnel, and launch crews were organized into detachments and began the move overseas.

Deployment

The preliminary work for the deployment began even before the training program was fully underway (not surprising given Grayback's compressed time scale). The first unit to go overseas was the 6926th RS(M). Its move began in June and was completed in August, involving 725 personnel. They went to ten tracking sites: Guam; Wake Island; Clark AB, Philippines; Okinawa; K-6, Korea; Chitose AB and Shiroi AB, Japan; Midway Island; Shemya Island in the Aleutians, and Elmendorf AFB, Alaska. From these widely dispersed sites, they would provide direction-finding bearings on the balloon's transmitters once they emerged from Communist airspace. Because the deployment began in June, the 6926th RS(M) did not participate in Moby Dick Hi. Rather, once the tracking sites were set up, crews at Chitose AB, Japan, and Kadena AB,

Okinawa, would send aloft transmitter-equipped balloons. The program, code-named Moby Dick Far East, would provide the training in balloon tracking. It would also supply information on wind currents and radio propagation characteristics in the Far East and Alaskan areas. (Under certain atmospheric conditions, radio signals can "skip" very long distances; at other times, all but nearby signals are drowned out by static.) Finally, the balloon launches would add considerably to the program's cover. The Moby Dick Far East balloon flights were originally scheduled to begin on August 1, 1955. This was pushed back to September 1. The launches began on September 7. The plan was for two balloons per day plus two five-day "saturation periods" of five balloons per day. On October 15, the launch crew at Chitose moved to K-6 AB, Korea. This gave better flight paths for direction-finding training. Training went well and by the end of October, 70 percent of objectives had been accomplished.[52,53,54]

The deployment of the 456th TCW and 1110th ASG began in early October. Because of the size of the move (1,763 total personnel and 49 aircraft), the deployment of the 456th TCW was split into two parts. The ground crews and some air crewmen (winch operators and pole handlers) would go by ships to their Pacific bases in early October. The aircraft would follow in November. The deployment began on October 5.[55] The first unit to move was the 745th TCS which left Charleston AFB by train for Seattle on October 9. It was followed on October 15 by the 746th TCS. The next day, the Wing headquarters and the remaining four squadrons (including Paul Lovrencic) left by a pair of troop trains for Parks AFB, California.

The train ride took three and a half days with only two very brief stops (20 minutes each) at Lincoln, Nebraska, and Salt Lake City for calisthenics. The train arrived at Parks AFB on October 20. The 523 wing personnel remained there for three days before they were moved by bus to San Francisco. They immediately boarded the troopship USNT *General A. E. Anderson,* which set sail on October 23, 1955.

Conditions aboard the ship were spartan. On the second day out, the ship's supply personnel at first failed to issue bed linens. A more serious problem was the lack of ventilation in the lower levels. Even after duffle bags blocking the vents were removed, the compartments were often uncomfortable. Another shortcoming was the poor recreation facilities. Two movies were shown each night and three bingo games were held each week. This could only accomodate a part of the troops. An attempt to organize a variety show fell through. Finally, ten musicians were found and organized into two bands—one jazz, the other western music—which alternated.

To keep the airmen busy, they were assigned various details by rank, such as KP, chipping paint, polishing brass, and guard duty (the latter in the sleeping quarters to prevent any pilfering). Lovrencic swept and mopped down the deck each morning. He can still recall the shrill piping and the call, "sweepers, sweepers, man your brooms, clean sweep down fore and aft." After they were finished, a rope was tied around the mops and they were thrown overboard to sit in the wake for a few minutes. When the rope was pulled back aboard, the mops would be clean. Sometimes the knot would be too loose and the mops would be lost. But no problem—"I don't know where the Navy got them, but they must have had a hold full of them—every morning there were new mops to use," Lovrencic said later. The airmen also learned that to make a brand new set of fatigues look a little used, they could be tied to a rope and dragged in the salt water for about an hour. When they were pulled in, the fatigues would be faded, making the wearer look like an "old timer."

The ship stopped at Okinawa to drop off the 744th personnel, then proceeded to Yokohama, Japan, arriving on November 10.[56] The personnel disembarked and were sent to their various destinations.

Lovrencic and the other members of his detachment boarded a Japanese troop train. Their destination was a last-minute change. Originally, they were to go to Iwo Jima. However, on September 25–26, Typhoon Louise hit the island with 109-mph winds, destroying 80 percent of the base's facilities. There was not enough time to rebuild so an alternate site was selected—Itazuke AB, Japan.[57]

When Lovrencic and the others arrived at Itazuke AB, they found they would be living in a tent city. On the first day, there were no blankets or sheets. They had to sleep on the cots in their old Air Force overcoats as blankets. As Lovrencic remembered, "And there was snow on the ground, it was quite cool and we didn't even have the pot belly stoves working." Despite the problems, Lovrencic liked it better than Iwo Jima would have been. "For a single, young kid, 19 years old in Japan it was a paradise."[58]

As the 456th TCW was heading west, the 1110th ASG was heading east toward its launch sites in Western Europe. The move began on October 10 and involved 743 men. One of these was T/Sgt. Robert L. Burch. He was assigned to the 1110th ASG in May and completed his training as a photo equipment technician in September 1955. He recalled being "sick" about leaving his wife and year-old son for a six-month overseas deployment. Burch and the launch crew he was assigned to went overseas by troop ship from Brooklyn; after ten days, the ship docked at Bremerhaven, West Germany. The personnel left for the launch sites. There were five sites: Gardermoen, Norway; Evanton, Scotland; Giebelstadt and Oberpfaffenhofen, West Germany; and Incirlik AB, Adana, Turkey. The latter was Burch's destination. The seven officers and 113 men of the Incirlik launch team were first taken to Bremen, then flown to Incirlik via Rome and Athens. They arrived at Incirlik on October 30.

Burch and seven other men lived in a hut about 12 by 14 feet. Clothes had to be washed in a bucket. Burch recalled, "There was a large commercial type washer, mounted on a small trailer, that was operated by a gasoline engine. The unit was seldom operational and we only had the one for the entire detachment. It was easier to do small loads in a 5 gallon bucket using our heater stove to boil the water."[59]

In contrast, members of the launch crew at Gardermoen, Norway, lived in a former German two-story wooden barracks. Unlike the other launch sites, use of Norway required a change in that nation's normal policy. The Norwegians do not allow foreign troops to be permanently stationed on its soil.

The final step in the deployment was the movement of the C-119 recovery aircraft. For the move, each squadron was split into a squadron and a detachment, each with eight or nine aircraft. Their destination and call signs were:

	744th	TCS	Okinawa	Ascot
Det. 1	744th	TCS	Itazuke AB, Japan	Center
	745th	TCS	Adak, Alaska	Clover
Det. 1	745th	TCS	Misawa AB, Japan	Easy
	746th	TCS	Kodiak, Alaska	Girlie
Det. 1	746th	TCS	Johnson AB, Japan	Mudhen

The Wing headquarters and the Recovery Operations Control Center (ROCC) were at Shiroi AB, Japan.[60]

The first unit to deploy was the 746th TCS. Its eight aircraft left Charleston AFB on November 2 and flew to McChord AFB, Washington, via a refueling stop at Ardmore AFB. After minor maintenance and crew rest, the aircraft left for their final duty station at Kodiak, Alaska. The last C-119 took off at 4:00 A.M. PST, November 4.[61]

It was on this long over-water leg across the Gulf of Alaska that

George Mathews, navigator on a C-119, learned one of its unpleasant characteristics: the plane could not be ditched. It had been tried, but never successfully owing to the high wing design of the plane. When the C-119 hit the water, the weight of the wing crushed the fuselage. (The underside of the fuselage was dragged back by the water, the top part was carried forward, collapsing it.) If ditching was out, parachuting was not that great an alternative. The crewmen were issued seat pack life rafts which clipped on the parachute. They lacked adequate exposure suits for protection against the cold water they would fly over. All the crew had were yellow "one size fits all" suits in packages hanging on the cargo compartment wall. As Mathews recalled, "I figured out that if we got in trouble I had to leave my seat, go down the ladder, unpack and don the exposure suit (no small trick), go back to my seat, put on my chute, attach the life raft then make my way to the rear of the aircraft and jump out the rear door. How the pilots were supposed to do all this and still fly the aircraft I never did figure out."[62]

Fortunately, there were no problems and the eight aircraft arrived at Kodiak. The next unit, the 745th TCS, left Charleston AFB on November 5 and followed the same route (Ardmore, McChord, Kodiak) before flying on to their final stop of Adak, Alaska. The units were deployed like stepping stones across a stream; with the "stepping stones" established, the Japanese-based units could deploy. Det. 1 745th TCS left on November 6, Det. 1 746th TCS on November 10, and Det. 1 744th TCS on November 13. Because of the long distance between Adak and the landing site at Misawa AB, Japan, several aircraft had to wait forty-eight hours at Adak for favorable winds. Once the aircraft had reached Misawa, they flew on to their final destination. The final unit, the 744th TCS, left on November 14 for Okinawa. Forty-five of the C-119s had left Adak by November 20. The final four left between November 23 and December 5. The only mishap during the deployment, ironically, happened on the ground. On November 13, *Mudhen 22*, a C-119 based at Johnson AB, Japan, was sitting on the ramp when a taxiing B-29 put a wing through its canopy. The aircraft was too badly damaged to be repaired in time for the project. This reduced the total number of recovery aircraft to forty-eight.[63] The deployment phase marked another change in the reconnaissance balloon program. The code name Grayback was dropped and replaced by the final one: Genetrix.

It was now December 1, the planned date for the start of operations. The people, balloons and aircraft were in place. They awaited only the authorization to begin launches.

Waiting

One of the first tasks the newly deployed squadrons faced was unpacking the 2,751,290 pounds of supplies and cargo sent over to support them. Lovrencic and the other crewmen unpacked and set up the engine docks and built the maintenance stands.[64] In all some 32 million pounds of equipment was moved overseas in a logistical program called Grand Union.[65]

Throughout December the aircraft and their crews flew practice recovery missions. These were similar to the training at Charleston: midair recoveries of practice gondolas, land pickups, and ocean recoveries. At Itazuke, the Air Force crash boat was used to take the practice cans out to sea and drop them. Ocean recovery was often difficult, especially for the Alaskan-based detachment, due to high winds, rough seas, and freezing weather.[66]

Mathews recalled the Navy at Kodiak was very helpful. The first thing they did after the squadrons arrived was to issue the crewmen Navy exposure suits. Called "poopie suits," they were individually fitted and worn at all times in flight. They were a big improvement over what the crew had earlier.[67]

The C-119s also worked with the Moby Dick Far East balloons. Starting on November 23, the balloons were fitted with VHF transceivers. This allowed the recovery aircraft to track, home in on, and intercept the balloons.[68] Between the start of operations and December 27, when it was concluded, a total of 211 Moby Dick Far East balloons were launched (97 from K-6, Korea). The training they provided was excellent with the commander giving the wing an overall rating of 95 percent by the end of December.

The crews were also making long-distance patrol flights. It was during one such mission that a near-international incident occurred. On December 30, *Easy 24* took off from Misawa AB and flew east on a course that kept it well clear of the Soviet-occupied Kuril Islands. During the flight, inclement weather closed in and the Loran radio beacon faded out—leaving dead reckoning as the only navigation means. Unbeknownst to the crew, winds 50 knots higher than forecast had pushed the aircraft off course toward the Kurils. As the aircraft flew back toward Japan, it was intercepted by two Russian MiGs. The Recovery Operations Control Center ordered the C-119 to head south and told them they had, as the wing's history put it, "penetrated an undesirable area." Following the incident, the patrol patterns were altered to keep the C-119s clear of Communist airspace.[69]

Activities on the ground were also underway. Since late October, command post exercises were conducted to test the communications network and train the personnel. Each exercise lasted five days. They included simulated balloon launches, tracking, fixing, and recovery operations. The actual command functions and procedures were used whenever possible. After each exercise there was a two- or three-day break to evaluate the results.

One activity had not been in the original plan. When the 66CT balloons were substituted, the recovery plan was reevaluated. Because they flew lower, the wind currents they rode would be faster. This meant they might reach the recovery zone in bad weather or at night, cross through, then pass beyond the area before the C-119s could reach them. It was important the balloons not go beyond Japan, as a gondola down in the open Pacific would probably not be found. The 456th TCW came up with the idea of ground cut-down stations. They were fitted with spare airborne cut-down equipment. They were built at Shiroi and each of the squadron bases except Johnson AB. A Yagi antenna added to the equipment's range. The ground stations covered an area from the northern tip of Formosa to the northern end of Japan and around Adak and Kodiak.[70,71]

In contrast, the situation at the launch sites was far different. As T/Sgt. Robert L. Burch recalled: "We promptly laid around our quarters for more than two months. . . . On Thanksgiving day we dug trenches for a sidewalk from our hut to the latrine and to the next hut."[72]

During the first ten days of January 1956, the 456th TCW began saturation tests of the Fuchu air/ground control station. This was ordered by Colonel Daniel, the wing commander, owing to his dissatisfaction with the very poor air/ground control of the recovery aircraft during December. The facilities were not adequate for the volume of traffic. To correct this, the four chief radio operators from the Japan- and Okinawa-based squadrons were added to the staff at the Fuchu air/ground station. The tests also showed the single control team at the ROCC was not adequate to handle aircraft from six squadrons. A second team was added.[73] This had been a time for final tests, to sort out the problems in preparation for the "big day" when balloon launches could begin.

It was now January 10, 1956 and the waiting was over.

6

Genetrix

In deciding whether to let the reconnaissance balloons be launched, President Eisenhower faced a dilemma. The U.S. needed information on Soviet military power, industrial strength, and future developments. Yet, at the same time, Eisenhower was seeking political agreements with the Soviets on a wide range of issues—a nuclear test ban, a halt in production of nuclear materials, Open Skies, and the reunification of Germany. With the fading of the Cold War there seemed some hope an accommodation could be reached.

The dilemma was that intelligence operations such as the reconnaissance balloons ran the risk of provoking the Soviets and causing a chill in relations and lessening the chances of agreement. Eisenhower and Secretary of State John Foster Dulles were both "rather allergic" to the balloons, feeling the political difficulties would not justify the results. Many in the administration felt it would take the Soviets about three weeks to "catch up with it" (i.e., develop an effective defense). Later on, in a conversation with the Joint Chiefs of Staff, Eisenhower noted that if the Soviets sent balloons over the U.S., he would think they might be discussing mobilizing.[1] The military felt Genetrix was important, valuable, and worth any difficulties. There is an anecdote about Eisenhower's decision. The final Grayback test flights had carried cameras to take intelligence-quality photos for evaluation. One of these balloons passed directly over Fitzsimons General Hospital outside Denver during the time the president was there for treatment after his September 24, 1955, heart attack. These photos were among those shown to the president when his approval was sought to begin operational launches. Eisenhower appreciated their striking clarity and the amount of information they provided. This apparently overcame his reluctance and he approved.[2]

Launch

The first moves were to establish the program's cover. On the afternoon of January 5, 1956, an urgent message was sent by the 1st Air Division to the launch team at K-6 AB, Korea. It ordered them to cancel a survey of launch sites in Japan and immediately move to Kadena AB on Okinawa and launch one balloon on January 9.

This was part of a cover plan called White Cloud. It involved the launching of ten WS-124A balloons each from Okinawa, Hawaii, and Alaska between January 9 and July 1956. By flying the two operations concurrently, the line between the genuine weather balloons (White Cloud) and the reconnaissance balloons (Genetrix) was blurred. The State Department had requested the first cover launch be made the day before the start of reconnaissance operations.

The first White Cloud launch went off as planned on January 9 despite bad weather and damaged equipment. It received press coverage.[3,4] The same day, the Air Force issued a press release which stated the Moby Dick program was being extended to Europe and the Far East. The balloons would carry "meteorological instruments, including cameras to photograph clouds."[5] The cover was now in place.

The launch order sparked a flurry of activity at the Western European launch sites. The crews at Incirlik, Turkey, were organized into twelve-hour shifts (0500 to 1700 and 1700 to 0500). T/Sgt. Robert L. Burch was assigned to the B/U section of the instrumentation section. He, A/1Cs Richard L. Candy, William T. Thorne, and David L. Douglas made up the 1700 to 0500 shift. The 0500 to 1700 shift was M/Sgt. Preston J. Culpepper, S/Sgt. Ben T. Dillahay, A/2Cs Joseph F. Godlewski and James B. Pulliam. 2nd Lt. Lloyd D. Mitchell and M/Sgt. Elvin B. Feigum were in command of the instrumentation section. Marty Staub was the Eastman Kodak Technical Representative at Incirlik, Turkey. He kept the cameras checked and loaded with film for both shifts.[6]

The five launch sites had a total of 1,300 of the 128TT balloons and 1,500 of the 66CT type on hand. The plan envisioned a total of 2,500 balloon launches. It was planned that once launches began, they would be made at the maximum rate and altitude in order to saturate or avoid

Soviet air defenses. All the balloons would carry the DMQ-1 camera gondola. The DMQ-2 ELINT package was not ready in time.

When approval was given to begin launches, USAF Headquarters had added several restrictions. Initially, only ten "effective" balloons were to be launched per day (an effective balloon was one that had been successfully launched, reached its preset altitude, and was believed to have entered Soviet airspace). Also, the maximum altitude of the balloons was to be 55,000 feet. The altitude restriction was significant because it affected the amount of hydrogen gas used to fill the balloon, the amount of ballast it could carry, and the lifetime. More significantly, the lower altitude made them more vulnerable to Soviet air defenses. (It is not clear whether these restrictions were due to operational considerations or were political decisions by the Eisenhower administration.)

One adjustment to the cameras had to be made owing to the substitution of the 66CT for the 128TT balloon and the lower altitude. Camera gondolas had their exposure rates set at one photo every 6.25 minutes. Originally, cameras for the 128TT balloons were to be set for an exposure rate of one every 12.5 minutes. This change compensated for the higher ground speed at 55,000 feet and insured the coverage would overlap.

In order to meet both the necessary lifetime of seven to eight days and the 55,000-foot altitude restriction, the 66CT balloons were set for an initial altitude of 46,500 feet. When they descended to 40,000 feet, ballast would be released to raise the balloon's altitude. For the 128TT balloons, the initial altitude was 50,000 feet and the ballasting altitude was 45,000 feet. As the flight progressed, the ballast would be used up, and the balloon would become lighter and climb to 55,000 feet.[7]

To ready the payload, the launch crew set the various timers that operated the on-board systems. The first of these was the safety circuit which would dump the ballast and separate the payload if the balloon was still below 15,000 feet thirty to forty minutes after launch. This prevented a leaking balloon from drifting into air lanes. The second timer activated the ballasting system 90 to 100 minutes after launch. After this, any time the balloon went below the preset minimum altitude, the fine steel shot ballast would be released.

Another timer turned on the camera. The time delay was based on weather estimates of when the balloon would be over Communist territory. This was to prevent the camera from photographing the launch site or friendly countries. After 126 hours, the timer would shut off the camera. Although this would prevent all the film from being used, it was necessary to safeguard the battery power supply. (Later, a battery would be added to allow continuous camera operation.)

The final timer turned on the HF radio tracking beacon. Timing was critical. It should not transmit while the balloon was over the U.S.S.R., as the Soviets could use their extensive direction-finding network to locate it. However, if delayed too long, there would not be enough time to locate the balloon for recovery. After analyzing weather data, the following times were selected—Incirlik: 50 hours, Evanton: 90 hours, Gardermoen: 84 hours, Giebelstadt and Oberpfaffenhofen: 80 hours. These would turn the radios on a few hours before the balloons reached the recovery zones.

Should the gondolas come down outside the zones, the launch crews also attached placards to the sides of the gondolas. One carried a multilingual message. In English it read:

> THIS BOX CAME FROM THE SKY
> IT IS HARMLESS
> IT HAS WEATHER DATA IN IT
> NOTIFY THE AUTHORITIES
> YOU WILL RECEIVE A
> VALUABLE REWARD IF YOU
> TURN IT IN AS IT IS

A second placard for illiterate finders showed the gondola descending by parachute, a peasant family loading it on a cart, taking it to a government fort, and receiving a bag of money and a present. (A third repeated the message in Russian but was not ready for the initial launches.)

The final step before the payload was launched was to connect the P-51 power plug to the suspension system cabling. This turned the control unit on.[8] Then the balloon was released. As it swung upward, the 6 x 6 truck carrying the payload was driven toward the balloon. When the balloon was directly above the truck, the payload was released and it was yanked upward.

Five years after the program began, after all the setbacks and disappointments, the first reconnaissance balloons were on their way.

Reconnaissance Balloons over Russia

On January 10, 1956, nine Genetrix balloons were launched—eight from Incirlik, Turkey, and one from Giebelstadt, West Germany. One of the balloons failed soon after launch. The other eight climbed into the winter sky and headed east. The timers activated the cameras and the balloons began photographing the endless steppes of Russia.

As they rode the winter jet stream, the balloons ran the gauntlet of Russian air defenses. The day fighter force was composed of MiG-15s and MiG-17s. The MiG-15 first flew in 1947 and was designed to destroy U.S. bombers. Although it caused heavy casualties among B-29s over North Korea, it was on the wrong end of an eleven to one kill ratio versus the F-86. It had a service ceiling of 47,980 feet, but at these altitudes it suffered from instability. The MiG-17, first flown in 1950, was a complete redesign based on Korean War experience and improved aerodynamic knowledge. The MiG-17 also was fitted with an afterburner and could reach 54,460 feet. Both carried a pair of 23mm cannons and one 37mm cannon firing solid shot, orange-colored tracers and explosive shells which detonated at 600 yards. The planes could also carry two rocket packs, each with sixteen 57mm air-to-air unguided rockets.[9]

The fighters were integrated with a ground-controlled intercept (GCI) network. This was adapted from the system used by the Germans in World War II. The fighters would circle a radio beacon, waiting for a target to enter their sector. Overlapping early warning radars picked up the targets. The bearings were relayed to GCI stations which directed the fighters to the targets. The pilots were kept on a short leash—the controllers told them when to climb, descend, and open fire. The fighters were also equipped with a device based on the German "Naxos" which allowed them to home in on bombers' radar transmissions.

Two Soviet antiaircraft guns also posed a threat to the Genetrix balloons. The KS-19 100mm gun could throw a 34.6-lb shell to a maximum altitude of 47,574 feet. Its maximum rate of fire was 15–20 rounds per minute. The fire was directed by a SON-9A Fire Can radar. The other was the huge KS-30 130mm gun. Its 49.4-lb shell could reach a remarkable 72,200 feet. The rate of fire was 10–12 rounds per minute. Fire control was by the SON-30 Fire Wheel radar. (Both these radars were based on U.S. SCR-584 radar supplied under Lend-Lease.) The guns could fire proximity-fused shells. This was a fuse fitted with a small radar set which detonated the shell at its nearest point to the target.

The data from the early warning radars was relayed to batteries. The battery's own fire control radar then picked up the target, aimed six guns automatically and fired a 2–3 shot burst from each gun. (The crews simply loaded the guns.) The batteries were located around nuclear weapons sites, headquarters, and key targets like factories and bridges. Batteries are normally positioned for interlocking coverage.

Although both the KS-19 and KS-30 guns could reach the altitudes at which the balloons floated, there were major shortcomings. At very high altitudes, the dispersion of the shells (i.e., the spread from the aim point) was considerable. Also, the KS-30 130mm gun had been introduced to service only the previous year and numbered very few (ultimately, it would be judged a failure owing to its bulk). Balancing the guns' inaccuracy were the large numbers of small, high-velocity fragments scattered by the exploding shells over a considerable area. Any one of these could penetrate the balloon and bring it down.

To indicate the seriousness with which the Soviets took air defense, these aircraft, radars and antiaircraft guns were under the control of a separate branch of the Soviet military—the Antiaircraft Defense of the Homeland (PVO-Strany). In the Warsaw Pact countries and Communist China, similar weapons, tactics, and organization were used.[10]

As the first wave of balloons drifted east, some presumably fell victim to the air defenses. Others fell to earth owing to hardware failures or balloons bursting. The survivors sailed on—each morning as the sun rose, the photo cell would turn on the camera. The sunlight would heat the gas, causing the balloon to rise. Later, the gas would cool, causing it to descend. At sunset the balloon would glow red, green, and blue in the darkening sky. The fading light would cause the photo cell to shut off the camera, the day's photo run complete. Periodically, ballast would be jettisoned to prevent the balloon from descending too low. Each day the cycle would repeat.

In the Far East and Alaska, the balloons' arrival was eagerly awaited. Each crew wanted to be the first to recover a gondola. The 456th TCW Weather Section, starting on January 11, began making forecasts of the balloons' locations and trajectories. Using these, the recovery aircraft would be directed to the estimated intercept point.[11]

On January 13, three Genetrix balloons switched on their HF radio tracking beacons. The ground stations picked up their signals and took bearings. The information was relayed to the ROCC and the balloons' locations were determined. C-119 recovery aircraft flew toward them in two-plane formations. One of these was Capt. Slaughter Mimms's aircraft, call sign Center 39. Over the recovery zone, Mimms's radio operator, A/1C Don Shannon, picked up the homing signal. The C-119 began climbing to 20,000 feet to make visual contact. At this altitude, the ground speed of the C-119 was only about 80 knots. The beaver tail door was opened and the crew began to extend and rig the poles. The cargo compartment was very cold. Lovrencic felt the crew was ill-equipped for these frigid conditions with the type of clothing they had been issued. At 20,000 feet the crew had to use oxygen. This was supplied from large, cumbersome "walk around" bottles. Each was good for about twenty minutes—less if one had to make physical exertions. Sometimes the crewmen just set the bottle aside, worked awhile, then took a few breaths of 100 percent oxygen and then went back to work. (A risky procedure as a person would remain conscious for only a few minutes.)

The pole handlers—Lovrencic, A/1Cs Paul A. Ellis, Jim Murphy and William B. Culpepper—by now had the poles and hooks rigged. The crew spotted the balloon as it floated at about 50,000 feet and Shannon transmitted the coded cut-down signal. The gondola released, the parachutes opened, and it began the descent toward the earth. The balloon, free of the weight, rose and burst into thousands of fragments.

Center 39 began flying figure eight patterns, making repeated passes at the drogue chute. Contact was finally made at 9,000 feet. The hooks caught the drogue chute and the winch played out, then stopped. The crew then began to reel in the gondola. This continued until the drogue chute was wound part way on to the winch. Because of the 100-foot line between the drogue chute and the gondola, the latter was still well behind the aircraft. The crew clipped a transfer cable from the floor onto a loop on the line. Then the winch was backed off and the drogue chute was removed. At this point the line to the gondola was being held by the transfer cable. The winch cable was now run to the forward end of the aircraft and around a wheel on the ceiling, and then to the back of the cargo compartment ceiling and around another wheel. The end was passed down from the ceiling through the loop the transfer cable was attached to. The winch operator, S/Sgt. Jim Muehlberger, then wound the winch up a little until it carried the weight of the gondola and the transfer cable went slack. The transfer cable was then removed and the winch was turned on and the line was pulled over the two wheels (which acted like a giant pulley) and onto the winch. The four main parachutes followed until they were almost to the winch. At this point the gondola was hanging just behind the aircraft. The crew simply reached out, grabbed it and pulled the gondola in. The beaver tail door was closed and the first recovery was complete. After they landed, the crew was met by wing commander Col. James L. Daniels and presented with a case of whiskey for their accomplishment.[12] The other two balloons were also successfully recovered by other aircraft. The score for January 13 was three for three. It had been a good day.[13]

Wave after Wave

Following behind the first wave were more balloons. The other launch sites were brought into operation: Oberpfaffenhofen, West Germany, on January 11 (five); Evanton, Scotland, on January 12 (one), and Gardermoen, Norway, on January 13 (three).[14] Other than number of launches to be made per day, the only restriction on launch operations had to do with the two West German bases, Giebelstadt and Oberpfaffenhofen. Because of their proximity to East Germany, 66CT balloons from these two sites were to be launched so that they would cross the border only during hours of darkness. This did not apply to 128TT balloons or to the other sites.[15]

The tally for the first week was nine each on January 10 and 11, eight on January 12, and ten each on January 13, 14, 15, and 16. It had taken only three days for the launch sites to reach the quota of ten launches per day.[16] At the other end of the flight path, awaiting the balloons that made it through, the 456th TCW maintained 24-hour patrols from all the bases. Both the aircraft and ground stations kept a constant listening watch on the Genetrix frequencies.[17]

The early recoveries had indicated two problems. As expected, some of the balloons arrived in the recovery zone during bad weather or at night when midair recovery was impossible. To assist in finding the balloons cut down over the ocean, a small UHF transmitter was attached to the side of each gondola. The beacon had a range of 100 miles and an operating lifetime of 48 hours. The problem was the beacons weren't working. Tests with recovered gondolas indicated they were not floating in the correct attitude and were rolling in the waves. To work, the beacon's batteries had to be immersed in salt water. If they were taken out of the water (say, by the gondola rolling over), they would fail after only a few minutes.[18] Without the guidance of the beacon, searchers would have to look for a small gondola amid a vast expanse of ocean. To assist in finding them, the 456th TCW aircraft dropped leaflets to fishermen asking them to return any floating gondolas they might find.[19]

The other problem was the water station. Although it was not fully tested, the water station was rigged on all the early launches. Because the beacons failed on the first few gondolas that came down at sea, the recovery aircraft could not attempt an ocean pickup. The gondolas were picked up by ships. When examined, it was found the water stations had not extended. At the same time, a "friendly national" was injured when he handled a squib used to extend the water station. This was from a gondola that failed near a launch site. Accordingly, the squib was removed as a hazard. Although the water station could no longer be activated, it was left on the gondola because its weight was needed so the gondola would float with the beacon battery under water.[20]

Despite these problems, Genetrix was off to a good start. The launch crews were meeting their quota, the balloons were making it through to the recovery zones and being picked up in acceptable numbers. It was time for a step-up in activities. On January 17, the launch quota was raised to twenty per day. The totals for the next eight days (the second week of the project) were:

January 17	20
January 18	18
January 19	19
January 20	18
January 21	20
January 22	16
January 23	21
January 24	21

(Starting on January 23, the Russian language placard was attached to the gondolas.)

As before, some of the balloons failed soon after launch. On January 23, a balloon was found near Hedemora, Sweden. The balloon's envelope covered several tall pine trees. The payload, including the camera gondola, was also found. Other balloons came down at Vormsund and Skarnes in Norway. Three more were found in Kent, England, and were turned over to the local police.[21]

The vast majority successfully crossed into Communist airspace. Although specific details are not available, it is not hard to imagine the reaction they produced: on a collective farm in East Germany, a milkmaid stared upward into the brightening morning sky at three balloons shimmering red and green like blazing full moons. In a small town in the Ural mountains, crowds gathered on street corners, and, ignoring the icy wind whipping through the dreary streets, looked upward at a shiny disk as it drifted slowly eastward. On a collective farm in Soviet Central Asia, a group of villagers awakened in their crude huts to find one of the snow-covered fields had now been wrapped in plastic from a fallen balloon. Farther east a balloon burst and the gondola parachuted into the deep pine forests of Siberia. A snow storm was raging, covering and hiding it from search parties, never to be found.

Despite the U.S. experience during Moby Dick Hi, Soviet radar had little difficulty in detecting the high-flying balloons. Detecting, however, was one thing; interception was quite another. The problem Eastern European, Soviet, and Chinese pilots faced was similar to that of the earlier RB-36s. The GCI ground controller would direct the MiGs to make a long climb toward the balloons as they floated at or above the plane's maximum ceiling. Once at maximum altitude, the MiG would have to fly at its best climb speed, straight and level, with the throttle firewalled to maintain it. The GCI controller would have to anticipate any maneuvers, lining the fighter up well before it reached the balloon. If the MiG had to turn, it would lose speed in the maneuver and descend. The MiG closed on the balloon at about 300 knots, giving the pilot only a few seconds to aim and fire. In those final few moments, as the balloon, a gleaming silver bubble against an indigo blue sky, grew in the windshield, the pilot tried to center it in the gunsight. Suddenly the nose of the MiG flashed fire as the large shells reached toward the thin plastic. Under the wings, the two pods erupted as thirty-two rockets were fired like a huge shotgun.

Sometimes the balloon would be ripped open or burst into orange flame and begin the long fall toward the earth. Other times the fighter would miss and, with most of its fuel used up in the climb, be unable to make another pass. The balloon would sail on, like a great white whale disdainful of the sharks swarming below it.

Although the balloons could not shoot back, attacking them was not risk free. The MiGs were flying on the edge of controllability, only a few knots above the stall speed. Abrupt maneuvers, such as a sharp last-second correction to line up on a balloon, could result in a sudden loss of airspeed and a stall. The MiG-15 was particularly vulnerable as it was longitudinally unstable. Abruptly hauling back on the stick could, without warning, flick the MiG-15 into a spin. The pilot had three turns to recover. If unsuccessful, the pilot ejected.[22,23]

There were losses due to operational causes as well. On January 21 a pair of MiGs made a hurried takeoff after two balloons over Hungary. One of the planes was flown by a Russian pilot, the other by a Hungarian. As they took off, the two fighters collided; the Hungarian pilot was killed but the Russian survived.

Despite the difficulties of intercepting the high-flying balloons, Soviet, Warsaw Pact, and Chinese fighters and antiaircraft guns were taking a toll. Of the 219 balloons launched in the first two weeks, about 76.2 percent had been lost. Launch problems, weather, and hardware failures accounted for many but intelligence reports had reached the West indicating some of the balloons had been lost to enemy fire. According to intelligence reports reaching the CIA from Bulgaria, a balloon was shot down by antiaircraft fire and landed on the former Royal Palance of Vranya near Sofia. It started a fire that did 12,000 Leva worth of damage. The palace was used as a convalescent home for scientists. Three other balloons were brought down in the area around Plovdiv in central Bulgaria.[24] One can only speculate if any fighter pilot had yet reached the coveted status of balloon "Ace" with five kills.

Yet the balloons were still getting through in significant numbers. Of the 219 balloons launched in the first two weeks, 52 had reached the recovery zone. The majority of them were recovered. As long as this continued, so would the project. The actual percentage varied on a day-to-day basis. During the second week of the project the percentages were:

January 17	10.0%
January 18	38.8%
January 19	46.3%
January 20	16.1%
January 21	45.0%
January 22	43.7%
January 23	9.5%
January 24	23.8%

By this time certain patterns had emerged. Most of the gondolas being recovered were from Incirlik, Turkey. The two West German sites were virtually tied for a distant second place. No balloons from Gardermoen, Norway had made it yet.[25] Several reasons could be suggested—Turkey was closest to the recovery zone, had better weather, and was an area where Soviet air defenses were thin. Balloons from Norway had to cross the full width of Russia's northern defense barrier. Additionally, if they drifted north the balloons would be lost amid the polar ice.

Among the recovery units, the most successful was Det. 1, 744th TCS at Itazuke AB, Japan. Best of the best was Capt. Slaughter Mimms's crew. After making the first successful midair recovery on January 13, 1956, a second followed several days later. The crew's third midair recovery was made on January 23. Additionally, they received credit for two "assists." The gondolas were cut free but they were unable to make the pickup. One of the gondolas landed in Japan and was recovered by a helicopter. It was brought back to Johnson AB. The other gondola came down at sea. After it landed, the crew dropped dye and smoke markers to pinpoint its location. They also saw a Japanese fishing boat heading toward the floating gondola. The C-119 made several low passes which chased it off. As Lovrencic recalled, "I believe the passes were so low you could see the whites of the eyes as some of the crewmen jumped overboard." A SA-16 amphibian landed and took the gondola aboard.[26] Once recovered, the gondolas would be processed then sent by air to the 15th Reconnaissance Technical Squadron at March AFB, California. The film was in the hands of the interpreters an average of 75 hours after recovery. The interpreters became the first westerners to see the interior of Russia.[27]

Not all recovery attempts were successful. The experiences of the Alaska-based units were particularly frustrating. George Mathews, the navigator on Capt. Harold E. Mitchell's crew flying out of Kodiak recalled:

> As [the balloons] began to show up a crew would be put on alert and if it got within range we would launch and go after it. It soon became apparent that something was wrong. We would launch for a recovery with the transmitting frequency and the cut down code, track the thing, find it (sometimes) and dial in the code which was supposed to cut it down. Nothing would happen. The balloon would go sailing on to the east. We would confirm we had the right balloon, had the proper code and were doing everything right but we could never cut the things down.
>
> This went on for some time with the same results. We never knew what went wrong. There was much speculation that the folks who didn't want us to catch the things figured out a way to render the balloon receivers inoperative or that the receivers were failing due to poor design or power failure but it is hard to believe that that many would have failed.[28]

Concern in the White House

During the first two weeks of the balloon flights, the Russians had made no public statements or protests. Then, on the morning of

January 24, 1956, the Soviet Embassy called the State Department requesting an appointment for the ambassador, Georgi M. Zaroubin, to meet President Eisenhower. It was explained he had a message from Premier Nikolai Bulganin for the president. There were no other details except it was "personal" and it did not deal with disarmament.

Word of the request was relayed to the White House via Press Secretary James C. Hagerty and Special Counsel Bernard Shanley. They told the president of the request when Eisenhower returned from lunch at 2 P.M. The president agreed to the meeting and asked Hagerty to get what information he could. Hagerty and Shanley called Secretary of State John Foster Dulles, told him the president had agreed and asked if he had any idea what it was about. Dulles said he did but could not explain over the phone. He also asked Hagerty to immediately come over to his office to discuss some matters he wanted to relay to the president before the meeting was definitely set.

When Hagerty arrived at the State Department, Dulles and Undersecretary of State Herbert Hoover, Jr., were waiting for him. Dulles explained that the message could be on any number of subjects, but both he and Hoover believed it would be a very strong protest over the reconnaissance balloons. He further expected the protest would be coupled with another attack on the Open Skies proposal (i.e., the balloons were another attempt by the U.S. to get military information over Russia and Open Skies was just more of the same). Dulles believed if it was a protest, the text would be released in Moscow simultaneously with the meeting and mark the start of a worldwide propaganda campaign making the usual charges of war-mongering, etc.

Despite this, Dulles explained to Hagerty, he strongly urged Eisenhower to have the meeting for reasons of diplomatic protocol. If the president met with the Soviet ambassador, the Russian government would be less able to brush off requests by the U.S. ambassador, Charles E. "Chip" Bohlen, to see Bulganin. Previously, if Bohlen had a message from Eisenhower for Bulganin, he was referred to the Foreign Minister, Molotov. Dulles also stressed the meeting should take place after the president's press conference set for 10:30 A.M. the next morning.

Hagerty relayed Dulles's recommendations to Eisenhower. The president commented:

> Foster may be right on his guess. I haven't thought too much of this balloon thing and I don't blame the Russians at all. I've always thought it was sort of a dirty trick. But that was the gamble we took when we made the decision and they ought to have a good answer ready for me if I have to use it when I see the

Ambassador. You call Foster and tell him that I want his suggestions for that answer over in my office in a sealed envelope no later than 9:30 tomorrow morning. Also tell Foster that I want him here with me when the Ambassador comes in.

Eisenhower also felt it had been timed deliberately, just before his meeting with British Prime Minister Anthony Eden—"That's the way they do things and we will have to handle it as carefully and delicately as we can." He quickly added the U.S. must never close the door on such messages and give them study even if convinced in advance they were only propaganda. Eisenhower agreed it would be best if the meeting was after the press conference and a time of 11:30 A.M. the next morning was set.[29]

At the State Department, work was underway on a response. Dulles suggested the Soviet ambassador be told the Secretary of State would prepare a formal reply to the protest. Dulles included a draft of such a response and a copy of the Air Force press release of January 9. As for tactics, Dulles suggested Eisenhower not be letter perfect on the subject. Rather, he should show only a newspaper reader's knowledge of the subject. Dulles also mentioned a Navy balloon which had been launched from Japan, crossed the Pacific, and was then over Texas. He concluded by saying Eisenhower should not make any substantive reaction until it had been studied.[30]

In short, Eisenhower and Dulles were sticking to the weather balloon cover story and were prepared to lie. One must remember the context: from time immemorial, no nation had admitted it spied on its enemies in peacetime. Athough nobody was, by the mid-1950s, so naive as to say, "Gentlemen do not read other people's mail," equally nobody was willing to admit they did. There was a very serious reason: spying in peacetime could be considered an act of war. If the U.S. was to *officially* admit it was spying on Russia, the Soviets could use this as a pretext to declare war. Thus the automatic denials and Eisenhower's reluctance to authorize airborne espionage operations.

The next day, January 25, everything was in readiness for the Soviet ambassador and the protest he was expected to bring. After a press conference staff meeting that morning, Hagerty saw the president again and told him of several other possibilities—a request by Bulganin and Khrushchev to visit the U.S., a seeming acceptance of a part of Open Skies (with a lot of strings), or an agreement to halt H-bomb tests. Eisenhower said they were possibilities, then smiled calmly and said, "Well, we'll know the answer in a few hours."[31]

At 9:30 A.M. Eisenhower received a call from Defense Secretary Charles Wilson. He said the people in the Pentagon thought the meeting would be a protest over the balloons and offered to get together information for the President if he wanted to use it in the response.[32]

Promptly at 11:30 A.M., Ambassador Zaroubin was shown into the president's office to confer with Eisenhower and Dulles. The 15-minute meeting was anticlimactic—the letter was a proposal for a 20-year Treaty of Friendship with the United States. After Zaroubin left, Eisenhower called Hagerty into the office. As he walked in, Eisenhower said, "Well, Jim, it wasn't what we thought. There is no mention of the balloons." Dulles said he was quite surprised, then laughed and added, "Maybe that's what you get for having somewhat of a guilty conscience." The president added he was sure the Russians knew about the balloons and they might bring it up at a later date.[33]

At 12:00 P.M., Eisenhower called Secretary of the Air Force Donald Quarles. He asked Quarles what he thought the total result was expected to be. Quarles gave a rather ambivalent answer, saying the balloon photos would be valuable and perhaps justify the whole effort. At the same time, Quarles said he would also be willing to call it off if outside reasons warranted. Eisenhower said he was going to ask very soon for a presentation from everybody in the government that put anything aloft so as to get an idea how provocative it was.[34]

Ironically, on January 25, the Air Force again raised the quota. There were now to be thirty launches per day.[35]

Death of the Whales

The daily totals for the next three days were:

January 25	30
January 26	26
January 27	19

On January 28, another increase to forty balloon launches per day was ordered. This would remain in effect until the end of the program. The totals for the rest of January were:

January 28	19
January 29	31
January 30	17
January 31	18

The launch sites were not reaching their daily quotas. The reason was not launch team problems or shortages of supplies, but the weather. Western Europe was in the grip of the worst winter weather in several years. The balloons were not to be launched in conditions of rain, fog, or icing. The worst weather was at Evanton, Scotland, while the best was at Incirlik, Turkey, as expected.[36] (Not surprisingly, the Incirlik crews held the record for most launches: 28 in 24 hours.)[37] Accordingly, a feasibility test was made of launches under more severe weather conditions. These were successful and the Genetrix balloons were cleared for launch in fog and light rain.

There was a far greater problem, however, one that threatened the program: the Russians had found ways to stop the balloons. On January 25, a total of thirty balloons had been launched. Of these, four (13.3%) made it to the recovery zone. The last of these arrived on February 1 and was visually and electronically tracked. The intention was to cut the gondola free once the balloon was over land. Before this could be done, the balloon descended below 30,000 feet and self-terminated. Despite this, a C-119 was able to make a midair recovery.[38]

After this, the balloons just stopped arriving. None of the 112 balloons launched between January 26 and 30 made it through. One weakness the Soviets were able to exploit was the balloons' tendency to "overballast." It was expected the Genetrix balloons would follow the normal flight profile of a Skyhook balloon. Warmed by the sun, the balloon would float at its maximum altitude throughout the day. At sunset the hydrogen gas would cool and the balloon would start to descend. When it reached a preset altitude, ballast would be jettisoned (about 7 percent of the gross load). This would halt the descent and it would remain at this altitude during the night. At sunrise the gas would be heated by the sun, expand, and the balloon would quickly rise to its maximum altitude. It would remain there until late afternoon when the cycle would repeat. Thus the balloon would have minimal vulnerability during the daylight hours.

The actual flight profile of the Genetrix balloons was different. Atmospheric disturbances were causing the balloon's altitude to vary. To compensate, the balloons jettisoned ballast two or three times per day. This used about 10 percent of the gross load every 24 hours (rather than the 7 percent planned). This high rate was aggravated by the narrow altitude limits. Only 5,000 to 6,000 feet separated the ballasting altitude and the 55,000-foot ceiling ordered by the Air Force. The net result of this was to cut the seven-to-eight-day lifetime of the balloon to only four to five days. When the balloon ran out of ballast, it could no longer compensate for the loss of hydrogen gas vented due to solar heating. As the balloon lost lift, it began to descend, picking up speed until it reached 30,000 feet and self-terminated. The shorter lifetime of four to five days meant the balloons were still over eastern Siberia when they came down.

A related problem was the balloons' altitude profile. As expected, the balloons rose rapidly after sunrise. Then, shortly after noon, the balloons began to cool and descended, arriving at their ballasting altitude with several hours of daylight left. This meant they were at maximum altitude for only a few hours per day. The rest of the time they were within reach of both fighters and antiaircraft guns.[39]

It may have taken the first two weeks for the Soviets to realize the weak points of the balloons' incorrect ballasting/altitude profile and then to work out tactics. Although their radar could detect the balloons, the Soviets had problems determining the position and exact altitude of high-altitude targets. With incomplete tracking data, it would take time for the pattern to be spotted. Once it was, a counter tactic was obvious—a dawn patrol trying to catch the balloons before they rose in the morning sunlight, then afternoon attacks on the balloons once they had descended again.

By the end of January, the 1st Air Division was not yet aware of the overballasting/altitude profile problem.[40] Instead, suspicion about the sudden increase in the loss rate was centered on the HF transmitter each balloon carried. The timers were turning them on well before they left Communist airspace. Soviet and Chinese direction-finding stations could fix the balloons' locations and the "Naxos" device on the MiGs would, once set for the balloons' frequencies, lead the fighters directly to them. In one case, a cluster of eighteen balloons was tracked over northern China heading directly for Japan. Only three made it to the recovery zone.[41]

Accordingly, on January 31, two of the frequencies used by the HF transmitters were dropped and a new one added. Also, the turn-on time was delayed by 12 hours for all launch sites except Incirlik, Turkey.[42]

The sudden drop-off in recoveries was quite apparent to the C-119 crews. Lovrencic recalled:

> There were many times where we would go up . . . and not make any contact at all with one of the balloons. Some of the flights . . . lasted as long as 12.5–13 hours and I still have the old flight log that shows proof of that—a C-119 flying

for 12.5–13 hours. Again ham sandwiches—I will never eat ham sandwiches again.[43]

The lack of balloons was having its greatest impact in Washington D.C. At 9:53 A.M., January 31, Secretary of State Dulles called Air Force Secretary Quarles. Dulles told him, with recoveries sharply down, he was not sure it was worth continuing. Quarles said they did not feel too disturbed. Although recoveries were not as high as hoped, it was expected they would lag behind launches. (Four of the balloons launched on January 25 were then entering the recovery zone.) Dulles said the subject might come up at the White House and he felt the Russians "are on to the game now." Quarles offered to provide a report which Dulles wanted by 12:30 P.M.[44]

Dulles's worries could only have increased over the next few days. After February 1, the recoveries stopped. At the launch sites things were not much better:

February 1	1
February 2	19
February 3	18
February 4	10

The sudden fall-off in the number of launches was due to bad weather. Because of this, the forty-per-day quota was not being met and the recovery crews were waiting in vain.

As during the training flights, the balloons' spectacular appearance attracted attention. On February 3, a Genitrix balloon passed over Oslo, Norway. Some thought it was a parachute; others wondered if it was a *flyvende tallerken* (flying saucer). Reports came in from Grorud, Oslo, Holmestrand, Larvik, and Porsgrunn between 11:30 A.M. and 2:00 P.M. In fact, the balloon had been launched from Gardermoen at 10:30 A.M. and drifted over the center of Oslo an hour later.

Dulles was closely monitoring the situation. On February 2 he received a call from his brother, Allen Dulles, the CIA director. He needed to know about the CIA's "counterpart of Genetrix," specifically, "whether they would permit any action in that area." (This was not a balloon, but an airplane—a very special one, then in its final stages of flight testing.)[45] The next day Dulles called W. Park Armstrong, Jr., Special Assistant for Research and Intelligence. Dulles said he was anxious to keep a close watch on whether the balloons were making it through and if there was any evidence of "diminishing returns." If it got to that point, Dulles wanted the flights stopped. Armstrong told him a few of the balloons had started to transmit but had not reached the recovery area yet. Dulles told him that both he and the president were nervous about it. He again repeated that if the reconnaissance balloons were failing to produce "substantial returns," he did not want to go on. The U.S. had found out what could be done about the "bugs" in the balloon. The conversation ended with both agreeing the time for protest was near.[46]

The Soviets Protest

On February 4, 1956, Soviet Deputy Foreign Minister Andrei A. Gromyko handed a protest note to U.S. ambassador Bohlen in Moscow. Separate notes were sent to Turkey and later to West Germany. The note to the U.S. complained of

> the launching by United States military organs from the territory of Western Germany, and also from United States Air Force bases situated on the territories of several nations bordering on the Soviet Union, of balloons into the air space of U.S.S.R.
>
> The apparatus suspended from the aerial spheres includes automatic photographic cameras for aerial photography, radio transmitters, radio receivers and other things.

The note continued:

> Investigation shows these spheres and their suspended apparatus are manufactured in the United States.

It charged the balloons were a

> gross violation of Soviet air space . . . contrary to obligations assumed by the U.S. government in accordance with the UN charter and incompatible with normal relations between states.
>
> The Soviet Union presents a decisive protest and demands that the government of the United States take measures for the prompt cessation of the impermissible activity of the American military organs.

The Soviets had more in mind. For several weeks Communist newspapers had been conducting a campaign against propaganda-carrying balloons launched by the American Free Europe Committee (a CIA front which also operated Radio Free Europe). The Soviets saw the opportunity to kill two birds (or balloons) with one stone. After saying they had protested in September 1955 about these flights, the Soviets complained:

According to data at the disposal of Soviet organs, the flights of these aerial spheres over territory of the Soviet Union have not only not ceased but have increased of late.

The Soviets also demanded these activities be stopped.[47]

The same day, the Air Force launched ten balloons. The situation remained critical—not enough balloons were being launched and none was making it through. In response to this (and presumably to Dulles's dissatisfaction with the lack of recoveries), the 1st Air Division sent an urgent message on February 5 to the launch sites. It said that the "entire operation must be pressed to the maximum extent possible. I want you to use every means possible to launch at the maximum rate from all sites. Unless results are obtained soon there will be no reason to continue the Operation."[48]

Despite the launch crews' best efforts and the eased weather restrictions, conditions remained bad and they were not able to meet the quota: they launched only twelve on February 5 and fifteen on February 6.

Time had run out.

The End of Genetrix

At 10:15 A.M., February 6, Eisenhower and Dulles met to discuss the Soviet protest and other matters. After recalling that both he and Dulles were "rather allergic" to it and doubted the results would justify the "inconvenience," the president then said he thought it was time to suspend the balloon launches. Dulles agreed but added it should be handled "so it would not look as though we had been caught with jam on our fingers." Dulles said an appropriate response to the Soviet protest would be prepared and sent.

At 12:12 P.M., Dulles called Air Force Secretary Quarles and told him of the president's decision. Dulles asked if the phone conversation was sufficient authority for him to proceed. Quarles said it was and the operation would be halted until further notice.[49,50] By the time the word reached the launch sites, fifteen more balloons had been launched. This brought the final total to 448 reconnaissance balloons.

While the launch crews stood down, the recovery crews and their aircraft were kept busy half a world away. Ironically, on the same day the project was closed down owing to the failure of the balloons to reach the recovery zone, a balloon entered the recovery area. It had been launched on January 31 and was the only survivor of the eighteen sent up on that day. The gondola was successfully recovered in midair.

On February 8, four balloons (out of the eighteen launched on February 3) entered the recovery zone. One of the balloons was visually and electronically tracked. The gondola was successfully cut down but when the midair recovery attempt was made, the drogue chute broke free from the main assembly and the gondola landed in the ocean. For the next three days recovery was attempted but was hampered by heavy seas and snow showers. The effort failed and contact was lost.

Another of the balloons was being tracked by a recovery aircraft when it self-terminated. The C-119 could not reach it and the gondola came down at sea. It was found by Japanese fishermen on February 15.

The third balloon which entered the recovery zone on February 8 was cut down by a C-119 during the night. Because a midair recovery was not possible in darkness, the gondola landed in trees on the northern end of Honshu, the largest Japanese island. Due to the terrain, deep snow and snow slides, it was too dangerous for the ground recovery team to go after it right away. Its recovery was put off temporarily to await better conditions. The fourth balloon was intercepted but no electronic contact could be made. A fighter shot the balloon down and its gondola was recovered by boat.[51]

Also on February 8, the U.S. responded to the Soviet protest. After noting an "apparent confusion between a publicized meteorological operation and previous Soviet allegations" concerning the propaganda balloons, the note denied any U.S. government involvement with them. As for the "weather" balloons, it said:

> The US Government is happy to supply information complementary to what is already public knowledge. Under US auspices, a meteorological survey is being carried out by the launching of balloons which are in effect miniature 'satellites' and which remain aloft for several days at a very considerable height placing them out of the range of commercial aircraft. A number of balloons have been launched in several parts of the world and many have been passing over the US. For example, a balloon sent up on January 8 in California, transited the US, the Atlantic Ocean, and the Eurasian Continent and was identified on January 20 transmitting homing signals from the Western Pacific.

A copy of the Air Force press release was included "for convenient reference."

The note further requested that the Soviet government return the gondolas that had "come into its possession," denied the balloons posed a hazard to air traffic, and said the U.S. government "would be happy to explain further the safety measures." Up to this point, the U.S. note had maintained the weather balloon cover story. Its final sentence, however, gave the Soviets what they wanted: "Provisionally, however, in order to avoid misunderstandings, and in view of the Soviet Government's objection, the US Government will seek to avoid the launching of additional balloons which, on the basis of known data, might transit the USSR."[52]

Although the Soviets had forced the U.S. to halt the reconnaissance balloon launches, they decided to exploit them for propaganda. On the evening of February 9, they put on a show at the Moscow residence of Foreign Minister Molotov. The driveway of the Spiridonvka Palace was draped with fifty or so balloon envelopes. In the courtyard were "tons of aluminum and plastic containers"—some of the captured gondolas. Western newsmen said they were "about the size and shape of the biggest home refrigerators."[53] The frozen winter night was floodlit by truck-mounted generators for the benefit of Soviet television and newsreels. In a conference room, several Soviet spokesmen explained the balloons' features and lashed out at the U.S. Foreign Ministry Press Chief Leonid Ilyichev attacked the balloons as a menace to aircraft and people on the ground and declared: "All such attempts by American military organs are an attempt to conduct a policy 'to brink of war' which has been condemned by peoples." A Soviet meteorological specialist, Col. A. V. Tarantsov, described the gondolas' technical features. He said the camera carried enough film to take 400 to 500 photos. The gondola was waterproof and carried orange dye to help spot it at sea. A radio locator beacon would also turn on when it landed in the ocean. Colonel Tarantsov showed a negative of a Turkish airfield. In addition to saying the balloons were being used for espionage, he claimed they could be used to carry germs.[54]

The display at the Spiridonvka Palace seems to have had three goals. The obvious one was to lambast the U.S. and increase Cold War tensions. The political support Eisenhower had gained from the Open Skies clearly rankled the Soviets. By attacking the balloons, the Soviets could seek both to undermine Eisenhower as peacemaker and to serve notice they would tolerate no attempts to learn of their military and industrial strength. The other two goals were related but also contradictory. One was to reassure the Russian people about Soviet air defenses. Ilyichev stressed that during January, "a great number of balloons" had been captured. At the same time the Soviets, as *Newsweek* put it, "exploited fully her opportunity to sow fear of the mysterious US craft, drifting soundless and unseen"[55] Unlike the U.S. with FUGO, the Soviets apparently saw fear as unifying.

While the political storm over Genetrix was developing, the 1st Air Division was making plans should a resumption of flights be authorized. Two ideas emerged. The first was to launch all the usable balloons at the maximum rate possible and at maximum altitude. The goal was to saturate Soviet defenses, rise above trouble, and to complete the full 2,500 flights as soon as possible. A Soviet fighter patrolling its sector could engage only one target at a time. Under this "stream" approach, for each balloon attacked many more would slip through. The flights could be completed by mid-April if a resumption was authorized prior to February 15.

The other alternative was to launch only the remaining 400 high-serial-number 128TT balloons. At 80,000 feet they would be above Soviet defenses. In addition to maximum altitude, the water station would be removed to reduce the radar return and make them harder to detect. With these measures it was felt the balloons might attract less attention and thus be acceptable. The proposals were sent to Air Force Headquarters on February 9, 1956, the same day as the Moscow press conference.[56]

At the same time, the 1st Air Division was analyzing the data from the recovered gondolas in order to find ways of reducing the loss rate. It was at this time the overballasting problems were first realized.[57]

After the recovery attempts of February 8, the 456th TCW air crews maintained the 24-hour patrols, waiting for any more "stragglers." These patrols continued for 48 hours after the last balloon was estimated to have reached the recovery area. None did. Subsequently, flights were restricted to daylight search missions for floating gondolas. The "sea drift" was computed based on the balloon's location when it came down, the ocean currents, and surface winds. It was still an impossible task. If the location was off by 60 miles, for instance, the drift direction would be 180° in error. The search flights were soon concluded and the bulk of February was concerned with midair recovery practice and navigation training.

Then, on February 21, radar picked up a balloon. Two C-119s, Girlie 64 and 67, took off to intercept if it proved to be a Genetrix balloon. Fighter aircraft were also alerted in the event a shoot-down was required. The C-119s caught up with the balloon but no electronic contact could be made. The balloon appeared to be a Genetrix so the fighters were scrambled. They shot the balloon down. All its parachutes were streamers and the payload fell into the sea. No debris could be spotted. It was subsequently determined that it had been a Navy balloon launched from Opamma, Japan.

Although the 456th TCW's last recovery proved a case of mistaken identity, gondolas were still being turned in by Japanese civilians. Three gondolas which had come down in January were found and returned by Japanese fishermen. On land, another three were found by Japanese nationals.[58]

When the reconnaissance balloon program was being planned, it was presumed the jet stream would remain favorable until at least May 1. On February 21, however, the 1st Air Division told Air Force Headquarters that trajectory information indicated the balloon flights could not be made after March 15. This added a note of urgency as the cutoff date was just over three weeks away.[59]

On February 24, Air Force Headquarters selected the second option, but with restrictions. Of the 400 balloons, 90 percent would be limited to a maximum altitude of 58,000 feet. Only the remaining 10 percent of the 128TT balloons would be allowed to fly at 80,000 feet. The proposal was sent on to Secretary Quarles with the request operations begin at the earliest possible date. On February 29, the Air Force was notified it had been turned down. It is a truism of intelligence that an operation cannot continue once it is publicized. Eisenhower's interest in balloon reconnaissance, limited to start with, had evaporated with the Soviet protest. There was also now an alternative.

On March 1, 1956, project Genetrix was formally terminated.

Summary

It was now time for an accounting. The five launch sites sent up a grand total of 448 balloons. The breakdown was:

Oberpfaffenhofen, Germany	88
Incirlik, Turkey	162
Gardermoen, Norway	32
Evanton, Scotland	88
Giebelstadt, Germany	78
Total:	448

Some of the balloons failed at launch or before they reached Communist airspace. From the available information, it appears approximately 379 actually crossed the border. Of these, the bulk, 235, were never seen or heard from again. Some drifted over the Arctic and were lost. Others presumably came down owing to minute holes in the balloons, the balloons bursting due to the extreme cold, or ballasting system failure. A small number may have been rendered silent by failure of the HF transmitter.

After all these causes have been eliminated, it is clear the majority of the balloons did not live long enough for the HF transmitters to come on. The preponderance of these losses was due to enemy action: MiGs and ground fire. The Soviets have not released any detailed information on their "battle of the balloons." It can be speculated some Warsaw Pact, Soviet and Chinese pilots reached "ace" status. Indeed, with the large numbers of balloons, it was possible the top scoring pilots' totals could rival those of World War I "balloon busters." It was believed the over-ballasting was a smaller loss factor.

Only 144 balloons lived long enough to transmit any signals (21 of these were termination signals). Of the remaining 123 that were tracked, half were shot down or fell victim to other causes. Thus, of the 448 which started the journey, only 66 made it to the recovery zone. As noted earlier, not all the balloons responded to cut-down signals. A total of 57 balloons were successfully cut down (37 by aircraft, 14 by ground stations, 5 self-terminated, and 1 was shot down by a friendly fighter).

C-119s made midair recovery attempts on nineteen balloons and were successful on sixteen. The total by squadron was:

Det. 1	744th TCS	Itazuke, Japan	8
Det. 1	746th TCS	Johnson, Japan	5
	744th TCS	Kadena, Okinawa	1
Det. 1	745th TCS	Misawa, Japan	1
	746th TCS	Kodiak, Alaska	1

The 745th TCS at Adak was unsuccessful. Mimms's crew total of three midair recoveries represented 37.5 percent of the squadron's total and 19 percent of all midair recoveries.

Of the rest, twenty-one gondolas were picked up by Japanese individuals and agencies, two each by the U.S. Army and Navy, and three by Air Force amphibians and helicopters. In all, forty-four gondolas were successfully recovered.

The launch sites of the recovered gondolas fell into a definite pattern:

Oberpfaffenhofen, Germany	6	7.0%
Incirlik, Turkey	30	18.5%
Gardermoen, Norway	0	0%
Evanton, Scotland	1	1.1%
Giebelstadt, Germany	7	9.0%

Incirlik, on the less defended southern border and closest of the sites to Japan, provided the vast majority of the recovered gondolas. Gardermoen was unsuccessful.

And so to the bottom line: forty gondolas returned photos. This amounted to 13,813 usable exposures. This covered 1,116,449 net square miles of Soviet and Chinese territory (8 percent of their total area). This was equivalent to 37 percent of the continental United States. The cost per square mile was $48.49. This was significantly cheaper than the cost of getting mapping coverage of the U.S., then or now.[60,61]

As three-fourths of the recovered gondolas came from Incirlik, Turkey, the coverage was concentrated in the areas of Siberia and China. There was scattered coverage of European Russia and Soviet Central Asia. Virtually all was of interior areas—out of reach of both the short-range penetration flights and the decade-old Turban photos. The most important facility discovered was a vast nuclear refining complex at Dodonovo in Siberia.[62]

Aftermath

For the U.S. and Russia, the aftermath of Genetrix was a sterile series of diplomatic and propaganda exchanges. For the men of the 1st Air Division, it was a time to pack up and go home.

The Soviets continued their propaganda attacks on the balloons after the February 9 press conference. However, they were handicapped by the fact that the same wind which carried U.S. balloons over Russia could also take Russian balloons over Western territory. On February 8, the U.S. Army said it had found a Soviet weather balloon in northern Japan the previous weekend. The balloon measured about 5 by 3.5 feet and carried a label in Russian reading, "Instrument to measure air current."[63] It was the U.S. ace in the hole.

On February 18, the Soviets rejected the U.S. response to their protest. The new note, handed to Ambassador Bohlen, offered to "prove" the balloons were for spying by exhibitions in Western capitals.[64] The U.S. response came on March 1. The U.S. note said that Russian balloons had overflown Alaska and noted sharply, "It is illogical that the Soviet government should desire one rule for itself and another for the rest of the world." The U.S. then sought to wash its hands of the matter by suggesting the United Nations work out "a joint program for the utilization" of weather balloons. The U.S. note also made four other points—demanded the return of the U.S. gondola in exchange for the Soviet weather balloons the U.S. had, declined the Soviet request to display the gondolas in the West, rejected Soviet charges the balloons were air hazards, and chided the Soviets for not publishing the January 9 press release.[65]

The next day, the Air Force said five Russian weather balloons had been found in Alaska over the previous three years. The latest had been found in the last few weeks.[66] On April 1, the Japanese National Police reported they had recovered four Russian balloons in the last several months.[67] Although the Soviets angrily denied their balloons had flown over Alaska, their propaganda had been blunted. As one headline put it, "So What's Your Gripe?"[68]

Still, the Soviets and their allies continued, if only for domestic reasons. Miniature versions of the Moscow press conference were held in Eastern Europe and China. On March 7, the Communist Chinese exhibited U.S. balloons.[69] On March 31, the Poles put on a similar display of a balloon which had been shot down by a MiG near Kutno. The camera was described as holding 714 feet of film. Eighty exposures had been taken which were described as showing details as small as railroad lines.[70] In early May, the Chinese put on another, more extensive display. Four or five balloons were used: several dismantled to show the cameras and radio gear, another complete payload which dominated the room. The photos of the pilots which shot them down were by the entrance. Some 160,000 people were described as having seen it in the previous three weeks.[71] In June, a Czech magazine carried a description of how a balloon was shot down. It included gun camera photos of the balloon and a happy "Officer Novak," the pilot, reporting "Tasks carried out." In August 1956, an American tourist reported to the CIA that his Czechoslovakian driver had offered to show him the captured balloons. The driver warned him to say he was English if anyone asked. The tourist was taken to a building and shown five balloons and "all sorts of photographic equipment." No other visitors were there at the time.[72]

As for the units of the 1st Air Division, the two months following the stand-down was a period of idleness. At Incirlik, Turkey, T/Sgt. Robert L. Burch and the other members of his section had nothing to do.[73] The 456th TCW aircraft continued to fly. George Mathews recalled:

> We flew long, 12 hour patrols, mostly down the chain, back up the Bering Sea, over to Pt Barrow, back down over Fairbanks, Anchorage and back to Kodiak. The weather at Kodiak was sometimes very bad and the approach was downright dangerous. The runway ran right off the water up to the base of Mount Barometer which was about 5000 feet high. Once you passed the radio beacon about 1/2 mile off the end of the runway there was no going around under IFR [instrument flight rules] conditions as there was no way to get around or over the mountain. A couple of times we returned after 12 hour patrols, low on gas and expecting good weather only to find it foul. With not enough gas to make it back to Anchorage we had no choice but to land which we did, a few times under zero/zero conditions. We also flew some cargo missions around Alaska but mostly we just killed time.[74]

Although the Genetrix launches had stopped, the future of balloon reconnaissance was still unclear. A second series of flights was planned for the winter of 1957. These would use very high-flying balloons. On March 13, President Eisenhower told his Chief of Staff, Col. Andrew Goodpaster, he was not interested in any more balloon projects. Goodpaster called General Twining to tell him of the cancellation. General Twining said he fully understood and that would be the end of the matter.[75]

With no future balloon reconnaissance missions planned, there was no need to maintain specialized units to support them. On March 26, the Strategic Air Command transferred overall control of the individual units of the 1st Air Division back to their parent commands (it was formally deactivated two months later).[76] At the same time, personnel of the 1110th ASG and 456th TCW began packing their supplies. Burch helped load the remaining balloon hardware on railroad cars. This was shipped to the Rome Air Force Depot in New York State. This work was completed by the end of April and it was time to leave. Before they left, Burch and the others had to turn in their maintenance notebooks they had kept during launch operations. (Burch was never told how many of the balloons had made it to Japan.)

For Burch the trip home was a free-for-all as the Air Force had left them to their own initiative as to finding their way back to their stateside assignments. Burch recalled that after leaving Turkey on April 30:

We hitched rides to Athens where we stayed a week. Then we got a ride to Frankfurt, stayed overnight, and took a train to Paris. From Paris we flew to McGuire AFB, N.J., via Shannon and Goose Bay. By then I was almost out of money, but I had enough for a bus ticket to Denver. I finally got home about the middle of May.[77]

In Japan, Lovrencic and the other ground and air crewmen repacked the 456th TCW's supplies. Soon after, in May, the aircraft began the long flight back to the U.S. with minimum crews. The other personnel, including Lovrencic, sailed back. Their troopship, the USNT *General Mann,* left Yokohama and sailed directly to Seattle. The trip took eighteen days and they arrived back in the U.S. in June.[78]

After a deployment lasting over seven months, most of the personnel went on leave before reporting to their new duty stations. The 456th TCW was to be deactivated and many of its personnel were to be absorbed by the newly formed 419th Troop Carrier Group based at Ardmore AFB. By July 1, most of the supplies and equipment had arrived. The usual farewell parties for officers and airmen were held at the Ardmore AFB picnic grounds. A formal deactivation ceremony was held on July 6, 1956. The Wing was presented with an Air Force Outstanding Unit Award. The 456th TCW officially passed into history on July 9, 1956.[79] So disappeared one of the most unusual units the Air Force had ever operated. The end of Genetrix also brought to a close the first stage in the United State's attempts to conduct aerial reconnaissance over the Soviet Union. It had been tentative, limited and sometimes crude, yet it marked the way for all that followed.

The first series of U-2 overflights was underway.

7

Melting Pot

The January/February 1956 Genetrix flights were the high point of U.S. reconnaissance balloon efforts. Never again would the launches be made on so large a scale. There remained, however, one final chapter. It was meant to correct some of the technical and operational shortcomings of Genetrix but would end with failure, anger, and another Soviet protest. In the summer of 1956, however, that was still two years in the future.

The first to follow the lead of the Genetrix balloons was an extraordinary aircraft with the innocuous title of "U-2." Its story actually began with Kelly Johnson's earlier CL-282 proposal to fit long-span wings to an XF-104 fuselage. This was to meet an Air Force request for a very high altitude reconnaissance aircraft. In mid-1954, the Air Force selected two aircraft: the Martin RB-57D (a long-winged version of the Canberra which had fared so badly in the skies above Kapustin Yar) to meet the short term need, and a new design, the Bell X-16 Bald Eagle, for the long run. Kelly Johnson's CL-282 proposal was rejected owing to duplication and use of an inferior J-73 engine. Despite this rejection, Johnson continued in-house studies and looked for support.

At the same time, a number of committees were looking at various aspects of U.S. military and weapons planning. One of these groups, under James R. Killian, president of MIT, looked at the possibility of Soviet surprise attack. They became interested in use of very high altitude aircraft to make clandestine reconnaissance of Communist territory. They looked at the RB-57, the X-16, and the unsuccessful CL-282 and Fairchild designs. The committee concluded the CL-282, with a J-57 jet engine, would be superior. Kelly Johnson also promised he could have the prototype in the air only eight months after the go-ahead (seven months before the X-16, even with the latter's head start).[1]

On November 24, 1954, the proposal was submitted to President Eisenhower. Thirty of the aircraft would cost about $35 million. Although under CIA direction, the cost was too great for it to be funded completely from the CIA's budget. Accordingly, the Department of Defense would contribute a substantial part. Before overflights were begun, another meeting would be held for final approval.[2] Allen Dulles, director of the CIA, selected Richard Bissell to run the project.

At Lockheed, Kelly Johnson and a select team of some fifty engineers began putting in 100-hour weeks. The CL-282 design was revised with longer fuselage and wings to improve range and altitude, and with a "bicycle" landing gear rather than skids. Code named "Aquatone," development of the aircraft was conducted in secrecy at Lockheed's Skunk Works. The secrecy had its strange aspects: one day Johnson returned to his Encino home to find two government checks totaling $1,256,000 in his mailbox.

With construction of the prototype underway, the search began for a test site. Johnson finally selected Groom Lake, a dry lake bed in Nevada near the nuclear proving ground. It was subsequently added to the area controlled by the Atomic Energy Commission to ensure security. Two hangars, office space, and living areas were built, and by July, Lockheed, Air Force, and CIA personnel began arriving. It was called, with a fine sense of irony, "Paradise Ranch" or simply "The Ranch."[3]

By this time, the prototype, "Article 341," was ready. On July 24, 1955, it was disassembled and loaded on two Douglas C-124 Globemasters for the flight to The Ranch. It was then reassembled and underwent preflight checkout. The pilot for the early test flights was Tony LeVier, Lockheed's chief test pilot (who for security used the pseudonym "Anthony Evans").[4]

Taxi tests began on August 1. On the second run, the aircraft lifted off. LeVier misjudged his altitude above the lake bed and made a heavy landing, blowing both main wheels. The next day, the tires had been replaced and two more runs were made. LeVier concluded the plane was ready for flight.

The first flight was made on August 4, 1955. After two unsuccessful attempts to start the engine, takeoff was made at 3:55 P.M. LeVier made several stall checks while the T-33 and C-47 chase planes watched.[5]

Problems appeared when he tried to land. LeVier had been advised to land with the nose wheels touching down first. When he tried, the aircraft skipped, then launched back into the air. Five times he tried with the same result. To make matters worse, a rain squall was approaching. Finally, LeVier tried landing it as a "tail dragger" (i.e., a plane with a tail wheel). He stalled the aircraft just above the ground and thumped down, ending the 41-minute first flight.[6] Ten minutes later there were two inches of rain on the lake bed.

Despite this "eventful" first flight, the test program went into high gear. Soon the U-2 was breaking the world altitude record of 65,890 feet set by a British Canberra. The U-2 could reach up to 80,000 feet and remain at this altitude for hours at a time. In late 1955/early 1956, three groups of U-2 pilots were recruited. They were Air Force pilots with extensive time in single-engine aircraft, exceptional pilot ratings, and top-secret clearances, and were reserve officers with indefinite enlistments attached to units being disbanded. After briefings and medical checks, they went to The Ranch for flight training in the U-2. It was an unforgiving aircraft—at certain altitudes, only 4 knots separated the maximum and minimum speeds.

The first CIA U-2 unit went overseas in the spring of 1956. Two U-2s, their pilots, and support personnel were sent to Lakenheath, England. They had to leave owing to the controversy over the death of a British frogman inspecting the hull of a Russian cruiser during its stay in an English harbor. In June they moved to Wiesbaden, West Germany.

The first U-2 overflight was of East Germany and Poland on June 20. CIA pilot Carl Overstreet made the flight; he had just returned from a short trip home and was the last to know. The route took him to Warsaw, Poland, then back to Berlin and Potsdam, East Germany, before landing back at Wiesbaden.

On July 2, Bissell saw Col. Andrew Goodpaster, the president's staff secretary, requesting Eisenhower's permission to start overflights. Goodpaster discussed it with Eisenhower the next day and he gave approval. The series was to last ten days, ending on July 14. Bissell was told at 2 P.M.[7]

On the Fourth of July, 1956, U-2 Article 347 took off for the first overflight of the Soviet Union. CIA pilot Hervey Stockman flew over East Berlin, across Poznan in northern Poland, and headed for Minsk. The U-2 then headed north toward Leningrad. Stockman saw MiG fighters below trying to reach him. Once the U-2 reached Leningrad, Stockman turned south and flew along the Baltic coast. The flight had taken eight hours and forty-five minutes.

The next flight would go to Moscow. Carmen Vito took off in Article 347 the morning of July 5. The overflight route went over Krakow, Poland, due east to Kiev, and then north toward Minsk. The cloud cover had been heavy, but began to clear as Vito headed to Moscow. As the U-2 followed the Minsk–Moscow railroad, MiGs tracked it. All other air traffic was grounded and several MiGs crashed in the process. Vito could see SA-1 Guild surface-to-air missile (SAM) sites around Moscow. They did not fire. The U-2 then covered the Baltic ports before the cloud cover closed in below it and Vito returned to Wiesbaden.

In all, five U-2 overflights had been made during the first series: one on July 4, two on July 5, and another two on July 9. They produced a wealth of information. The heavily defended areas of Moscow and Leningrad, industrial areas, atomic plants, rocket sites, and aircraft storage sites had all been photographed. The most important result was to show that the Bomber Gap fears were unjustified. One photo showed nearly the entire Soviet force of Mya-4 bombers lined up at a single airfield. Enough areas had been covered to show there were no others; the negative could be proven. The U-2 photos indicated the Soviets had only fifty Mya-4s and TU-95s. This was fewer than the earlier estimates and far below the U.S. bomber force. The Bomber Gap had vanished.[8,9]

It had been hoped the U-2 flew too high for Soviet radar to pick up. On most training flights over the U.S., only one or two radar sites would pick up the aircraft. Over Russia, not only was the U-2 picked up, it was also tracked.[10] This underlined the discovery of the Genetrix balloons—Soviet radar was much more capable than the U.S. had thought.

The U-2 had overcome one shortcoming of the balloons: it flew above the reach of Soviet air defenses. There remained the political problem, however—Eisenhower's reluctance to authorize espionage flights over the Soviet Union. On July 10, Eisenhower said he was very close to deciding not to continue.[11] At the same time, the Soviets protested the flights. The note said the July 4 flight path was Minsk, Vilngas [sic], Kaunas, and Kaliningrad. One of the July 5 overflights was given as Brest, Pinsk, Baranovichi, Kaunas, and Kaliningrad.[12] In response, the U-2 overflights were put on hold for the time being.

The halt lasted four months. In the meantime, the second group of U-

2 pilots had completed their training and deployed to Incirlik, Turkey. Eisenhower authorized a series of overflights in November. One of these was the first overflight out of Turkey. The pilot who made the flight was Francis Gary Powers.[13]

In the wake of the U-2's success, Eisenhower ordered, in December 1956, a halt to all Air Force and Navy short-range overflights of Russia.[14] Although penetrations of Eastern European airspace could continue (and would through the 1960s), the skies over Russia would be the province of the CIA's U-2s. The third and final group of U-2 pilots was, at this same time, completing its training. In early 1957, they were deployed to Atsugi, Japan. The Wiesbaden unit was also on the move, transferring to Giebelstadt, West Germany (like Incirlik, this was also an old Genetrix launch site).

Ash Can and Grab Bag

After the hectic launch activities of January and early February 1956, the rest of the year was quiet for the 1110th Air Support Group. It was late spring before the launch crews arrived back at Lowry AFB. Three detachments were set up at Lowry, Vincent AFB (Yuma, Arizona) and Larson AFB, Washington. The 1110th ASG's first balloon launch since coming home was not made until December 4, 1956. It lifted off at 5:13 P.M. MST from Lowry and was found the next day by the Pennsylvania State Police at Gallett, Pa.[15]

The 1110th ASG gained two new missions in 1957. One was Moby Dick V. This involved flying high-altitude constant-level balloons from Lowry AFB. They were launched in an attempt to have them pass over a predesignated area at a set time. It was a continuation of the Moby Dick program. The operational altitudes were 50,000, 60,000, and 80,000 feet with three balloons launched per week. The balloons varied from 66 to 128 feet in diameter (presumably old 66CT and 128TT balloons left over from Genetrix). The payload also varied from 700 up to 1,000 pounds.

The other mission was an intelligence-gathering project. In this case, "gathering" was the right word. With the start of the Cold War, it was vitally important the U.S. know if the Russians had exploded their own A-bomb. The only means available at the time was to pick up the fall-out. In the spring of 1948, several WB-29 weather planes were fitted with large scoops. The air the scoops gathered passed through filters which would trap any fallout particles. The WB-29s, attached to a unit called AFOAT-1, were soon flying patrols off the Soviet Pacific coast. Between May 1948 and the start of September 1949, the filters showed unusually high levels of radiation 111 times. Each time it proved to be from natural sources such as volcanic eruptions, earthquakes, or normal fluctuations in background radiation.

On September 3, a WB-29, flying from Japan to Alaska, found high levels of radiation. More planes were sent out and they also returned filters with radioactive particles. In one case, the reading was 1,000 counts per minute; anything over 50 was abnormal. Scientists at Los Alamos and the Naval Research Laboratory determined the specific isotopes could only have been produced by an atomic explosion. It was estimated to have taken place between August 26 and 29 in Soviet Asia. (The test actually took place at Semipalatinsk on August 29). The WB-29 continued to make atmospheric sampling flights into the early 1950s, supplemented by fighters. Starting in 1953, B-57s were used to collect fallout.

The recovered material, a fine dust, could also indicate the design features of the bomb. Chemical analysis would indicate the nuclear materials, metals, and explosives used. Examination of the isotopes and other fallout products would indicate the efficiency of the weapon, that is, how much energy was released per gram of nuclear material versus the theoretical maximum if it was completely converted into energy. Taken together, the size and weight could be estimated for the complete weapon in its bomb casing. The diameter was set by the bomb mechanism, the length by the speed at which the bomb was dropped. The higher the speed, the longer (more streamlined) the casing would have to be. Thus from a small quantity of dust, a schematic of the weapon could be deduced. It was determined, for instance, that the Soviets' first A-bomb was similar in design to the weapon dropped on Nagasaki.

Atmospheric sampling also provided a clue to the most important intelligence question of all—the number of nuclear weapons in the Soviet stockpile. A reactor used to produce the plutonium for nuclear weapons also gave off the isotope krypton 85. This was vented into the atmosphere and was carried on the wind. As the U.S. knew how much krypton 85 was given off by Western reactors, any excess was from Russian reactors. This would allow an estimate to be made of Soviet plutonium production.[16]

Soviet weapons production took place at "Kyshtym 40" near Sverdlovsk in the Ural mountains. The complex sprawled across a wide area. The reactors, plutonium separation plants, and radioactive waste storage areas were on the southern shore of Lake Kyzyltash. To the north about twenty miles were the nuclear weapons production facilities. Here the bombs underwent final assembly.[17]

The ability to reach altitudes above those of aircraft made balloons an ideal means of sampling fallout. The development program began in March 1955 at Goodfellow AFB, Texas. Six General Mills personnel conducted the initial test flights. These early tests were successful, and during 1956 sampling flights were begun from São Paulo, Brazil, and French AFB in the Canal Zone. The transfer to control of the 1110th ASG began in September 1956 when the first two Air Force personnel—Capt. William B. Skinner and A/1C Glen H. King—started training at Goodfellow AFB. They were joined by six airmen later that month.

The January 16, 1957, operational plan directed the 1110th ASG to begin support launches for the project from Lowry, Larson, and Vincent AFBs. One flight per month was to be made from each base to 50,000, 65,000, 80,000, and 90,000 feet. Because a recovery helicopter was not available, no launches were made from Vincent AFB. WS-119L equipment was used in modified form. The long main bar and two ballast boxes were eliminated. Instead, a short bar and one ballast box were carried. The WS-119L control box was modified with an on/off control for the blower motor of the fallout collector. The sampling equipment was attached to the bar. The modified WS-119L equipment was tested in two launches from Lowry AFB on January 30 and February 13, 1957. Both were successful, and the way was now clear to use the leftover WS-119L hardware. By the end of February, a total of fifteen launches (ten successful and five failures) had been made from Lowry and Larson AFBs.

On April 1, 1957, the 1110th ASG took over operation of the fallout-monitoring balloons. There were two separate but related projects: Ash Can involved the collection of particulate debris—the actual fallout from the bomb; Grab Bag gathered whole air samples (including, one presumes, krypton 85). One flight to each of the four altitudes was to be made each month for both projects. The eight flight sets per month were made from three areas: 30° N, 8° N, and 25° S. This would provide a worldwide sample of radioactive material in the atmosphere.[18]

The balloons used for the Ash Can/Grab Bag flights ranged in size from 46 to 128 feet in diameter. The payload was 300 pounds. Flight time for the initial launches was two hours. When the mission was completed, the balloon used a novel method to descend to earth. Rather than cutting loose and parachuting to a landing, a vent near the apex of the balloon was opened and the helium gas allowed to escape. The payload remained attached to the balloon.[19]

With the new mission, the 1110th ASG was given control of three units which had conducted the General Mills test flights. (The launch crews were, up to this point, attached to the 1008th Special Weapons Squadron.) The units and their locations were: Det. 158, São Paulo, Brazil; Det. 159, Coco Solo Naval Station, Canal Zone; Det. 160, Goodfellow AFB; Det. 161, Lowry AFB; Det. 162, Larson AFB; and Det. 163, Vincent AFB.

Each unit had its own problems. The Goodfellow AFB crew made eight launches during April but had only two successes owing to bad weather. June was better: five tries, four successes. The Coco Solo launch crew had to cope with terrain: 25 percent landed in the jungle and could not be found. To be recovered, the balloons had to come down at sea. Even so, if they were not picked up within ten minutes, the filter paper would become wet and would have to be dried out before being mailed. A more general problem was controlling the altitude of the balloons. The 1110th ASG found the balloons were actually floating 8,000 to 13,000 feet higher than planned. The inaccurate wind reports made trajectory forecasts impossible.

During the spring, the supply of helium began to run low. Air Force Headquarters ordered a feasibility study of flying both Ash Can and Grab Bag collection units on a single balloon. Several modifications were developed in which the Ash Can blower fed both the units. This was tested and used operationally. Interestingly, if the Grab Bag payload worked while the Ash Can unit failed, a reflight would not be made. Clearly the Grab Bag's whole air sample was deemed more valuable.

Between January and the end of June 1957, a total of fifty-seven Grab Bag missions were launched with thirty-one successes. Fifty Ash Can flights were conducted; exactly half were successful. The Ash Can/Grab Bag flights continued in 1958, but with changes. Det. 163 (Vincent AFB) closed down and Det. 162 (Larson AFB) moved to Sioux City, Iowa. The first launches from Sioux City were planned for July 1. Part of the Ash Can/Grab Bag effort was constant improvements to the equipment. One particularly important modification was called "trapping." This used liquid hydrogen to transfer the air sample from the polyethylene bags into sturdier containers for descent and landing. There were also changes in rigging, collection equipment, and radio gear. Of more significance to the personnel was the change of the unit's name: it was now the 1110th Balloon Activities Group.[20]

There was much fallout for Grab Bag/Ash Can and the 1110th BAG to collect. Between 1949 and 1955, the Soviets had made ten nuclear tests. In 1956 alone, they exploded seven weapons. They made thirteen tests in 1957 and another twenty-five in 1958. (The 1958 total was nearly as many as all the previous Soviet tests put together.)[21] Despite this increase in the pace of nuclear testing, the availability of fissionable material would impose a bottleneck on Soviet nuclear warhead production until 1966.[22] Presumably, this information was based in part on the Ash Can and Grab Bag flights. Another source was U-2 photos of Soviet uranium mining facilities.

U-2 Overflights Continue

In 1957, the number of U-2 overflights increased. Although they covered many targets, increasingly they were directed at a new threat: Soviet ICBMs. Development of the Soviet R-7 ICBM began in the last years of Stalin's life. In August 1955, the first construction work started on the launch pad in the desert of Central Asia. Because this area, east of the Aral Sea, was not covered by the Genetrix balloons, the work was not discovered. Construction continued through 1956 and was completed in December. In March 1957, the first flight-model R-7 began checkout. It was rolled out to the pad on May 5. Final tests were conducted for the next ten days. The launch was made at 7:00 P.M. Moscow time on May 15, 1957. The missile failed 50 seconds into the flight. Two more launches followed during the spring and summer. They also failed, exploding on the pad or just after liftoff.[23]

This activity attracted the CIA's attention. Although the general area was known, the exact site was not. President Eisenhower authorized a series of U-2 overflights with the launch site as a priority target. The mission tracks were aligned on the major rail lines in the area.[24] As the U-2s set off on their quest, the CIA put together what it had on the area. Three decades later, Arthur Lundahl, chief photo interpreter of the CIA, described the process: "Some cases where we had literally pieced together bits of folklore, mapping, information, traveler's reports . . . we would have stuck all these little bits of information on a map and make a great melange of things."[25]

In June, a U-2 flying out of Pakistan found the site. According to one account, the pilot was flying along the assigned track when he saw something unusual in the distance. The pilots were authorized to deviate from their courses in such instances. It was the launch site and its huge flame pit. The pictures were beautiful, and five days later Lundahl's photo interpreters had put together a cardboard model of the launch site, showing the facilities and surrounding access roads.[26] Checking on a 1939 German Mil-Geo map, the CIA found the launch pad was built at the end of a 15-mile rail spur extending out into the desert from the main Moscow–Tashkent rail line. It had originally been built to support open-pit mining areas (probably worked by political prisoners of the Great Purge). One of the old quarries was apparently used as the flame pit. At the base of the rail spur was the small rail stop of Tyuratam. This was the name given to the launch site.[27,28]

Lundahl described the meaning of the U-2 photos, such as those of Tyuratam: "... one look at the aerial photos of that place, literally wiped out most of that folklore and gave us hard, crisp information that was measurable and reaffirmable by anybody who wanted to look at the pictures. It was really like seeing the dawn after a long dark night of ignorance."[29]

The string of R-7 launch failures was finally broken on August 3 when one flew 3,500 nautical miles to the impact zone on the Kamchatka Peninsula. On August 26, the Soviets announced the launch. A second followed on September 7. On hand at Tyuratam to witness the successful flight was Communist Party Secretary Nikita Khrushchev.[30]

In the wake of the two successes, Khrushchev authorized the launching of earth satellites using the R-7 as booster. The first, Sputnik 1, went into orbit on October 4, 1957. As the first man-made object placed into orbit, it had a tremendous impact on the West. For Americans, proud of their technological accomplishments and frontier heritage, the news that the final frontier had been opened by their Cold War adversaries was bitter. This was followed a month later, on November 3, by the orbiting of Sputnik 2 which carried a dog named Laika.

Behind the scientific and human accomplishment, there was considerable military significance. Only two U.S. Atlas ICBMs had been launched and both ended in failure. Although many more test flights would be needed before the Soviet ICBM, dubbed the SS-6 Sapwood by NATO, was an operational weapon, it was clear that the Soviets had gained a considerable lead in rocketry. The opening of space had impact in many fields, including reconnaissance.

WS-461L

As all this was going on, work resumed on balloon reconnaissance. The halt following the Genetrix operational flights lasted a year. During that time, the WS-119L hardware was in storage, presumably in some type of stand-by status. On January 30, 1957, headquarters of the Air Research and Development Command ordered the transfer of all remaining WS-119L funding to a new balloon project designated WS-461L. All manpower, facilities, test aircraft, and other resources freed up by the change were to go to the new program. The initial funding was $50,000 for a study of the weather data produced by the WS-119L flights. Priority of the project was 1-A. It was to be managed by the Cambridge Research Center.[31]

The WS-461L would differ in several important ways from the earlier WS-119L. Its operational altitude would be 100,000 feet and the balloon would fly for nearly a month. Both were considerably more than Genetrix. Equipment from WS-119L would be used wherever possible. The priority effort was seen as developing a new, higher-resolution camera (had the original one been used, resolution would be lost owing to the balloon's higher altitude). The HYAC-1 panoramic camera was a ground-breaking design. The camera had a 12-inch focal length, f/5 lens which was pivoted. As the lens swung back and forth, it "painted" the image on the film, which was held on a cylindrical focal plane. This provided high resolution over a 120° field. The only moving part was the pivoting lens. The camera carried 1,000 feet of 70-mm film. It was only 30.5 inches high, 27.5 inches long, and 10 inches deep. The Itek Corporation built forty HYAC-1 cameras in early 1958. The most striking change was in the flight profile. Genetrix had ridden the winter jet stream west to east. WS-461L would be launched during the summer when the air currents were in the opposite direction: east to west. The balloon would be capable of flying nearly around the world. That balloon technology existed in the late 1950s to allow a global flight will come as a surprise to many. The WS-461L used a complex relationship between the temperature of the gas inside the balloon and that of the outside atmosphere. As long as the gas inside a balloon is warmer than the outside atmosphere, the balloon will have excess lift. At night, the gas cools and the balloon will descend until it reaches a level at which the atmosphere is cooler. (In the stratosphere, the air is cooler as one goes lower.) The various elements must be balanced. The balloon must not absorb too much heat from the sun during the day or the gas will expand too much and be lost. Conversely, the balloon must retain heat during the night or it will drop too low. If the factors are correct, a balloon can fly around the world in the tropics and midlatitudes during the summer with minimal use of ballast. The procedure was first theorized in the early 1950s by scientists at the University of Minnesota and was tested in the mid-1950s by the Cambridge Research Center. That the procedure worked was completely classified. The meteorological feasibility of the project was determined by RAND. Development was to be completed by March 31, 1958. To do this, the specifications for the final system had to be released as soon as possible to allow sufficient production lead time. $750,000 was released for the program on May 14, 1957.[32]

This funding allowed the Air Force to undertake test flights. Before they could be made, however, Eisenhower's permission was needed. On June 26, 1957, at 2:15 P.M., President Eisenhower and Secretary of State Dulles met to discuss the project. Dulles's notes on the conversation read:

> I said that I had been asked to approve of some test balloon flights by the Air Force. These were designed to go around the world at high altitude in a westerly direction. The initial flights would be limited in numbers and without photographic equipment. If, however, the flights were successful, then they would be followed, presumably next year when weather conditions were appropriate, by balloons with photographic equipment.
>
> The President said he strongly disapproved of this project, certainly at this time, and asked me to inform the Air Force accordingly. He expressed the view that projects of this kind ought to be cleared at a political level before they were far advanced.[33]

This would seem to be the end of WS-461L. Yet, only seven days later, on July 3, Eisenhower met with Defense Secretary Charles Wilson, Deputy Defense Secretary Donald A. Quarles, and Secretary of State Dulles. Quarles outlined the project: 100,000-foot altitude, one-month lifetime, and improved equipment. Wilson said the project involved only $750,000. Department of Defense had asked the State Department if it was all right to circumnavigate the world while avoiding the Soviet Union. The president said "he would be delighted to have one tried." It should not go over Russia. Eisenhower also recommended the U.S. invite scientists to participate in the observations.[34]

From "strongly disapproved" to "delighted" in only a week—quite a change in attitude on Eisenhower's part. In fact, it was one of a number of examples of Eisenhower having second thoughts concerning reconnaissance operations over the Soviet Union. It was a pattern that would grow as time went on and one from which WS-461L would not be exempt.

The around-the-world test flights were soon underway and proved very successful. The first two balloons came close to a full circumnavigation while using as little as 39 pounds of ballast.

The test flights did not end with the coming of winter and the new year. The Cambridge Research Center's official history for 1958 mentions "large numbers" of balloons being launched "capable of about two weeks' sustained flight at altitudes of 100,000 feet"—presumably WS-461L test flights. The launches were not made from a land base but rather at sea from Military Sea Transportation Service aircraft carriers off the California coast. Launches were presumably handled by members of the 1110th Balloon Activities Group. The balloons would drift across the North American continent, collecting weather data. Some of the data were transmitted by radio while other measurements were recorded on-board for analysis after the gondola was recovered. As with the earlier Moby Dick balloons, tracking provided information on stratospheric winds. The altitude was measured and recorded on-board along with air temperatures at the different altitudes at which the balloon floated. The balloons were programmed to change altitude over time. This allowed calculation of stratospheric wind shears.

Another experiment carried by many of the gondolas was a sensing element called a "black ball." As the name suggests, it was a spherical black infrared absorber. The sunlight heated it up; when this was compared to the air temperature, the atmospheric heat balance could be determined. Other instruments measured the earth's albedo (reflectivity) and sky brightness.

Safety measures similar to those first developed for Moby Dick were used on these flights. If the balloons failed to reach 50,000 feet in 100 minutes after launch or whenever it later descended below 50,000 feet, the gondola would automatically be cut free and land by parachute.

The balloons drifted across North America until they reached the east coast. Normally the gondolas would land in the Atlantic Ocean. Recovery was by ship, although WB-50 weather aircraft assisted in the search for the floating gondolas. The gondolas carried a homing beacon to guide the search ship and planes. In the event the gondola came down on land, its parachute was colored orange and white for visibility. A number of gondolas were found by private citizens. The tests were successful and the balloons were considered to have "reached a high level of reliability."[35]

Although the emphasis in the Cambridge Research Center history was on weather and atmospheric studies, the use of aircraft carriers as the launch platform implies they were only ride-along experiments on WS-461L test flights. Such shipboard launches were to become part of the flight profile for the operational launches. This had both advantages and shortcomings. On the plus side, there was no need to involve other countries, avoiding political or security problems. A ship's mobility meant the balloons would not be tied to fixed bases. Countering this was a relatively low launch rate. The flight deck of a carrier is small compared to the acres of parking apron of an air base. Only one or two balloons per day could be launched, far below the better than one per hour rate of a skilled launch crew at a land base. During June 1955, as preparations for overseas deployment were underway, the Air Force explored the possibility of using an aircraft carrier as an alternate launch site. It was hoped this would avoid the operational difficulty caused by the bad European winter weather. There were several problems, however: the ship would also be subject to bad weather, supply difficulties, and the Navy had no carriers which could be spared from their normal commitments.[36] Aircraft could not take off or land with a Skyhook balloon stretched out across most of the flight deck. However, in contrast to Genetrix, the plan for WS-461L envisioned a much smaller scale of launches. Also, a Military Sea Transportation Service carrier would be used rather than a Navy fleet carrier. As the MSTS carriers were used only for transporting aircraft back and forth across the Pacific, they could more easily be spared.

Eisenhower Decides

By the spring of 1958, the WS-461L hardware was ready for Russian skies. Before launches could begin, however, Eisenhower's approval was needed. The reconnaissance situation had changed in the year since work began on WS-461L. The U-2 overflight program had come to a near-total halt. An overflight of the Soviet Far East on March 2, 1958, had resulted in a protest. In response, Eisenhower ordered further flights halted at once.[37,38] Although Eisenhower was willing to approve individual flights, they were few and far between. This meant probing flights were limited to the fringes of the Communist bloc.

Over Eastern Europe, for instance, North American RF-100A "Slick Chick" aircraft were used. They would take off from a base in West Germany, such as Hahn, climb and accelerate to supersonic speed before crossing the East/West border. The photo run was a straight supersonic dash for maximum speed. Reaching a predetermined point, the RF-100 would begin a climbing turn, then dive and dash back for the border. The flights were called "Keyhole" missions owing to their shape.[39]

In the Far East, Nationalist Chinese pilots were making similar flights over Communist China's coastal areas. Republic RF-84F Thunderflash aircraft were used for these missions. At the same time, Nationalist Chinese crews were being trained to fly RB-57D reconnaissance aircraft. With a maximum altitude of 66,000 feet, they would be above the reach of Communist Chinese MiG-15 and MiG-17 fighters. This would allow deeper overflights than the subsonic low-altitude RF-84Fs could make. The RB-57Ds would not be ready until the fall of 1958.[40,41]

As for Russia, except for the odd U-2 overflight, intelligence activity was limited to ELINT aircraft flying outside Soviet airspace. Their information was very valuable; for instance, U-2s were able to record telemetry from Soviet ICBM tests. This gave an insight into the design of the missiles, the test goals and the results.[42]

All of this could shed no light on the most pressing intelligence question facing the U.S. in early 1958: the number of Soviet ICBMs to be deployed. In the wake of the Sputnik launches, it was realized that for the first time the U.S. was now vulnerable to direct attack. Adding to the supercharged emotional environment was the realization just how vulnerable the U.S. was. There were no radars able to spot incoming warheads; U.S. bombers were not on alert, able to take off on short notice. The specter of Pearl Harbor returned.

The Air Force estimated the Soviets would have their first ICBMs deployed by the end of 1958, 500 by mid-1960, and 1,000 by mid-1961. The CIA estimated the first ten SS-6 ICBMs would be operational by early 1959, 100 by mid-1960, and 500 in mid-1961. These production rates, 500 ICBMs per year into the mid-1960s in the Air Force estimate, were far higher than the U.S. planned. If true, there would be a gap between the numbers of U.S. and Soviet ICBMs—a missile gap. The missile gap controversy would be the central question for U.S. intelligence for the next three years.[43]

On May 16, 1958, at 6 P.M., a meeting was held in the White House to discuss the WS-461L program. On hand were the president, Secretary of State John Foster Dulles, Chairman of the Joint Chiefs of Staff Gen. Nathan F. Twining, Vice Chairman Gen. Curtis LeMay, CIA Director Allen Dulles, Special Assistant for Science and Technology Dr. James R. Killian, Jr., and Colonel Gremmier of the Air Force. The meeting had been arranged by Secretary of State Dulles. They were operating under a deadline. In order for the balloons to be ready for launch under the proper weather conditions, approval had to be given by June 1, if not earlier. If this was not done, the summer wind currents would be missed and launches delayed a year. Eisenhower reviewed the plans but deferred his decision until Secretary of State Dulles could send him the reactions of several outside experts.[44]

Three days later, on May 19, Eisenhower told Dulles his decision was negative. Dulles informed Chief of Staff Brig. Gen. Andrew Goodpaster, who relayed word of the decision to the others at the meeting. Clearly, Eisenhower's earlier "allergy" to balloon reconnaissance had not changed.[45] But tomorrow was another day.

June 25—another meeting, same subject. The Air Force again asked permission to launch the WS-461L balloons. President Eisenhower was assured the balloons would not be spotted by the Soviets. Department of Defense Secretary Quarles also told him the chances of the balloons being detected were small and the chances of identification or a shoot-down practically nil. Floating at 100,000 feet, they were out of reach of even the U-2, then the highest-flying aircraft in the world. The Soviet SA-2 Guildline SAM, then in development, was apparently not seen as a danger. Eisenhower reluctantly agreed.[46] But time was fleeting; it was three weeks past the June 1 deadline. Preparations began, to set sail on what was to be the last chapter in a century and a half of balloon reconnaissance.

Melting Pot

The ship chosen as launch platform for the WS-461L balloons was the USS *Windham Bay* (TCVU-92). It was a World War II escort carrier which had been brought out of moth balls in late 1950 to serve as an aircraft transport vessel. Since that date, it had made numerous West Coast–Japan resupply voyages in support of fleet carriers in the western Pacific. With a flight deck 475 feet long and 85 feet wide, the USS

Windham Bay had ample room for the WS-461L balloon envelope.[47,48]

In late June 1958, the ship was moored at Pier 3 South at NAS Alameda. The first word that it was to undertake the launchings, code named "Melting Pot," was a message from Air Force Headquarters on June 23, apparently ordering preparations to begin in the event Eisenhower approved. A follow-up message arrived the next day. On June 25, Eisenhower gave the go-ahead. The next day, another message was sent to the USS *Windham Bay*, apparently notes of the final approval. The ship received its sailing orders on June 27. The next day, the first of the launch personnel boarded the ship. By the morning of June 30, the remainder of the group and their cargo were on the ship. It was made up of the unit commander Maj. Robert Anderson, three officers, sixteen airmen and eight civilian technicians. (The names of all launch crewmen have been changed owing to the events to follow.)

With all in readiness, the USS *Windham Bay* cast off from the pier at 10:54 A.M. PST. It sailed under the Oakland Bay Bridge, past Alcatraz Island, and at 11:59, under the Golden Gate Bridge and into the open ocean. For the next two days, the USS *Windham Bay* headed west toward the launch area of latitude 37° N and longitude 150° W. This was northeast of the Hawaiian Islands (roughly, south of Alaska and even with San Francisco). The ship arrived at the launch area early on the morning of July 2.[49]

Preparations for the first launchings were begun. The payload (camera, gondola, control unit, radio transmitter and receiver, and ballast box) was mounted on a support stand on the rear part of the flight deck. Its appearance was similar to the WS-119L unit. The spreader bar was longer and the various "boxes" were more spread out. A major difference, one that would set in motion the events to follow, was that the WS-461L had two cut-down systems for the camera gondola: a radio command system as on WS-119L and a preset timer. This would run for 400 hours (16.67 days) before dropping the gondola. This feature may have been added as a backup to the radio cut-down system which had failed repeatedly during Genetrix.[50]

The balloon envelope was laid out on a ground cloth on the flight deck. Hydrogen gas cylinders on a large cart were used to inflate the balloon. As the inflation process started, the USS *Windham Bay* began sailing with the wind, matching its speed and direction. Thus the wind over the deck was zero—dead calm.

The launch of the first operational WS-461L balloon, designated S-423, was made at 11:52 A.M. at 37°58′ N and 136°28.8′ W. It climbed into the sky and soon reached its ceiling of 100,000 feet. The westerly winds, if all went as planned, would carry the balloon over Japan, and then into Communist airspace in the area of China. The balloon would continue across China, then over southern Russia, and finally reemerge more than two weeks later over the Mediterranean or Western Europe. Its journey was about 10,500 miles long and was equivalent to 40 percent of the way around the world. This and the balloons that followed were pathfinders, or cover launches for the camera-carrying balloons. They could show the speed and direction of the upper air wind currents.

With the first launch completed, the ship headed north toward latitude 39° N for the next launch. The S-424 balloon was launched at 4:47 P.M., the same day, at a position of 39°04′ N and 136°30′ W. Once the launch was completed, the USS *Windham Bay* again headed northwest while preparations continued. The next morning, the ship ran into light rain and fog which did not clear until after 11:30 A.M. The ship increased its speed at 1:01 P.M., July 3, in preparation to launch S-425. The maneuvering for zero wind began at 1:49 P.M. but the balloon was not released until 4:03 P.M. The launch point was at 43°14.2′ N and 141°39.4′ W. The same evening, an injury to one of the launch crewmen occurred. A/2C George D. Palmer was carrying ballast cans into the Athletic Gear Locker. The cans tipped, wedging his left hand against the bulkhead and bruising a finger. This time, the injury was minor and Palmer returned to duty.

A second launch location, called area Bravo, around 50° N latitude, was now to be used. The ship continued northwest until it reached an area near 49° N and 141° W.

The launch of S-426 was made at 2:59 P.M. on July 4 after an hour and a half of preparations. The launch point was at 48°12′ N and 144°36′ W. The most northerly launch yet, the upper air currents would carry the balloon across Siberia, Central Asia, the Ukraine, Poland, and, finally, over Western Europe. Once its operation and trajectory were confirmed a half hour after launch, the ship headed west for its next launch point. The trip was at 5 knots as two of the four boilers were shut down to conserve fuel oil.[51]

After the hectic pace of four launches in three days, the weekend of July 5 and 6 was relaxed. The ship had to delay for the next scheduled launch so between 3 and 5 P.M. on Sunday, July 6, it laid to and the crew fished.

Monday, July 7, it was back to the business at hand. The morning saw poor weather as the ship sailed toward the launch point of 48° N and 152° W. Twice, fog caused extra lookouts to be posted and the foghorn sounded. Conditions remained bad as launch preparations for S-427 began at 10:26 A.M. Soon, however, it was clear that the ship could not compensate for the high wind speed. At 10:51 A.M., the attempt was canceled.

The fog returned during the early morning of July 8 but cleared soon after 8:00 A.M. The launch crew moved quickly to take advantage of the improved weather. At 8:47 A.M., the ship began maneuvering, the S-427 balloon was inflated and, at 10:54 A.M., it was released at 48°02′ N and 153°40′ W.

The fog closed in that afternoon and remained throughout the night and into the morning of July 9. Despite the bad weather, the launch crew pressed on in hopes of an improvement. At 10:35 A.M., the ship began sailing with the wind but nine minutes later it was apparent that weather conditions were unfavorable and S-428 would not be launched that day. The fog closed in again, not clearing until nearly noon. By that time, it was too late. The ship remained in the area.

The next morning, July 10, conditions were much better. The ship began maneuvering at 8:00 A.M. and S-428 lifted off 2 hours and 9 minutes later at 48° N and 154°16.8′ W. Originally, the plan was to remain in the same area for the next day's launch. A few minutes after noon it became clear S-428 was malfunctioning. The USS *Windham Bay* turned toward it and increased speed to 16 knots. By 12:20 P.M., it was underneath the high-flying balloon and a radio signal was transmitted to cut the gondola free. The balloon rose, burst, and the remaining payload descended under a separate parachute. Two minutes later, the payload was sighted in the water. A whaleboat was lowered and the payload was taken aboard at 12:42 P.M. It was back aboard the USS *Windham Bay* a few minutes later. After an examination, it was decided to search for the gondola. The ship headed toward the computed location of the S-428 gondola. On the way, it passed the balloon floating in the water. At 5:40 P.M., it began sailing various courses, trying to pick up the homing radio beacon on the gondola. Five minutes later, its bearing had been determined and the ship headed toward the gondola. At 6:24 P.M., lookouts spotted the gondola floating in the water. A whaleboat was lowered, and at 7:03, its crew recovered the gondola. Once it was aboard, the USS *Windham Bay* headed back to the launch area to try again the next morning.

When sunrise came on July 11, the wind was too strong and the morning launch attempt was canceled. The ship proceeded to an area where the weather would be more favorable. This proved correct and S-429 was launched at 4:15 P.M. (48°05′ N and 150°58′ W).

It was now time to launch the three HYAC-1 camera-carrying balloons. S-430 was the first, launched at 7:58 A.M. on July 12 (47°58′ N and 146°39′ W), S-431 followed at 4:16 P.M. on July 13 (50°41.5′ N and 155°20′ W), and S-432 brought the series, and U.S. balloon reconnaissance, to a close at 3:03 P.M. on July 14 (50°22′ N and 156°55′ W). The launches had gone perfectly but during preparations the timers on these three balloons had been set for 400 hours—something *not* authorized by Eisenhower's orders. This should have been sufficient time for them to drift across Russia, Poland, East Germany and then out of Communist airspace. But Eisenhower's delay in approving the project meant the launches were made two weeks after the weather window had closed. The forecast the launch positions were based on was no longer valid, as the upper wind currents were weakening.

During this series, another launch crewman had been injured. During the evening of July 12, Major Anderson, the unit commander, broke his knee when it struck the edge of a watertight door. He was put on the sick list. Presumably, Capt. Neville F. Stockton took over command.

After the launch of S-432 on July 14, the ship remained in the area pending a determination if another launch was needed at the same location. For the past several days the weather had been favorable. The fog had always cleared off before launch time. After the S-432 launch, the fog closed in again. On July 15, the ship headed for 49°30′ N and 151°30′ W for a possible launch. In the meantime, to the northwest of the ship, a storm had developed which lashed the ship with rain and high seas. That afternoon, the USS *Windham Bay* turned to the southwest and increased speed to clear the storm area. During the evening, the launch gear on the flight deck was covered for protection. The bad weather continued through the night.

With the dawn, things were clearer, both literally and figuratively. The ship had left the storm behind; the only significant weather was the by-now-familiar fog banks. More importantly, the question of more camera-carrying balloon launches had been decided—no more were needed and the shop could leave area Bravo. So at 7:00 A.M. on July 16, the USS *Windham Bay* altered course slightly and headed toward 39°30′ N and 144° W for a final series of "cover" launches and then home to San Francisco. The voyage to the final launch area took two days, the ship arriving during the morning of July 18.

The final launch operations were routine; S-433 was launched at 10:11 A.M. at 39°15.5′ N and 144°38′ W, S-434 followed on July 19 at 1:58 P.M. (37°57′ N and 136°18′ W), and the 13th and final launch, S-435, was made at 9:06 A.M. on July 20 (37°06′ N and 131°05′ W). This brought the launch phase of Operation Melting Pot to a close. The USS *Windham Bay* headed east toward San Francisco.

The ship arrived just before noon the next day. It passed under the Golden Gate Bridge at 12:19 P.M. and tied up at Pier 3 South, NAS Alameda, an hour later. The launch crew left the ship at 1:38 P.M. A week and a day later, the storm would break around them.[52]

The Storm Breaks

In November 1957, after sending Federal troops to enforce integration of Little Rock High School and after the launching of the first two Sputniks, Eisenhower wrote to a friend, "Since July 25th of 1956, when Nasser announced the nationalization of the Suez, I cannot remember a day that has not brought its major or minor crisis." He noted later, "crisis had now become 'normalcy'." Things did not change in 1958.

The Middle East continued to be unstable. In early May, Arab-Christian rivalries in Lebanon broke out in armed conflict. Then, on July 14 (the day S-432 was launched), a coup overthrew the government of Iraq. The pro-Western king, the crown prince and the premier were murdered by the street mobs and pro-Nasser army. In Jordan, King Hussein was threatened by a similar plot. There were also fears Israel might invade if Hussein fell and that Kuwait and Saudi Arabia might also become unstable. The area seemed to be drifting toward chaos. President Camille Chamoun of Lebanon requested the intervention of U.S. troops. Eisenhower agreed, and on July 15, U.S. Marines landed and took up positions in Beirut and the airport. Two days later, British paratroopers went into Jordan to bolster King Hussein's government.

The Soviets protested the moves, vetoed a proposal for a U.N. peacekeeping force to go into Lebanon, and proposed a summit meeting of the U.S., Britain, France, Russia, and India to settle the matter. The U.S. and Britain refused, saying any such effort should be within the

U.N. Khrushchev then repeated his call for a summit and sought to blame the U.S. for a refusal to negotiate. By the end of July, the situation had stabilized. Presidential elections were held in Lebanon to settle the dispute. In Iraq, government officials expressed an interest in establishing good relations with the U.S. and Britain. The level of uncertainty and instability was lower.[53]

All the while, the S-430, 431 and 432 balloons were drifting west across Russia, their timers clicking off the passing hours. It was now the last days of July and they were not going to make it. The timer of S-430 turned on the radio tracking beacon. The fixes showed it was over Poland. Soon after, the 400 hours were up and the camera gondola was cut free.

Word the balloon was coming down in Poland was relayed to Washington D.C. late in the evening of July 28—CIA Director Allen Dulles was told at 11 P.M. Eisenhower was informed the next morning, July 29. He was in a meeting with Secretary of State Dulles, who had just returned from a meeting of the Baghdad Pact members about the Middle East situation. General Goodpaster came in and told them the balloons were coming down in Poland.[54] Eisenhower became extremely angry. Dulles said later the president was as angry as he had ever seen him. Eisenhower said they had all let him down in a most terrible way. He criticized Dulles because he had agreed to the project, thinking it was properly safeguarded. He also ordered General Goodpaster to impound all money for the project.

By noon, Dulles was making phone calls for more information. At 12:25 P.M., he called Hugh S. Cumming, Jr., the Special Assistant for Intelligence. Cumming told Dulles, to quote the phone log, "the AF Officer was stupid and without authority set it at 400 hours instead of by command to bring it down and it dropped at 400 hours—the airspeed was miscalculated." (The balloon's location was indicated by radio signals.) Dulles said the loss meant they would never try anything like this again. Cumming said it was shocking. He did not know what action had been taken in regard to the Air Force officer but they would have to pick up the pieces. Dulles concluded by saying it could not have happened at a worse time—an apparent reference to the Middle East crisis.

At 12:29 P.M., Dulles called Department of Defense Secretary Quarles. Dulles told him of the president's reaction to the news. Quarles said he also should be criticized and felt critical of his own actions. He noted, on the other hand, this was one of the chances one takes with intelligence operations. Dulles was not impressed and responded that the chances were not estimated very well. Dulles also recalled somebody saying if the balloon were up for a day or two, there was no chance it would come down until commanded. Quarles said that was how the balloons should have been programmed. Dulles said the most important thing at the moment was to give out an "innocuous" cover statement.

Quarles called back several hours later to say a press release had already been made "on the 25th" (presumably June 25, the day Eisenhower approved the launches). He said he had the strong impression "no useful purpose" could be accomplished by adding to the earlier release. Dulles said he had not been aware of the release and said making a second one would "look like a guilty conscience." Dulles next asked what was carried by the balloons. Quarles said cameras. The Soviets would get the photos, depending on the gondola's condition on landing. Dulles and Quarles finally decided the best approach was to sit tight—to await the Soviet response.[55]

S-431 dropped the next day, July 30, also inside Communist airspace. No Soviet reaction was noted to its fall or that of S-430 the day before. The third balloon, S-432, came down during the afternoon of July 31.[56]

The same day S-432 was lost, Eisenhower sent a top secret memorandum to the Secretary of Defense. It read:

> There is disturbing evidence of a deterioration in the processes of discipline and responsibility within the Armed Forces. Setting aside earlier instances, I refer to recent occurrences which have special seriousness because of their operational character or connection. They include, in particular, unauthorized decisions which have apparently resulted in certain balloons falling within the territory of the Communist bloc, a reported violation of the Soviet border in the Caspian Sea area by one of our reconnaissance aircraft following a route that contravened my standing orders, and statements resulting in the disclosure of the location of certain of our atomic weapons storage and assembly sites within the United States.
>
> The harm done by this type of thing to the conduct of our international affairs, and to our national security, is obvious.
>
> I believe it is essential that action be taken at once, with provision for the appropriate degree of security, to fix responsibility in these instances through formal investigation and report, and to institute a general tightening of discipline and command and executive responsibility within the defense establishment.[57]

The memo reflected an atmosphere of increasing frustration. The launch of the Sputniks and the emerging missile gap controversy were generating demands for increased defense spending. Eisenhower refused, both for strategic reasons and, more importantly, because this threatened his goal of balancing the budget—an increasingly single-minded priority. Eisenhower felt the national mood of fear was unjustified, yet his efforts to ease public concerns fell on deaf ears and were attacked as penny pinching or as inadequate. Events had taken on a life of their own, outpacing Eisenhower's ability to shape or control them.

The balloon crisis faded in the early days of August. There had been no Soviet response, either public or private, to the fall of the balloons. Events were also pushing them aside. A new crisis was developing in the Far East over Quemoy and Matsu islands. These were two large off-shore islands held by the Nationalist Chinese. They were separated by only a few miles from the Communist mainland. Gen. Chiang Kai-shek believed they were critical to the safety of Formosa and, against the advice of the U.S., built up their garrisons. By the summer of 1958, there were 100,000 troops (one-third of his total ground forces) on the two islands.[58]

During early 1958, the Communist Chinese requested aircraft, long-range artillery, and air force advisers from the Russians to attack the islands and then "liberate" Formosa.[59] The preliminaries to the Formosa Strait crisis got underway even as the balloons were coming down. Late July saw increased Communist air activity over the straits.[60]

On July 31, even as S-432 was coming down and the Middle East crisis was still unfolding, Khrushchev left for four days of meetings with Mao Tse-tung. Khrushchev agreed to the attack but, it appears in retrospect, with strings. Within days of the meeting, intelligence reports indicated military airfields and artillery emplacements were being set up on the coast near the islands. By mid-August, it was clear a move against the islands could soon begin.[61]

The attack began on August 23 with a massive artillery bombardment. Some 20,000 shells hit Quemoy and Matsu. Over 400 guns battered the islands around the clock. Quemoy was hit with 120,000 shells in one week. A blockade prevented resupply of the islands as the Communist Chinese attempted to starve the Nationalists out. As the shells fell like rain, radio stations and loudspeakers on the mainland broadcast calls to "surrender," "return to the fatherland," and "kill U.S. advisors" because "the island is doomed."[62]

The choices facing Eisenhower were grim. If the U.S. did not intervene, the Communist Chinese would see the way clear to invade the islands and threaten Formosa. Its loss would put Japan, the Philippines, Thailand, Okinawa, and Vietnam at risk in the years to follow. Both Eisenhower and Dulles believed U.S. support for the Nationalists would prevent the Communist Chinese from going beyond the shelling and blockade. Should this fail, however, and the Chinese invade, the U.S. would have to resort to the use of tactical nuclear weapons to destroy the Communist air bases.

For the moment, Eisenhower ordered an increase in U.S. naval forces in the strait and Air Force units on Formosa. They were directed to be ready to escort Nationalist Chinese resupply convoys. The U.S. also made it clear it was willing to go to the brink should Communist Chinese actions require it.[63]

In the midst of the Formosa Strait crisis, a new incident occurred involving an intelligence operation. On September 2, 1958, a Lockheed C-130A-II Hercules of the 7406th Combat Support Squadron took off from Incirlik, Turkey. The transport had been modified to receive Soviet radio transmissions. On board was a crew of seventeen. They were to fly northeast toward Trabzon on the Black Sea coast, then turn southeast and fly to the Turkish city of Van, and finally return to Incirlik via the same route. The Trabzon–Van leg of the flight was parallel to the southern Russian border. The aircraft was to stay 100 miles from the border. The day was cloudy and the aircraft had to navigate using radio beacons. As reconstructed later, the aircraft actually homed on radio beacons in the Soviet Black Sea cities of Batumi and Poti. These decoy beacons were more powerful than Trabzon's beacon, only one kilocycle off Trabzon's frequency, and directly in line with the flight path between Incirlik and Trabzon. The decoy beacon pulled the C-130A-II east of the planned course. When the crew made the turn at what they thought was Trabzon, the aircraft then switched to the radio beacon at Van. In fact, it was flying toward another powerful decoy beacon near Yerevan in Soviet Armenia. Its frequency was 15 kilocycles off that of Van's beacon and its power drowned out the Turkish beacon at all but short ranges. The aircraft, led on by the decoy, crossed the Soviet border and into a deliberate trap.[64]

A ground ELINT station in Turkey picked up the radio transmissions of the five MiGs as they jumped the helpless transport:

> "I see the target, a large one."
> "Its altitude is 100 [10,000 m] as you said."
> "I am 201. I see the target. Attack! I am 201. I am attacking the target."

"Attack, attack, 218, attack."
"The target is a transport, four engined."
"Target speed is 300 [kilometers]. I am going along with it. It is turning toward the fence [border]."
"There's a hit!"
"The target is burning, 582."
"The target is banking."
"It is going towards the fence."
"Open fire!"
"218, are you attacking?"
"Yes, yes I . . ."
"The target is burning."
"The tail assembly is falling off the target."
"82, do you see me? I am in front of the target."
"Look!"
"Oh?"
"Look at him. He will not get away. He is already falling . . . ."
"Yes, he is falling. I will finish him off, boys. I will finish him off on the run. The target has lost control, it is going down."
"Now the target will fall."
"82, a little to the right."
"The target has turned over."
"The target is falling."
"Form up."[65]

An eyewitness on the ground saw two of the MiGs fire on the C-130A-II, blowing its right wing off. The aircraft hit the ground near a group of villagers. They ran to the scene and tried to rescue any survivors. Before they reached the aircraft, there was an explosion and it burst into flame. The villagers were forced to stay back until the fire died down. When it had burned out, they probed through the wreckage and found eighteen bodies, twelve of which were burned beyond recognition. (There were only seventeen crewmen; presumably this was an error by the source, a miscount of the mangled bodies, or a Soviet citizen killed by the falling debris.) An hour after the crash, a group of ten government vehicles arrived at the site and a number of officials made a thorough search of the wreckage. The source of the report said they found a large mass of melted gold in the plane's interior.[66]

The Soviets Protest

Following the ambush of the C-130A-II, events came tumbling one after another. The next day, September 3, 1958, the Soviets protested the balloon overflights of July. The Soviet Deputy Foreign Minister, Georgi N. Zarubin, handed the note to U.S. Chargé d'Affaires Richard H. Davis. It said:

> Several balloons carrying equipment which included automatic cameras for aerial photography, a receiving and transmitting radio set, etc, have been brought down in the air space of the Soviet Union lately. An examination of the equipment showed that it had been manufactured in the USA and that the balloons are being launched by the US Air Force. This is shown, in particular, by the insignias on various parts of the equipment.

The Soviets repeated their earlier objections to the balloons, calling them "a gross violation" and "a violation of the general accepted principle of international law which accords each state full and exclusive sovereignty over the air space above its territory." The note concluded:

> The Soviet government again protests to the US government against the launching of American balloons over the territory of the USSR and hopes that the US government will take immediate measures to stop such actions by American authorities.[67]

The question arises why the Soviets took so long to make a public protest. It had been five weeks since the balloons came down in Poland, and, despite what the note implied, the launchings had already stopped. The Soviet press did not "hype" the note—Pravda carried it on page 3, while Izvestia had it on page 2. One possibility is the timing was to maintain tension as the Formosa Strait crisis eased. Three days later, on September 6, Communist Chinese Premier Chou En-lai said he had agreed to resume ambassadorial talks in Warsaw with the U.S. It was the first break in the crisis.[68]

The U.S. responded to the Soviet protest note on the same day. It said the Soviet complaint had been investigated and the balloons were apparently those recently launched by the U.S. Air Force. These were high-altitude weather research balloons. The cameras were for photographing cloud formations and other weather phenomena. The U.S. requested the return of the balloons and also asked about the fate of the crew of the C-130.[69] Although the ELINT intercept indicated it had been shot down, the U.S. did not know if any of the crew had survived. (The eyewitness account of the bodies being removed from the wreckage did not reach the CIA until late November.)

The following day, September 7, the U.S. Navy escorted a convoy to Quemoy. The U.S. escort ships stayed three miles off the Communist

Chinese coast (the U.S. only recognized a three-mile limit; the Chinese claimed twelve miles). This first convoy drew no fire, a second one was badly hit and one Nationalist Chinese cargo ship was set afire. The other ships were driven off; the U.S. ships were not fired on. It was clear the Chinese "blockade by land shell fire" was still effective.[70]

The same day, Khrushchev sent a curiously ambivalent letter to Eisenhower. Although it said an attack on Communist China "is an attack on the Soviet Union," he added that "we have not the least doubt that the Chinese people will strike back at the aggressor in a fitting manner." This and other statements implied that, while the Soviets were willing to supply weapons and advisers, the Communist Chinese did not have a blank check to risk nuclear war with the U.S.[71]

On September 12, the Soviets responded to the U.S. request for information on the C-130. The note said an investigation team had "found the wreckage of a burned plane 55 km northwest of the city of Yerevan. They also found the remains of bodies there, from which it can be assumed that the six members of the crew were killed." The note claimed the flight "deliberately violated the state border of the Soviet Union" and protested "against the new gross violation." There was no accounting for the other eleven crewmen or even an admission the Soviets had shot it down.[72]

Starting on September 14, after nearly a week of failure, the Nationalists broke the blockade. Supplies were finally able to reach the islands. This included three 8-in. howitzers which were used for counter battery fire against the mainland guns. Amphibious tanks, landing craft, junks, and aircraft were used to bring in the supplies.[73] Clearly, the Chinese had failed in their attempts to starve out the islands.

It was only at this point, when the threat of nuclear war had passed, that Khrushchev extended nuclear protection to the Chinese. In a September 19 letter, he said if the U.S. attacked Communist China with nuclear weapons, the Soviets would respond "by the same means." It is worth noting the two letters came only after the negotiations had begun and the crisis had started to ease.[74]

At the end of September, the issue of the C-130 crew remained unresolved. Six bodies were returned on September 24. They were mutilated in the crash and only four could be positively identified. The Soviets refused a U.S. request to see the wreckage or additional information on the other crewmen.[75]

By the end of September, enough supplies had been built up on

Quemoy and Matsu so air drops alone would be sufficient. The Communist Chinese attempt to win air superiority over the islands had, by this time, ended in a stunning failure. Between late July and early October, the Nationalist Chinese claimed to have destroyed thirty-one MiGs with the loss of only two of their own aircraft. This was a kill ratio of nearly sixteen to one. During the latter stages of the conflict, the Nationalist Air Force used Sidewinder air-to-air missiles. Of the first five fired, four destroyed their targets.[76,77]

On October 5, the Communist Chinese admitted defeat. The Defense Minister announced they would cease firing on the Quemoy convoys if the U.S. would stop providing escorts. The shelling stopped, the U.S. stopped providing convoy escorts, and the Nationalists continued to pour in supplies.[78]

Showtime

Not until October 11 did the Soviets again raise the balloon issue. A press conference was called by the Soviet Foreign Ministry. In the hall were a large segment of the plastic balloon and the orange and white parachute attached to the wall. Hanging in front of them was a complete WS-461L payload. A. Ya. Popov, the acting press director of the Foreign Ministry, made an opening statement. He said, in part:

> In recent times several balloons have been brought down in the air space of the USSR; the equipment suspended from these balloons, as you could see for yourselves, includes automatic instruments. The containers suspended from the balloons house an aerial camera with a large supply of film and a control unit; a narrow-gauge camera which records the readings of the instruments and is designed to determine the coordinates of the aerial photos; a transmitting and receiving radio set and an automatically jettisoned ballast.

Popov then introduced Col. A. V. Tarantsov, who described the balloon's technical features. He had also done this for the February 1956 press conference. He noted:

> These new specimens of American aerial reconnaissance equipment show technical improvements that considerably increase their photo reconnaissance capabilities.
>
> These include the use of a camera and film of great sensitivity assuring photographs from altitudes of 30 to 35 km, which clearly show up individual objects, such as planes on an air field.

Concerning the on-board systems, Tarantsov said:

> A special program is employed to control the radio, whereby the transmitter operates while over US territory, shuts off when it approaches the borders of the Soviet Union, and switches on again when it leaves the USSR.
>
> The radio's receiver system, which picks up signals ordering it to drop the equipment on land (or in water), has been considerably complicated so as to make a forced landing of the balloon over the territory being reconnoitered as difficult as possible.

This was apparently a reference to the cut-down code signal which prevented the balloon's flight from being terminated by a strong radio transmission or a deliberate attempt. No mention was made of the fact that the balloons had come down owing to the on-board timer instead of being shot down as the Soviets implied. Any propaganda benefit the Soviets could have gained from this would have been canceled out by the admission that the balloons had floated too high for Soviet air defenses to reach. Tarantsov concluded by saying:

> Thus the technical aspects of the new American aerostats' equipment, as well as the programming of the apparatus, show indisputably that it is being used not for scientific purposes but for conducting secret aerial reconnaissance photography.

Tarantsov also showed film and prints taken from one of the balloons' cameras.[79]

Again the question was "why now?" It had been two and a half months since the balloons had come down and over a month since the public protest. In 1956, the protest and press conference had been only a few days apart. There were two possibly interrelated reasons, one international, the other domestic. The cease-fire had eased the Formosa Strait crisis. By making an issue of the balloons, the Soviets may have wanted to keep the crisis atmosphere alive.

It also had domestic aspects. The Soviet press was in the midst of a week-long spy scare campaign. Military newspapers warned soldiers and sailors to keep silent. Civilians were told foreign enemies took advantage of people who overindulged in vodka. The Soviets also launched a bitter personal attack on Capt. Joseph R. Ulatoski, assistant to the U.S. military attaché in Moscow: they accused him of stealing a letter containing military information.[80] Spy balloons floating silent and unseen would reinforce the siege mentality the Soviet government sought to foster.

In comparison to the 1956 series, the Soviet efforts in 1958 were low-key. There were no public displays of the captured gondolas in Eastern Europe or China. A follow-up article in the October 24 *Izvestia* was a complaint about the Western coverage of the press conference and said, in part:

> It can be assumed that the correspondents sent in reports on the October 11 press conference. But if so, these were never published. Only a few newspapers printed a brief Reuters report, and these tucked it away on a back page.
>
> The press organs which did print a report from their Moscow correspondents . . . tried to falsify the facts.[81]

The protest is ironic—the *New York Times* carried an article on the balloon press conference on page 1; *Pravda*'s account appeared on page 5.

The Formosa Strait crisis ended in farce. After extending the cease-fire, the Communist Chinese announced they would resume firing on Nationalist convoys—but only on odd-numbered days. Any resupply on even days would not be attacked. Eisenhower later wrote, "I wondered if we were in a Gilbert and Sullivan war."[82]

Less satisfying was the outcome of the C-130 incident. The U.S. made a repeated request to the Soviets as to the fate of the other eleven crewmen. When no response was made, the U.S. made public, in February 1959, the tape of the MiGs shooting the C-130 down. The Soviets called it a "fake" and a "gross forgery" but offered no proof or new information.[83]

Aftermath

Eisenhower's anger at the loss of the three balloons meant no more operational flights were made. The remaining WS-461L hardware was put into storage. It was apparently kept on stand-by readiness should a need arise.

Throughout 1958 and 1959, sporadic U-2 overflights of Russia were made. These were to determine the actual number of SS-6 ICBMs the Soviets had deployed. This was the central question in the missile gap controversy. The flights were made along major rail lines and to suspected ICBM sites. As the SS-6 was too large to move by roads, it was hoped the missiles could be "caught" in transit. Even if no ICBM sites were confirmed, this would give a general idea of the level of deployment. The problem was that no missiles were spotted and no ICBM bases confirmed. Although, in the CIA's view, this indicated only a low number had been deployed, it was not possible to "prove the negative." This was due, in part, to the limited number of overflights, the relatively small area covered, and the intransigence of the Air Force in holding to its high estimates.

The hunt for ICBM sites continued in 1960. Eisenhower authorized an overflight for late April 1960. One of its targets was a suspected ICBM complex at Plesetsk in northwest Russia. The overflight was made on May 1, its pilot was Francis Gary Powers, and it was not successful. The loss of the U-2 meant the missile gap controversy was still open.[84] (This and other related matters will be dealt with in the next chapter.)

The WS-461L program was formally terminated in 1961.[85] The equipment was put in dead storage. Ironically, the following year it was nearly sent into action again. During the summer and early fall of 1962, the Soviets suddenly increased arms shipments to Cuba. This raised fears that the Soviets were planning to set up nuclear armed ballistic missiles on the island. Up to this point, U-2s flown by CIA pilots were used to monitor developments. The arms shipments, however, included SA-2 Guideline surface-to-air missiles similar to those which shot down Power's U-2 and a Nationalist Chinese-operated U-2 on September 9, 1962. The loss of a U-2 over Cuba would probably mean the end of Cuban overflights. Among the options looked at during the first week of October were reconnaissance balloons. It was soon clear there was no substitute for the U-2.[86] Because of the SAMs, Air Force pilots were to be used for subsequent overflights. The target area for the next mission was San Cristobal, Cuba. It was at the center of a trapezoidal pattern of SAM sites. This was similar to the pattern of sites used to defend ballistic missile sites inside Russia. The overflight was made on October 14. When the photos were analyzed, they showed an SS-4 medium-range ballistic missile site. It was the start of the Cuban missile crisis.[87]

The WS-461L flights of 1958 were the swan song of the 1110th Balloon Activities Group. Its phase-out began in 1959 and it was closed down on January 1, 1960.[88] Its main mission, the Ash Can/Grab Bag, was continued by other units during the massive Soviet nuclear tests of 1961–1962.

It was during one of these flights that a bizarre incident occurred. One of the balloons descended toward a tree. Under the tree was a hunter. The Skyhook balloon landed in the tree and the thousands of square feet of plastic settled down on the hunter. It took him several minutes to get out from under the balloon.[89]

With the signing of the Test Ban Treaty, which ended above-ground nuclear testing, the sampling was shifted to Chinese nuclear weapons.

Many of the ex-1110th personnel continue launching balloons at NASA's National Scientific Balloon Facility at Palestine, Texas. The bulk of the activities are during several weeks in the spring and fall when the stratospheric winds die down. The balloons do not drift far from the launch site. It is not unusual to see more than one balloon floating in the blue Texas sky. The balloons are far different from those used during Genetrix and Melting Pot. They may be 800 feet long, have a volume of 34 million cubic feet, and be able to carry a 3,100-lb gamma ray telescope to over 130,000 feet. The altitude-controlled balloon pioneered by WS-461L is now in fairly common use. It is known by the acronym RACOON (RAdiation COntrolled balloON). In 1973, a 64-foot balloon was launched from Australia. The balloon drifted around the world twice in five weeks before landing near Brisbane, only nine miles from the launch site. Some things have not changed. Despite forty years of plastics development, the huge size and heavy payloads mean the balloons still burst from time to time. When the balloons are cut down, the payloads still tend to land in thick woods filled with brush, saplings, and snakes.[90,91]

The WS-461L hardware was in storage at Norton AFB in 1968. At the time, it was still considered sensitive.[92] The history of balloon reconnaissance extended from the French Revolution through the American Civil War, two World Wars, the Cold War, to the trauma of the 1960s.

It was now complete.

8

Conclusions

To assess the Air Force's experiences with lighter-than-air reconnaissance, it is important to remember the context—the intelligence situation, technology, and politics. The goal of Genetrix was pioneer reconnaissance. The balloons' cameras would photograph the land passing below as they rode the jet stream. They could not cover a small specific target area. In the context of the early 1950s, this did not matter. Russia was a blank—coverage of any area was a plus. It was to answer the most basic question of intelligence: what was there?

In regard to technology the picture is confused. Ballooning (and balloon reconnaissance) was a very old technology—over 170 years by the time the first Genetrix balloon headed east. Yet, at the same time, plastic Skyhook balloons represented a very new technology. The first Skyhook had been launched a little over eight years before. Moreover, they had undergone a tremendous growth in payload and flight time: from 70 pounds and a day or so to almost 1,500 pounds and over a week aloft. Given this, the high failure rate of the early Moby Dick Hi flights and the overballasting problem would not be unexpected.

The long development delay, from the winter of 1951–52 to 1955–56, caused another technological comparison, one not favorable to the balloons. Because of the delays, the balloons did not go aloft until nearly the eve of the start of U-2 operations. The contrast between the flexibility and precise coverage of the U-2 and the randomly drifting balloons was not favorable to Genetrix. Yet, when the reconnaissance balloon program began in late 1950, an aircraft with the performance of the U-2 did not seem possible before the end of the decade. The seeds were there but it took the brilliance and drive of Kelly Johnson to bring it to reality. Still, it seems unfortunate it was not possible to hold more closely to the original Gopher schedule.

Another factor was the limitations placed on the balloons. This adversely affected the program's effectiveness. The 55,000-foot ceiling placed on the balloons threw away their primary advantage: the ability to rise above Soviet MiGs. It meant the loss rate would be high. In retrospect, this was the poorest decision of the program. The very few WS-461L/Melting Pot launches meant only a small area could be covered (even if the three balloons had not been lost due to the cut-down timers).

The final factor was President Eisenhower's fears about the Soviet's response to the balloons and the U-2 overflights. Time after time Eisenhower would say that if the Soviets were to do the same, the U.S. would be on the brink of war. He felt and feared the Soviets would react in a similar manner.[1–4] Eisenhower's concern was whether the photos were worth the risk of starting World War III.

This concern limited both the number and usefulness of the balloons and the U-2 overflights. As Paul Worthman noted:

> The USSR overflight program was curiously tentative. . . . The caution can be illustrated two ways, rather easily. If you plot all U-2 overflights of the USSR on a single map, the limitations of the effort are almost shocking. The second evidence is knowing that from early 1958 to April 1960, practically *no* overflights of the USSR were made (one uses the word 'practically' because some of the overflights were so shallow as to scarcely qualify).[5]

From his description, it appears some of the U-2 "overflights" were little more than the earlier short-range penetration flights. It also implied the gross area covered was on a par with that of Genetrix. Of course, the U-2 covered specifically selected areas, which made a considerable difference.

Outside factors adversely affecting the performance of balloon reconnaissance are one of the constants of its history. Whether General Burnside's refusal to allow Lowe to fly before Fredericksburg, positioning the *Santiago* too close to Spanish lines, or the limitations on altitude and number of launches per day for Genetrix, they have extracted a price. Contrast this with the first U-2 overflights. These were not brief, tentative, shallow penetrations. Rather, they went directly to Moscow and Leningrad. The first time was the safest, and one never knew how long the opportunity would last.

The political controversy the balloons caused was also a preview of the U-2 incident. With both the 1956 and 1958 series, the U.S. maintained the weather balloon cover story. This had several built-in advantages. The cover story had "plausible deniability." The U.S. had been flying the Moby Dick weather balloons for years. Genetrix and Melting Pot could easily be made to appear to be just more of the same. Appearances were enough.

When the U-2 began overflights, a similar cover story was prepared in the event one was shot down or crashed. The U-2 was a civilian weather plane which had crossed the border after the pilot reported problems with the oxygen system. When Francis Gary Power's U-2 failed to reach Norway, the cover story was released. Khrushchev was able to turn the cover story into a trap. First the Soviets announced only that the aircraft had been shot down—nothing more. Then, several days later, after the U.S. had denied the flight had been a deliberate attempt to violate Soviet airspace, Khrushchev publicly announced Powers had been captured alive and had admitted he had been spying.

Eisenhower was made to appear he was not in charge of the U.S. government. Khrushchev may have wanted to undermine his prestige before the Paris summit meeting or simply to bully him. Eisenhower turned the tables by making the unprecedented admission that he had personally authorized the overflights and that the U.S. spied.[6]

Assessment

What, then, was the assessment of balloon reconnaissance? Opinions run the spectrum. One of the harshest was by CIA official Herbert Scoville who called it a "disaster." This was perhaps influenced as much by the competition the balloons presented to the U-2 as by their shortcomings.[7] Robert Burch, one of the 1110th ASG launch crewmen, said, "From what I heard later, our efforts were really of little value. . . . I really don't believe we did much good for the Intelligence community."[8] More upbeat was the Air Force's official report:

> Weapons System 119L was a reasonably effective means of obtaining pioneer reconnaissance at comparatively small cost.
>
> The type of photography obtained affords an excellent source for pioneer reconnaissance, but due to limiting factors, detailed analysis of new intelligence is difficult.
>
> More specific knowledge of balloon performance must be obtained, and design influenced thereby, in order to obtain everything possible from this weapons system.[9]

Finally, at a meeting with President Eisenhower on February 10, 1956, Gen. Nathan Twining said the information the balloons acquired would be very valuable for the future.[10]

In retrospect it seems fair to say that despite its promise and achievements, balloon reconnaissance, owing to technical problems and the limitations imposed on the launch rate and altitude, was not able to meet the U.S. need for information on Russia. But it was the first step. Such first steps are frequently tentative with many stumbles. What is important is where those steps lead. So it was with balloon reconnaissance.

In January 1958, after the launch of the first two Russian Sputniks, President Eisenhower authorized development of the Discoverer reconnaissance satellite. To speed development, existing hardware would be used. The Thor intermediate-range ballistic missile was used as booster with an Agena upper stage. The camera the satellite carried was the HYAC-1 used on WS-461L. Presumably, the lens system was modified to compensate for the higher altitude of the satellite (150 miles vs. 100,000 feet for the balloon). The camera used on Discoverer had a ground resolution of 10 to 15 feet. The camera was fitted to the forward end of the Agena. The film was returned to earth with a reentry capsule based on the technology developed for ballistic missile warheads. It was at the front of the Agena, ahead of the Genetrix camera. The exposed film was fed through the back of the capsule, onto a take-up reel.

Once the photo run was complete, the film would be loaded into the reentry capsule. It would then separate, fire a retro-rocket, and descend toward a recovery zone near Hawaii. After the reentry heating was over, the capsule would deploy a parachute. Because the capsule could easily be lost at sea, it would be recovered in midair. The recovery gear was the same as that used for the Genetrix missions. The aircraft were some of the beaver tail C-119s modified for the 456th TCW. Many of the pilots and crewmen were also from the 456th TCW.[11]

The first Discoverer launch was made on February 28, 1959. The Thor-Agena placed Discoverer 1 into orbit but the Agena began to tumble. This was the start of an 18-month-long "bad streak." Each of the first twelve Discoverers suffered a variety of failures: booster malfunctions which prevented the satellite from reaching orbit, loss of attitude control which caused it to tumble, and failure of the capsule to de-orbit properly. It was not until Discoverer 13 (launched August 10, 1960) that all the steps were correctly accomplished. The capsule was recovered from the Pacific Ocean after the midair recovery attempt failed.

The next launch, Discoverer 14 (August 18, 1960), carried a Genetrix camera. Its target was a suspected Soviet ICBM site at Plesetsk in northwest Russia. The launch was successful, and the next day the capsule separated and reentered. As it descended under the parachute, one of the C-119 recovery aircraft picked up the capsule's recovery beacon. The aircraft was S/N 51-8037 which had been based at Itazuke AB, Japan, during the Genetrix flights. Its aircraft commander was Capt. Harold E. Mitchell who had been part of the Kodiak detachment. On the third try, the loops caught the parachute and the capsule was reeled aboard. This was the first midair recovery of a space capsule. Its photos were dark and of poor quality but showed rail lines not present on World War II maps of the area. Two more capsules were recovered by the end of the year but these photos were poor, apparently because of clouds.

The early months of 1961 saw another bad streak as four Discoverers failed. However, between June and September, four capsules were successfully recovered. All had taken excellent photos of suspected Soviet ICBM sites. Only the Plesetsk site showed any missiles. The four SS-6 ICBMs were all the Russians had. The missile gap was over.

The Discoverer satellites could do what the early penetration flights, reconnaissance balloons, or the U-2 could not: cover any specific area inside the Soviet bloc at will, limited only by weather, film supply, and satellite availability. Accordingly, the Discoverer, under the designation "Program 162," became the standard area surveillance satellite used by the U.S. during the early 1960s. By the final mission in April 1964, a total of seventy-eight Discoverer/Program 162 launches had been made. Its success was due in part to the preliminary work done by the Genetrix program in the area of camera development and midair recovery. As Paul Worthman, who worked on both early balloon reconnaissance development and Discoverer, noted, "We were all very grateful that there had once been a lighter than Air Force."[12,13]

The Soviets also developed reconnaissance satellites at the end of the 1950s. They used the Vostok manned spacecraft as the basis for their reconnaissance satellite. It was composed of two parts: a spherical reentry capsule and the service module. The reconnaissance camera replaced the cosmonaut and his ejector seat. Their first attempt ended in a launch failure during late 1961. The next try, Cosmos 4 on April 26, 1962, was successful. It reentered and landed in Central Asia three days later. Four more Soviet reconnaissance satellites followed by the end of 1963. Within a year, the Soviet reconnaissance satellites were operational.[14]

The Age of Surveillance had arrived.

Source Notes

Chapter 1

1. Donald Dale Jackson, *The Aeronauts,* (New York: Time-Life Books, 1980), Chapter 1.
2. Tom D. Crouch, *The Eagle Aloft: Two Centuries of the Balloon in America,* (Washington, D.C.: Smithsonian Institution Press, 1983), Chapter 1.
3. Jackson, *The Aeronauts,* 75–81.
4. Crouch, *Eagle Aloft,* 336–338.
5. Robert C. Mikesh, *Balloon Bomb Attacks on North America,* (Fallbrook, Calif.: Aero Publishers, 1982), 3.
6. Bruce Catton, *The Coming Fury,* (New York: Doubleday & Co., 1961).
7. Crouch, *Eagle Aloft,* 335–350.
8. Ibid., 350–353.
9. Catton, *The Coming Fury,* 458, 462, 466.
10. Crouch, *Eagle Aloft,* 352, 353.
11. Jackson, *The Aeronauts,* 86.
12. Crouch, *Eagle Aloft,* 343, 344, 354–356.
13. Jackson, *The Aeronauts,* 87.
14. Crouch, *Eagle Aloft,* 363.
15. Ibid., 364, 365.
16. Ibid., 357–369.
17. Bruce Catton, *The American Heritage Short History of the Civil War,* (New York: Dell, 1960), 54, 55, 63–65.
18. Bruce Catton, *Terrible Swift Sword,* (New York: Pocket Books, 1963), 254–261.
19. Crouch, *Eagle Aloft,* 375–386.
20. Ibid., 356, 357, 381, 382.
21. *Lighter-Than-Air Flight,* Lt. Col. C. V. Glines USAF, ed., (New York: Franklin Watts Inc., 1965), 110–114.
22. Crouch, *Eagle Aloft,* 386.
23. Catton, *Terrible Swift Sword,* 256–257, 267–269, 273–278.
24. Crouch, *Eagle Aloft,* 386–391.
25. Jackson, *The Aeronauts,* 88, 89.
26. Catton, *Terrible Swift Sword,* 296–299, 301–306.
27. *Lighter-Than-Air Flight,* 115–118.

28. Catton, *Terrible Swift Sword,* 302, 303, 308–321.
29. *Lighter-Than-Air Flight,* 117.
30. Crouch, *Eagle Aloft,* 394, 395.
31. *Lighter-Than-Air Flight,* 117, 118.
32. Crouch, *Eagle Aloft,* 397, 398.
33. Catton, *Terrible Swift Sword,* 343–353, 397–412, 424–437.
34. Catton, *Short History of the Civil War,* 85–96, 103. To put the 6,000 killed at Antietam in perspective, this was four times the number of U.S. soldiers killed in the June 6, 1944, invasion of Europe and twice the number killed in the War of 1812, the Mexican War, and the Spanish-American War *combined.*
35. Bruce Catton, *Never Call Retreat,* (New York: Pocket Books, 1965), 14–20.
36. Crouch, *Eagle Aloft,* 380, 394, 395, 398–404.
37. Catton, *Never Call Retreat,* 117–127.
38. Crouch, *Eagle Aloft,* 394, 395.
39. Ibid., 405–407.
40. Catton, *Never Call Retreat,* 139–149.
41. Crouch, *Eagle Aloft,* 408–411.
42. Ibid., 394, 395.
43. Ibid., 336, 412, 413. Lowe left ballooning in 1866 to embark on a series of business ventures. In later years, he moved to California and built a narrow-gauge railroad up the San Gabriel mountains east of Los Angeles to the peak of Mount Lowe. He was also a founder of Cal Tech and one of the richest men in California. A descendant also played a role in the history of flight—his granddaughter was Florence Leontine Lowe, better known as Pancho Barnes, race pilot, test pilot, Hollywood stunt pilot, and operator of the Happy Bottom Riding Club near Edwards AFB.
44. John W. R. Taylor, Michael J. H. Taylor, and David Mondey, *Air Facts and Feats,* (New York: The Continents Publishing Group, 1973), 202.
45. Crouch, *Eagle Aloft,* 422–424.
46. *Lighter-Than-Air Flight,* 122–127.
47. Jackson, *The Aeronauts,* 91, 92, 96, 97.
48. Taylor, Taylor, and Mondey, *Air Facts and Feats,* 204.
49. Walter Raleigh, *The War in the Air, Vol. 1,* (Oxford: Oxford University Press, 1922), 147–150.
50. This was not the only military balloon in action at the time. In 1884, the French used a balloon to help in the capture of the town of Dienbienphu in French Indo-China: Jackson, *The Aeronauts,* 93.
51. Raleigh, *War in the Air, Vol. 1,* 150–152.
52. *Lighter-Than-Air Flight,* 128, 129.
53. John M. Blum, *The National Experience Part Two: A History of the United States since 1865,* (San Diego: Harcourt Brace Jovanovich, 1985), 531–535.
54. Crouch, *Eagle Aloft,* 524–527.
55. *Lighter-Than-Air Flight,* 130.
56. Crouch, *Eagle Aloft,* 525–527.
57. Raleigh, *War in the Air, Vol. 1,* 153, 154.
58. Jackson, *The Aeronauts,* 93, 95.
59. Raleigh, *War in the Air, Vol. 1,* 459, 460.
60. Aaron Norman, *The Great Air War,* (New York: MacMillan, 1968), 329.
61. Crouch, *Eagle Aloft,* 527.
62. Robert O. Paxton, *Europe in the Twentieth Century,* (New York: Harcourt Brace Jovanovich, 1975), Chapter 2, 3.

63. Gordon A. Craig, *Europe, 1815–1914,* (Hinsdale, Ill.: The Dryden Press, 1972), Chapter 19.
64. Norman, *The Great Air War,* 329, 330.
65. Paxton, *Europe in the Twentieth Century,* 86, 87.
66. H. A. Jones, *The War in the Air, IV, (Oxford: Oxford University Press, 1934), 127.*
67. H. A. Jones, *The War in the Air, II,* (Oxford: Oxford University Press, 1928), 194.
68. Jones, *War in the Air, IV,* 150, 151.
69. Paxton, *Europe in the Twentieth Century,* 87–89.
70. Thomas R. Funderburk, *The Fighters, the Men and Machines of the First Air War,* (New York: Grosset & Dunlap, 1965), 36.
71. David C. Cooke, *Sky Battle: 1914–1918,* (New York: W. W. Norton, 1970), 77.
72. Ron Wallace Clarke, "Rockets," *Fly Past,* (July 1985): 37.
73. Funderburk, *The Fighters,* 161.
74. Cooke, *Sky Battle: 1914–1918,* 182.
75. Ezra Bowen, *Knights of the Air,* (New York: Time-Life Books, 1980), 82, 83.
76. Funderburk, *The Fighters,* 190, 191.
77. Martin Caidin, *The Silken Angels,* (New York: J. B. Lippincott Co., 1964), 36, 38, 40–45.
78. Paxton, *Europe in the Twentieth Century,* 127, 132, 133, 135, 143, 144.
79. Bowen, *Knights of the Air,* 171.
80. Cooke, *Sky Battle: 1914–1918,* 256, 258–261.
81. Paxton, *Europe in the Twentieth Century,* 145.
82. Jackson, *The Aeronauts,* 100.
83. *Lighter-Than-Air Flight,* 133, 134. Observation balloons continued to be part of the world's armed forces into the 1920s. Artillery-spotting duties would subsequently be taken over by light aircraft. Yet balloons did not disappear entirely. The German Wehrmacht made some use of observation balloons during World War II. The balloons were manufactured by Riedinger at Augsburg. The design was somewhat longer and thinner-looking than those of World War I. Called a *Fesselballon,* they were 112 feet long, 32.4 feet in diameter, and had a volume of 49,449 cubic feet of hydrogen. Two observers (three in a squeeze) rode in the basket up to 6,562 feet above the ground. Like their World War I predecessors, they made visual observations and oblique photography. Two balloons were attached to an artillery observation battalion. Some units used six trucks, carrying twenty-eight hydrogen cylinders each, with others for the winches and cables. Each battery had four 20mm cannons for antiaircraft protection. At least two independent balloon batteries (101 and 102) existed. German balloons were used at Sedan, France, in 1940 and, starting a year later, on the Eastern Front, specifically the Balkans (Greece, Yugoslavia and Albania). German units in this area were fighting partisans who lacked air support. (The balloons could not have survived in a sky filled with P-51s or P-47s.) By 1944, the observation balloon units had been disbanded.[84]
84. "Balloons in the Balkans," *World War II Investigator,* (June 1988): 18, 19. Currently, several unmanned observation balloons are stationed on the U.S./Mexico border. Resembling the World War I balloons, they have a bulge on their underside which houses a radar antenna which tracks low-flying drug-carrying aircraft. The only other current observation balloon program is an Israeli electronic intelligence (ELINT) balloon called Stratus. The listening equipment is carried aboard the balloon and the signals are relayed down the mooring line to the main computer and operator's console.[85]

85. "COMINT balloon operational," *Flight International,* (17 June 1989): 28.

Chapter 2

1. John M. Blum, *The National Experience Part Two: A History of the United States since 1865,* (San Diego: Harcourt Brace Jovanovich, 1985).
2. *Japan at War,* (New York: Time-Life Books, 1980).
3. James J. Halley, "Operation Outward," *Aviation News Magazine,* (31 October–13 November 1986): 590, 591.
4. Mitsuo Fuchida et al., *Readers Digest Story of World War II,* (Pleasantville, N.Y.: Readers Digest Association, 1969), 120–129, 516.
5. David Johnson, *The London Blitz,* (New York: Stein and Day, 1984), 28.
6. A more famous example of a nation being reluctant to use a new weapon lest it be turned against them was radar jamming chaff. The U.S., Britain and Germany all independently discovered aluminum strips could jam radar. But all were slow to use it. Alfred Price, *The History of U.S. Electronic Warfare, Vol. 1,* (Westford, Mass.: The Association of Old Crows, 1984), 32, 62, 63, 83, 90, 91.
7. Halley, "Operation Outward," 590, 591.
8. Robert C. Mikesh, *Balloon Bomb Attacks on North America,* (Fallbrook, Calif.: Aero Publishers, 1982), 3.
9. Bert Webber, *Silent Siege,* (Fairfield, Wash.: Ye Galleon Press, 1983), 378.
10. Webber, *Silent Siege,* 235, 236.
11. Mikesh, *Balloon Bomb Attacks,* 6.
12. Webber, *Silent Siege,* 237, 238, 245.
13. Ibid., 238–241, 245, 252, 286.
14. Mikesh, *Balloon Bomb Attacks,* 4, 7–9.
15. Webber, *Silent Siege,* 263.
16. Mikesh, *Balloon Bomb Attacks,* 9, 11, 14.
17. Webber, *Silent Siege,* 238–243, 257.
18. Mikesh, *Balloon Bomb Attacks,* 11–17, 61.
19. Ibid., 45–47, 54.
20. Ibid., 58–61.
21. Webber, *Silent Siege,* 249.
22. Mikesh, *Balloon Bomb Attacks,* 22, 23.
23. Webber, *Silent Siege,* 259–263.
24. Mikesh, *Balloon Bomb Attacks,* 28.
25. Webber, *Silent Siege,* 262–263.
26. Ibid., 263, 266–271, 329.
27. Mikesh, *Balloon Bomb Attacks,* 28–34.
28. Gordon Wright, *The Ordeal of Total War,* (New York: Harper Torchbooks, 1968), 250.
29. "What Next, Please," *Time,* (1 January 1945): 14.
30. "Balloon Mystery," *Newsweek,* (1 January 1945): 36.
31. Mikesh, *Balloon Bomb Attacks,* 25–27.
32. "Trial Balloons?" *Newsweek,* (15 January 1945): 40, 41.
33. Webber, *Silent Siege,* 330.
34. Ibid., 274.
35. Ibid., 244, 253–255.

36. Mikesh, *Balloon Bomb Attacks,* 23, 63.
37. Webber, *Silent Siege,* 256.
38. Mikesh, *Balloon Bomb Attacks,* 16.
39. Webber, *Silent Siege,* 378.
40. Ibid., 278.
41. "Hanford," *After the Battle,* (#41): 9–10.
42. Lansing Lamont, *Day of Trinity,* (New York: Atheneum, 1965), 58, 98, 133, 151–153.
43. Webber, *Silent Siege,* 278–280.
44. Ibid., 265, 337.
45. Mikesh, *Balloon Bomb Attacks,* 28–30.
46. Keith Wheeler, *Bombers over Japan,* (New York: Time-Life Books, 1982), 167, 168.
47. *Japan at War,* 161–164.
48. Wheeler, *Bombers over Japan,* 168–170, 175, 176.
49. Mikesh, *Balloon Bomb Attacks,* 38.
50. Webber, *Silent Siege,* 255.
51. Ibid., 342, 343.
52. Mikesh, *Balloon Bomb Attacks,* 29.
53. Webber, *Silent Siege,* 280–282.
54. Ibid., 224–233, 282.
55. Ibid., 346, 347.
56. Ibid., 264, 265.
57. Mikesh, *Balloon Bomb Attacks,* 34, 36.
58. Philip J. Klass, *UFOs Explained,* (New York: Random House, 1974), 89, 90.
59. Mikesh, *Balloon Bomb Attacks,* 36.
60. Webber, *Silent Siege,* 252, 328–353.
61. *Japan at War,* 62–65, 95, 109, 117.
62. Wright, *The Ordeal of Total War 1939–1945,* 265.
63. Webber, *Silent Siege,* 307, 308.
64. Ibid., 350–353.

Chapter 3

1. Gordon Wright, *The Ordeal of Total War 1939–1945,* (New York: Harper Torchbooks, 1968), 224, 225.
2. William Taubman, *Stalin's American Policy,* (New York: W. W. Norton, 1982).
3. Thomas B. Cochran, William M. Arkin, and Milton M. Hoenig, *U.S. Nuclear Forces and Capabilities,* (Cambridge, Mass.: Ballinger, 1984), 15.
4. "The Story Behind Plastic Balloons," General Mills Public Relations Department, September 1957, 2.
5. Otto C. Winzen, "Exploring the Sky by Proxy," *Progress Thru Research* (Winter 1948): 5.
6. Tom D. Crouch, *The Eagle Aloft: Two Centuries of the Balloon in America,* (Washington, D.C.: Smithsonian Institution Press, 1983), 639, 640.
7. George L. Christian, "Skyhooks May Become Space Platforms," *Aviation Week,* (10 October 1955): 52, 53.
8. "Flying High," *Progress Thru Research,* (Spring 1951): 18.
9. "How to Build a Better Skyhook," *Progress Thru Research,* (Fall 1952): 1.

10. Christian, "Skyhooks May Become Space Platforms," 47.
11. "Flying High," 15.
12. Crouch, *Eagle Aloft,* 640.
13. Cmdr. Ed Melton, "Twenty-Five Years of Skyhook," *Naval Research Reviews,* (February 1973): 1.
14. Crouch, *Eagle Aloft,* 641.
15. Christian, "Skyhooks May Become Space Platforms," 53.
16. Letters to the Editor, *Aviation Week,* (19 December 1955).
17. Crouch, *Eagle Aloft,* 641, 642.
18. Donald H. Menzel and Lyle G. Boyd, *The World of Flying Saucers,* (New York: Doubleday, 1963), 13, 14, 26–28.
19. Edward J. Ruppelt, *The Report on Unidentified Flying Objects,* (New York: Doubleday, 1956), 16–19.
20. John A. Keel, "The Man Who Invented Flying Saucers," *Whole Earth Review,* (Fall 1986): 54–61.
21. Menzel and Boyd, *World of Flying Saucers,* 15–21.
22. *Project Blue Book,* Brad Steiger, ed., (New York: Ballantine Books, 1976), 44.
23. Mantell accident report, Headquarters Air Force Inspection and Safety Center, Norton AFB.
24. Ruppelt, *Report on Unidentified Flying Objects,* 31–33.
25. Menzel and Boyd, *World of Flying Saucers,* 33–35.
26. Mantell accident report.
27. Menzel and Boyd, *World of Flying Saucers,* 35.
28. Ruppelt, *Report on Unidentified Flying Objects,* 37.
29. Mantell accident report.
30. Ruppelt, *Report on Unidentified Flying Objects,* 35.
31. Robert H. Wood, "A Navy Answer on 'Saucers'," *Aviation Week,* (26 March 1951): 82.
32. Robert H. Wood, "Saucers, Secrecy & Security," *Aviation Week,* (19 February 1951): 50.
33. Winzen, "Exploring the Sky by Proxy," 6.
34. "Plastic Balloons to Carry Instruments Higher," *Science News Letter,* (23 July 1949): 54.
35. Wood, "A Navy Answer on 'Saucers'," 82.
36. Richard Wilson, "A Nuclear Physicist Exposes Flying Saucers," *Look,* (27 February 1951): 60–64.
37. Wood, "A Navy Answer on 'Saucers'," 82.
38. Wilson, "A Nuclear Physicist Exposes Flying Saucers," 60–64.
39. Ruppelt, *Report on Unidentified Flying Objects,* 35–39.
40. David R. Saunders and R. Roger Harkins, *UFOs? Yes!* (New York: Signet Books, 1968), 65.
41. Wilson, "A Nuclear Physicist Exposes Flying Saucers," 60–64.
42. "Saucers? No, Skyhooks," *Newsweek,* (26 February 1951):17.
43. Wood, "Saucers, Secrecy & Security," 50.
44. "How to Build a Better Skyhook," 3.
45. Wood, "A Navy Answer on 'Saucers'," 82.
46. Melton, "Twenty-Five Years of Skyhook," 1.
47. "Flying Saucers," *Aviation Week,* (February 19, 1951): 13.
48. Douglas Botting, *The Giant Airships,* (Alexandria, Va.: Time-Life Books, 1980), 79.
49. Winzen, "Exploring the Sky by Proxy," 2.
50. "How to Build a Better Skyhook," 5.
51. Christian, "Skyhook May Become Space Platforms," 47.

52. "How to Build a Better Skyhook," 5.
53. Lt. Col. David G. Simons and Don A. Schanche, *Man High,* (New York: Avon, 1960), 54, 60, 126.
54. Winzen, "Exploring the Sky by Proxy," 2.
55. "Flying High," 15.
56. Edwin J. Kirschner, *Aerospace Balloons from Montgolfiere to Space,* (Fallbrook, Calif.: Aero Publishers, 1985), 18, 19.
57. "Moby Dick Balloons Explore Upper Air," *Aviation Week,* (24 August 1953): 29.
58. Lloyd Mallan, *Men, Rockets and Space Rats,* (New York: Julian Messner Inc., 1955), 192–194.
59. Scientific Study of Unidentified Flying Objects, Edward U. Condon, Project Director, (New York: Bantam Books, 1969), 757, 758.
60. "Flying High," 15.
61. "Cosmic Ray Mystery," *Science News Letter,* (6 September 1952): 159.
62. Mallan, *Men, Rockets and Space Rats,* 177, 180.
63. Simons and Schanche, *Man High,* 16.
64. "Letters to the editor," *Smithsonian,* (March 1987): 22.
65. Winzen, "Exploring the Sky by Proxy," 6.
66. "Flying High," 15.
67. Eloise Engle and Arnold Lott, *Man in Flight: Biomedical Achievement in Aerospace,* (Annapolis: Leeward Publication, 1979), 17.
68. Simons and Schanche, *Man High,* 50.

Chapter 4

1. Memorandum for Record: To establish requirements for development of a reconnaissance capability by use of recoverable free-balloons, 3 October 1950, Modern Military Branch, National Archives.
2. Dino A. Brugioni, "The Tyuratam Enigma," *Air Force Magazine,* (March 1984): 108.
3. Jeffrey Richelson, *American Espionage and the Soviet Target,* (New York: Morrow, 1987), 101–104.
4. Paul F. Crickmore, *Lockheed SR-71 Blackbird,* (London: Osprey Publishing Limited, 1986), 9.
5. Richelson, *American Espionage,* 110, 111.
6. Research Publications Inc., State Department 146, 1982.
7. Michael R. Beschloss, *Mayday,* (New York: Harper & Row, 1986), 77, 78.
8. Memorandum for Record: To establish requirements for development of a reconnaissance capability by use of recoverable free-balloons, 3 October 1950, Modern Military Branch, National Archives.
9. W. W. Rostow, *Open Skies,* (Austin: University of Texas Press, 1982), 189, 190.
10. Brig. Gen. George W. Goddard and Dewitt S. Copp, *Overview,* (New York: Doubleday, 1969), 384.
11. Memorandum for Record: Use of Free Balloons to Secure Electronic Information, 17 October 1950, Modern Military Branch, National Archives.
12. Statement of Suggested Military Characteristics, Modern Military Branch, National Archives.
13. Memo to Commanding General Air Material Command: Subject Photo Recon-

naissance Balloons, 6 November 1950, Modern Military Branch, National Archives.

14. Memorandum for Record: Use of Free Balloons to Secure Electronic Information, 17 October 1950, Modern Military Branch, National Archives.
15. Memorandum for Record: To request information on the progress to date of Project Gopher, 5 April 1951, Modern Military Branch, National Archives.
16. Memorandum for Record: Status Report of Project Gopher, 29 November 1951, Modern Military Branch, National Archives.
17. "How to Build a Better Skyhook," *Progress Thru Research,* (Fall 1952): 1–5.
18. Memo: Use of Free Balloons to Secure Electronic Information, 24 April 1951, Modern Military Branch, National Archives.
19. Memorandum for Record: Status Report of Project Gopher, 29 November 1951, Modern Military Branch, National Archives.
20. Rostow, *Open Skies,* 189, 190.
21. "Whales in the Sky," *Newsweek,* (15 October 1951): 54, 55.
22. Rostow, *Open Skies,* 189, 190.
23. "Whales in the Sky," 54, 55.
24. Rostow, *Open Skies,* 190, 191.
25. "Moby Dick" (History from Cambridge Research Center).
26. Charlotte Knight, "A Report on our 'Flying Saucer' Balloons," *Collier's,* (11 June 1954): 53, 54.
27. George L. Christian, "Skyhooks May Become Space Platforms," *Aviation Week,* (10 October 1955): 49.
28. "Moby Dick" (History from Cambridge Research Center).
29. "Project Moby Dick" (History from Atmospheric Devices Laboratory).
30. Knight, "A Report on Our 'Flying Saucer' Balloons," 54.
31. "Moby Dick Balloons Explore Upper Air," *Aviation Week,* (24 August 1953): 24.
32. R. W. Koch, "The CIA's Death Valley Albatross," *Air Classics,* (April 1979): 72.
33. Wright Air Development Center Technical Report 53-52, "Status of Air Force Project GOPHER," 6 March 1953, Microfilm Roll #30857, Air Force Historical Research Center, Maxwell AFB, Alabama.
34. Edward J. Ruppelt, *The Report on Unidentified Flying Objects,* (Garden City, Doubleday & Co., 1956), 141, 173.
35. Donald H. Menzel and Lyle G. Boyde, *The World of Flying Saucers,* (Garden City, Doubleday & Co., 1963), 155–157.
36. Ruppelt, *Report on Unidentified Flying Objects,* Chapter 12.
37. *Project Blue Book,* Brad Steiger, ed., (New York: Ballantine Books, 1976), 400, 401.
38. Carrollton Press, CIA, 1979, 16A.
39. Walt Andrus, "Air Intelligence Report No. 100-203-79," *MUFON UFO Journal,* (July 1979): 8.
40. *Project Blue Book,* 397.
41. Menzel and Boyd, *World of Flying Saucers,* 134–135, 155–160.
42. Ruppelt, *Report on Unidentified Flying Objects,* 169, 170.
43. "Moby Dick Balloons Explore Upper Air," 30.
44. Aeronautics and Astronautics, 1915–60, (NASA 1961), 71.
45. "Project Moby Dick" (History from Atmospheric Devices Laboratory).
46. Knight, "A Report on Our 'Flying Saucer' Balloons," 55.
47. "Project Moby Dick" (History from Atmospheric Devices Laboratory).
48. "Moby Dick" (History from Cambridge Research Center).
49. "Project Moby Dick" (History from Atmospheric Devices Laboratory).
50. "Skyhooks May Become Space Platforms," 47.

51. "The Story Behind Plastic Balloons," 6.
52. "Moby Dick" (History from Cambridge Research Center).
53. "Project Moby Dick" (History from Atmospheric Devices Laboratory).
54. "Moby Dick Balloons Explore Upper Air," 29, 30.
55. History of the 1110th Air Support Squadron, 1 July 1954–31 December 1954, Microfilm Roll MO 109, Air Force Historical Research Center, Maxwell AFB, Alabama.
56. "Moby Dick Balloons Explore Upper Air," 29.
57. Knight, "A Report on Our 'Flying Saucer' Balloons," 52.
58. "Moby Dick" (History from Cambridge Research Center).
59. "Moby Dick Balloons Explore Upper Air," 29.
60. "Project Moby Dick" (History from Atmospheric Devices Laboratory).
61. "Moby Dick" (History from Cambridge Research Center).
62. Knight, "A Report on Our 'Flying Saucer' Balloons," 54.
63. "Moby Dick" (History from Cambridge Research Center).
64. Frederick A. Johnsen, *Thundering Peacemaker,* (Tacoma, Wash.: Bomber Books, 1978), 4, 5, 10–12.
65. Edward W. Van Orman, "One Thousand on Top," *Airpower,* (March 1987): 16, 20, 22, 38.
66. Richelson, *American Espionage,* 107.
67. "Skywriters," *Aeroplane Monthly,* (February 1983): 106.
68. Robert Trimble, "The L. A. Tornados," *Air Classics,* (November 1974): 29, 31, 64, 65.
69. William Green, *The World Guide to Combat Airplanes—2,* (New York: Doubleday, 1967).
70. David A. Anderton, *Strategic Air Command,* (New York: Scribner's, 1975), 265.
71. Lou Drendel and Tom Y'Blood, *B-47 Stratojet in Action,* (Warren, Mich.: Squadron/Signal, 1976), 31.
72. Richelson, *American Espionage,* 108, 109.
73. Ibid., 101, 108.
74. Carrollton Press, 267A, 1979.
75. Richelson, *American Espionage,* 107, 108.
76. Dick van der Aart, *Aerial Espionage,* (Shrewsbury, England: Airlife Publishing Ltd., 1985), 18, 19.Archives.
77. Beschloss, *Mayday,* 76, 78, 79.
78. Subject: Future Development Action—GOPHER Project To Director of Requirements DCS/D, 17 April 1953, Modern Military Branch, National Archives.
79. Rostow, *Open Skies,* 191, 192.
80. Subject: Future Development Action—GOPHER Project To Director of Requirements DCS/D, 17 April 1953, Modern Military Branch, National Archives.
81. Memorandum for Record, Problem: To determine the feasibility of assigning to USAFSS a new mission of locating and tracking high altitude balloons, 21 January 1953, Modern Military Branch, National Archives.
82. Subject: Future Development Action—GOPHER Project To Director of Requirements DCS/D, 17 April 1953, Modern Military Branch, National Archives.
83. Anton Antonov-Ovseyenko, *The Time Of Stalin,* (New York: Harper Colophon Books, 1981), 313–318.
84. William Taubman, *Stalin's American Policy,* (New York: W. W. Norton, 1982), 230–233.
85. Memorandum for: Mr. Ayer, Subject: Project Gopher Developments, 11 June 1953, Modern Military Branch, National Archives.
86. Future Development Action—Gopher Project Director of Research & Develop-

ment, DCS/D *THRU* Director of Intelligence DCS/O, 9 June 1953, Modern Military Branch, National Archives.

87. Memorandum for: Mr. Ayer, Subject: Status of "Grandson," Modern Military Branch, National Archives.
88. Memorandum for the Record, Problem: To take action on a Memorandum to General Samford from Mr. Ayer, dated 22 December 1953, regarding political acceptability of Project GRANDSON, December 1953, Modern Military Branch, National Archives.
89. Memorandum for: Frederick Ayer, Jr., Subject: Project GRANDSON, Modern Military Branch, National Archives.
90. Rostow, *Open Skies,* 192.
91. Specialized Reconnaissance Operations, From: Deputy Director for Collection & Dissemination, Directorate of Intelligence DCS/O, 23 October 1953, Modern Military Branch, National Archives.
92. Military Characteristics for A Balloon Pioneer Reconnaissance System, 4 October 1954, Modern Military Branch, National Archives.
93. Special Purpose Reconnaissance Vehicle, From: Collection Operations Division Deputy Director for Collection & Dissemination, Directorate of Intelligence, 30 March 1953, Modern Military Branch, National Archives.
94. Richelson, *American Espionage,* 115, 121–123.
95. Military Characteristics for a Balloon Pioneer Reconnaissance System, 4 October 1954, Modern Military Branch, National Archives.
96. Memorandum for Record, Problem: To determine the feasibility of assigning to USAFSS a new mission of locating and tracking high altitude balloons, 21 January 1953, Modern Military Branch, National Archives.
97. Military Characteristics for a Balloon Pioneer Reconnaissance System, 4 October 1954, Modern Military Branch, National Archives.
98. Fundamentals of Aerospace Weapons Systems, (Washington, D.C.: U.S. Government Printing Office, 1961), 138–151.
99. Memo to Commanding General, Air Resupply and Communications Service, Subject: Request for Liaison Officer, 1 December 1952, Modern Military Branch, National Archives.
100. Military Characteristics for a Balloon Pioneer Reconnaissance System, 4 October 1954, Modern Military Branch, National Archives.
101. Report: Description and Evaluation of the Meteorological Operations Associated with Phase VI Tests (Operation "Flying Cloud"), Air Research and Development Command, 1 February 1953.
102. Andrew Brookes, *V-Force, the History of Britain's Airborne Deterrent,* (London: Janes, 1982), 36–38, 74–76.
103. Rostow, *Open Skies,* 3–9, 22–25, 26–32, 48–50, 52–58, 64, 79–80.

Chapter 5

1. *History of the 456th Troop Carrier Wing and Project 119-L, 1 January 1955 thru 9 July 1956,* (Tactical Air Command, n.d.), Introduction.
2. *History of 1st Air Division, Historical Study No. 62,* (Headquarters Strategic Air Command, November 1956), 10.
3. Tape: Paul M. Lovrencic to Curtis Peebles, 5 September 1987.

4. *History of the 456th Troop Carrier Wing, 1 January–30 June 1955,* (Tactical Air Command, n.d.), 8.
5. Tape: Lovrencic to Peebles, 5 September 1987. All American Engineering has an interesting history. It began as part of All American Aviation in 1937. This was the last all airmail only airlines. It used a novel pickup and delivery system. The mail bags were on a rope suspended between two poles. The aircraft would fly low and pick up the bag in flight. (Drops were done in a similar way.) All American Aviation served small towns in the Allegheny Mountains that lacked airports; the pickup was the only way they could have the advantages of airmail. During World War II, the company built a pickup system that allowed low-flying C-47s to pull a glider off the ground and into the air. Following the war, costs of the airmail pickup service were too high, and All American was unable to get permission to have a dual pickup/passenger airline. In 1948, the airmail effort was ended and All American became a conventional airline. In 1953, it was renamed Allegheny Airlines (later USAir). All American Engineering was spun off as an independent company. Its background, with the pickup gear, made it a natural choice for the balloon recovery equipment. (For a full account, see W. David Lewis and William F. Trimble, *The Airway to Everywhere,* Pittsburgh: University of Pittsburgh Press, 1988.)
6. *History of the 456th Troop Carrier Wing, 1 January–30 June 1955,* 5–7.
7. Letter: George Mathews to Curtis Peebles, 29 September 1986.
8. *History of the 456th Troop Carrier Wing, 1 January–30 June 1955,* 9, 10.
9. *History of 1st Air Division, Historical Study No. 62,* 10, 11.
10. Tapes: Lovrencic to Peebles, 5 September 1987 and 8 April 1988.
11. Letter: Mathews to Peebles, 29 September 1986.
12. Standard Operating Procedure Number 6, Operations Standards and Criteria in Water Recovery, 2 June 1955.
13. *History of the 456th Troop Carrier Wing, 1 January–30 June 1955,* 10, 11.
14. Letter: Mathews to Peebles, 29 September 1986.
15. *History of the 456th Troop Carrier Wing, 1 January–30 June 1955,* 11.
16. Tape: Lovrencic to Peebles, 5 September 1987.
17. *1st Air Division (Meteorological Survey), Final Report Project 119L,* (Strategic Air Command, n.d.), 12, 13, 19.
18. *History of 1st Air Division, Historical Study No. 62,* 11, 12.
19. Colonel John Knotch, USAF Ret., "Before the U-2," *Gung Ho,* (April 1983): 25, 69.
20. *1st Air Division (Meteorological Survey), Final Report Project 119L,* 19.
21. Memo: Subject—Recovery of Meteorological Equipment, 24 January 1956. The dimensions are given for "Type 1" and "Type 2," presumably DMQ-1 and 2.
22. *History of the 456th Troop Carrier Wing and Project 119L, 1 January 1955 through 9 July 1956,* "Code Names."
23. *1st Air Division (Meteorological Survey), Final Report Project 119L,* 12–14.
24. *History of 1st Air Division, Historical Study No. 62,* 11–17.
25. *Denver Post,* 17 August 1955, 1.
26. *1st Air Division (Meteorological Survey), Final Report Project 119L,* 14.
27. Foreign Nuclear Detonations—Through 31 December 1981, Department of Energy.
28. Philip J. Klass, *Secret Sentries in Space,* (New York: Random House, 1971), 4–9.
29. John Prados, *The Soviet Estimate,* (New York: The Dial Press, 1982), 41–43.
30. Wayne R. Austerman, "Ramming: The Final Option," *Airpower,* (May 1987): 10–19, 54, 55.
31. Research Publications Inc. CIA 1544, 1984.
32. Jeffrey Richelson, *American Espionage and the Soviet Targets,* (New York: William

Morrow and Co., 1987), 86.
33. *History of the 456th Troop Carrier Wing, 1 January–30 June 1955,* 2, 4, 10, 11.
34. *History of 1st Air Division, Historical Study No. 62,* 19.
35. Tape: Lovrencic to Peebles, 5 September 1987.
36. *History of the 456th Troop Carrier Wing and Project 119-L, 1 January 1955 thru 9 July 1956,* Summary and Analysis—Project Genetrix, 14.
37. Letter: Mathews to Peebles, 29 September 1986.
38. *History of the 456th Troop Carrier Wing and Project 119-L, 1 January 1955 thru 9 July 1956,* Summary and Analysis—Project Genetrix, 14.
39. C-119F Accident Report, Headquarters Air Force Inspection and Safety Center, Norton AFB.
40. Letter: Mathews to Peebles, 29 September 1986.
41. *History of the 456th Troop Carrier Wing and Project 119-L, 1 January 1955 thru 9 July 1956,* Summary and Analysis—Project Genetrix, 21.
42. *History of 1st Air Division, Historical Study No. 62,* 18, 19.
43. Letter: Mathews to Peebles, 29 September 1986.
44. *Denver Post,* 12 September 1955, no page.
45. *Denver Post,* 14 September 1955, 3.
46. Log of Advance Party Detachment 1 746th Troop Carrier Squadron, 15 September 1955. An "interesting article" about "an incident involving a C-119, a space object and parachuting airmen over Indiana" appeared in the September 13, 1955, issue of *Stars and Stripes.*
47. *History of the 456th Troop Carrier Wing and Project 119-L, 1 January 1955 thru 9 July 1956,* Summary and Analysis—Project Genetrix, 13, 14.
48. *History of 1st Air Division, Historical Study No. 62,* 31.
49. *History of the 456th Troop Carrier Wing and Project 119-L, 1 January 1955 thru 9 July 1956,* Summary and Analysis—Project Genetrix, 13, 14. Unfortunately, sources disagree about the numbers of balloons launched and recovered. *1st Air Division (Meteorological Survey),* page 13, states 162 WS-119L balloons were launched during Moby Dick Hi and 12 gondolas were recovered out of 39 tries. *History of 1st Air Division,* page 19, states 55 attempts were made with 42 balloons cut down and 12 successfully recovered. The numbers in the *History of the 456th Troop Carrier Wing . . . 1 January thru 9 July 1956* are used as there is more specific information.
50. *History of 1st Air Division, Historical Study No. 62,* 19, 20.
51. *History of the 456th Troop Carrier Wing and Project 119-L, 1 January 1955 thru 9 July 1956,* Summary and Analysis—Project Genetrix, 16–18.
52. *1st Air Division (Meteorological Survey), Final Report Project 119-L, 15, 16.*
53. *History of 1st Air Division, Historical Study No. 62,* 21.
54. *History of the 456th Troop Carrier Wing and Project 119-L, 1 January 1955 thru 9 July 1956,* Vol. II, Section I, II, III.
55. *1st Air Division (Meteorological Survey), Final Report Project 119-L, 16.*
56. *History of the 456th Troop Carrier Wing and Project 119-L, 1 January 1955 thru 9 July 1956,* Overseas Processing, 4–7.
57. Ibid., Chapter III: Operations and Training, 4.
58. Tape: Lovrencic to Peebles, 5 September 1987.
59. Letters: Robert Burch to Curtis Peebles, 21 September 1986 and 23 March 1988.
60. *History of the 456th Troop Carrier Wing and Project 119-L, 1 January 1955 thru 9 July 1956,* Vol. II, Section I, 7.
61. Ibid., Chapter III: Operations and Training, 13.
62. Letter: Mathews to Peebles, 29 September 1986.
63. *History of the 456th Troop Carrier Wing and Project 119-L, 1 January 1955 thru 9*

July 1956, Chapter III: Operations and Training, 13–16, and Vol. II, 6. For some reason, all the code names used on WS-119L began with a "G" (Gopher, Grandson, Grayback, and Genetrix).
64. Tape: Lovrencic to Peebles, 5 September 1987.
65. *1st Air Division (Meteorological Survey), Final Report Project 119-L, 16.*
66. *History of the 456th Troop Carrier Wing and Project 119-L, 1 January 1955 thru 9 July 1956,* Vol. II, Section III, 10.
67. Letter: Mathews to Peebles, 29 September 1986.
68. *1st Air Division (Meteorological Survey), Final Report Project 119-L, 15.*
69. *History of the 456th Troop Carrier Wing and Project 119-L, 1 January 1955 thru 9 July 1956,* Vol. II, Section II, III and IV, 7–13.
70. *1st Air Division (Meteorological Survey), Final Report Project 119-L, 16, 17.*
71. *History of the 456th Troop Carrier Wing and Project 119-L, 1 January 1955 thru 9 July 1956,* Vol. II, Section I, 4.
72. Letter: Burch to Peebles, 29 September 1986.
73. *History of the 456th Troop Carrier Wing and Project 119-L, 1 January 1955 thru 9 July 1956,* Chapter III: Operations and Training, 19, 20.

Chapter 6

1. Memorandum of conversation with the President, 6 February 1956, 10:15 A.M., Meetings with the President, Jan–July 1956, Box 4, JFD Papers, Dwight D. Eisenhower Library. Memorandum for Record—Conference of Joint Chiefs of Staff with the President, 10 February 1956.
2. Letter: James A. Winker to Curtis Peebles, 31 May 1988.
3. *1st Air Division (Meteorological Survey) Final Report Project 119L,* 17, 18.
4. *History of the 456th Troop Carrier Wing and Project 119L, 1 January 1955 thru 9 July 1956,* Chapter III: Operations and Training, 25.
5. Press Release by Headquarters U.S. Air Force Simultaneously with Start of Operation, 9 January 1956.
6. Letter, Robert L. Burch to Curtis Peebles, 21 September 1986.
7. *1st Air Division (Meteorological Survey) Final Report Project 119L,* 17–19, 23, 27.
8. Part III—Present Mission, 7–9, 13–15. Mimeographed document from files of R. W. Koch.
9. William Green and Gordon Swanborough, *The Observer's Soviet Aircraft Directory,* (New York: Frederick Warne & Co., 1975), 159–165.
10. David C. Isby, *Weapons and Tactics of the Soviet Army,* (London: Jane's, 1981), 221–232.
11. *History of the 456th Troop Carrier Wing and Project 119L, 1 January 1955 thru 9 July 1956,* Chapter III: Operations and Training, 21, 37, 38.
12. Tape: Paul M. Lovrencic to Curtis Peebles, 5 September 1987.
13. *History of the 456th Troop Carrier Wing and Project 119L, 1 January 1955 thru 9 July 1956,* Chapter III, 19, 20.
14. Ibid., Chapter II, Section V, 13.
15. *1st Air Division (Meteorological Survey) Final Report Project 119L,* 19.
16. *History of the 456th Troop Carrier Wing and Project 119L, 1 January 1955 thru 9 July 1956,* Chapter II, Section V, 14.
17. Ibid., Chapter III: Operations and Training, 21.
18. Locator Beacon, 2. Mimeographed document from files of R. W. Koch.

19. *History of the 456th Troop Carrier Wing and Project 119L, 1 January 1955 thru 9 July 1956,* Chapter III: Operations and Training, 25.
20. *1st Air Division (Meteorological Survey) Final Report Project 119L,* 22, 23.
21. *Dagens Nyheter* [Swedish newspaper], 8 March 1956. *Aftenposten* [Norwegian newspaper], 11 February 1956, translated by Svein Tonning.
22. "Pontius," "MiG-15 the Last Word," *Air Progress,* (June 1971): 51–54, 72, 73.
23. Chuck Yeager and Leo Janos, *Yeager,* (New York: Bantam Books, 1985), 205–210. Chuck Yeager flew a MiG-15 whose pilot defected from North Korea. "Pontius" flew a Pakistani Air Force MiG-15 UTI two-seat trainer. Both commented on its sometimes vicious flight characteristics. In the lack of any detailed descriptions of balloon interceptions, the author has reconstructed the foregoing based on basic aerodynamics and known Soviet procedures.
24. James C. Hagerty, Daily Log, 24 January 1956, Dwight D. Eisenhower Library. Given the instability of the MiG-15, one can only wonder if any balloons became MiG aces. *Aftenposten* [Norwegian newspaper], 4 and 11 February 1956, translated by Svein Tonning. CIA Report, "Balloons over Bulgaria," 17 April 1956.
25. *History of the 456th Troop Carrier Wing and Project 119L, 1 January 1955 thru 9 July 1956,* Vol. II, Section I, 15.
26. Tapes: Lovrencic to Peebles, 5 September 1987 and 8 April 1988.
27. *1st Air Division (Meteorological Survey) Final Report Project 119L,* 22.
28. Letter: George Mathews to Curtis Peebles, 29 September 1986.
29. Hagerty, Daily Log, 24 January 1956.
30. Memorandum for the President, Subject: Call of the Soviet Ambassador, 24 January 1956. Dwight D. Eisenhower Library.
31. Hagerty, Daily Log, 25 January 1956.
32. Telephone Calls, 25 January 1956, Dwight D. Eisenhower Library.
33. Hagerty, Daily Log, 25 January 1956.
34. Telephone Calls, 25 January 1956, Dwight D. Eisenhower Library.
35. *1st Air Division (Meteorological Survey) Final Report Project 119L,* 20.
36. Ibid.
37. Letter: Burch to Peebles, 21 September 1986.
38. *History of the 456th Troop Carrier Wing and Project 119L, 1 January 1955 thru 9 July 1956,* Chapter III: Operations and Training, 27, and Vol. II, Section V, 13, 14.
39. *1st Air Division (Meteorological Survey) Final Report Project 119L,* 23.
40. *History of 1st Air Division, Historical Study No. 62,* Headquarters Strategic Air Command, November 1956, 53, 54.
41. *1st Air Division (Meteorological Survey) Final Report Project 119L,* 26.
42. Part II Prior to Moby Dick Far East, 8, 9. Mimeographed document from files of R. W. Koch.
43. Tape: Lovrencic to Peebles, 5 September 1987.
44. John Foster Dulles, Phone Log, 31 January 1956, Dwight D. Eisenhower Library.
45. Dulles, Phone Log, 2 February 1956.
46. Dulles, Phone Log, 3 February 1956.
47. *Los Angeles Times,* 6 February 1956, 1, 13.
48. *History of 1st Air Division, Historical Study No. 62,* 49.
49. Dulles, Phone Log, 6 February 1956.
50. Memorandum for the Files, 6 February 1956, W. B. Macomber, Jr., Dwight D. Eisenhower Library.
51. *History of the 456th Troop Carrier Wing and Project 119L, 1 January 1955 thru 9 July 1956,* Chapter III: Operations and Training, 28, and Vol. II, Section V, 14.
52. Memorandum for Col. A. J. Goodpaster, 8 February 1956 (text of State Department note), Dwight D. Eisenhower Library.

53. "How Far Up Is Home?" *Newsweek,* (20 February 1956): 22, 23.
54. *Los Angeles Times,* 10 February 1956, 1.
55. "How Far Up Is Home?" 22, 23.
56. *1st Air Division (Meteorological Survey) Final Report Project 119L,* 25. A weight would be added to compensate for the missing water station so the gondola would float in the proper attitude without rolling.
57. *History of 1st Air Division, Historical Study No. 62,* 53, 54.
58. *History of the 456th Troop Carrier Wing and Project 119L, 1 January 1955 thru 9 July 1956,* Chapter III: Operations and Training, 29–31, and Vol. II, Section V, 18.
59. *History of 1st Air Division, Historical Study No. 62,* 53.
60. *History of the 456th Troop Carrier Wing and Project 119L, 1 January 1955 thru 9 July 1956,* Vol. II, Section V, 13–15. Merton E. Davies and William R. Harris, *RAND's Role in the Evolution of Balloon and Satellite Observation Systems and Related U.S. Space Technology,* (Santa Monica: RAND, 1988), 61.
61. *1st Air Division (Meteorological Survey) Final Report Project 119L,* 22, 25–27. Unfortunately there is disagreement between sources on the total number of Genetrix balloons launched. The *History of the 456th Troop Carrier Wing . . . 1 January 1955 thru 9 July 1956* states that 448 balloons were launched, 66 entered the recovery zone, and 44 were successfully recovered. *1st Air Division (Meteorological Survey)* gives the following, as of March 5, 1956:

516	launched
117	known failures
12	did not enter Soviet airspace
387	operational systems
144	heard to transmit
67	entered recovery area
44	recovered

Subsequently, 8 more gondolas were found near the launch sites.As *History of the 456th Troop Carrier Wing* gives the 448 total both by launch site *and* by each day, this figure is used. It is possible *1st Air Division (Meteorological Survey)* included some of the Moby Dick Far East/White Cloud launches (it uses the phrase, "During the operation period . . ."). As the numbers of balloons entering the recovery zone are broken down by each day in *History of the 456th Troop Carrier Wing,* the number 66 has been used. The two sources have been combined to form a hybrid estimate of the balloons' ultimate fate.

62. Jeffrey Richelson, *American Espionage and the Soviet Target,* (New York: William Morrow and Company, 1987), 139.
63. *South Bay Daily Breeze,* 8 February 1956, 1.
64. *Los Angeles Times,* 19 February 1956, 25.
65. Ibid., 2 March 1956, 1.
66. Ibid., 3 March 1956, 8.
67. Ibid., 1 April 1956, 27.
68. Ibid., 2 March 1956, 1.
69. *Los Angeles Mirror News,* 7 March 1956, 6.
70. *Stars & Stripes,* 31 March 1956.
71. *New York Times,* 5 May 1956.
72. "Czechs 'Kill' One Balloon," *Aviation Week,* (18 June 1956): 55. CIA Report, "Captured U.S. Balloons Shown to Tourist/Popular Attitudes and Morale," 20 September 1956.
73. Letter: Burch to Peebles, 21 September 1986.
74. Letter: Mathews to Peebles, 29 September 1986.

75. Memorandum for the Record, 13 March 1956, Dwight D. Eisenhower Library.
76. *1st Air Division (Meteorological Survey) Final Report Project 119L,* 25.
77. Letter: Burch to Peebles, 21 September 1986.
78. Tape: Lovrencic to Peebles, 5 September 1987.
79. *History of the 456th Troop Carrier Wing and Project 119L, 1 January 1955 thru 9 July 1956,* Chapter 1, 12, 13. There was a postscript to the Genetrix story. One of the balloons passed over northern Russia and came down in the Arctic Ocean. For the next two years it floated, the fiberglass box able to withstand icy water and polar storms. The gondola finally washed ashore on Iceland. It was found by Dick Philbrick who had worked on the project. He was able to have it sent back to the U.S. Despite what it had gone through, the film survived and proved to be some of the best photos of the program.[80]
80. Brigadier General George W. Goddard and Dewitt S. Copp, *Overview,* (Garden City, N.Y.: Doubleday, 1969), 385.

Chapter 7

1. Jay Miller, *Lockheed U-2,* (Austin, Tex.: Aerofax Inc., 1983), 12, 13.
2. Research Publications Inc., White House 704, 1983.
3. Clarence L. "Kelly" Johnson with Maggie Smith, *Kelly: More Than My Share of It All,* (Washington, D.C.: Smithsonian Institution Press, 1985), 120–123.
4. Orin Humphries, "High Flight," *Wings,* (June 1983): 12.
5. Skip Holm, "Artical Airborne," *Air Progress Aviation Review,* 1986, 25–29.
6. Kenneth W. Weir, "The U-2 Story," *Society of Experimental Test Pilots,* 1978 Report to the Aerospace Profession, 186, 187. It was after the first test flight the aircraft got its name. LeVier was climbing out when he saw Johnson and "saluted" him with an obscene gesture and mumbled something about Kelly trying to kill him. (Johnson had advised him to land on the nose wheel first.) Kelly responded with the same gesture and "You Too!" LeVier answered "You Did." The U-2/"You Too" label stuck.
7. Carrollton Press, 333C, 1979.
8. Miller, *Lockheed U-2,* 25, 26, 106.
9. Jeffrey Richelson, *American Espionage and the Soviet Target,* (New York: William Morrow and Co., 1987), 141–144. U-2 Article 347/Sn#56-6680 had a long and interesting life. In 1958 it was transferred to the 4080th Strategic Reconnaissance Wing, the Air Force's U-2 unit. It apparently was transferred back to the CIA at some point in the late 1950s/early 1960s and converted to a U-2 B before 1962. In the fall of 1962, it was apparently a U-2 E (one of 18 aircraft fitted with improved ECM equipment). It is believed to have been the aircraft used by Major Steve Heyser to make his overflight of the Soviet MRBM site at San Cristobal, Cuba. It was later modified to a U-2 F (with midair refueling and two large "ram's horn" ELINT antennae). By 1964 it had been transferred back to Air Force control. (U-2s frequently bounced back and forth between the Air Force and CIA.) Between 1964 and 1968, it flew missions over Vietnam. In the fall of 1964, it was painted black, the first Air Force U-2 to carry this finish. In 1975 it was deployed in Europe. When all the early U-2s were retired from service in 1980, it was given to the National Air and Space Museum. It was placed on display in mid-1986.
10. Transcript of "The Chicago Show," 30 April 1970, WLS-TV, 9.

11. Carrollton Press, 333D, 1979.
12. Chris Pocock, *Dragon Lady,* (Shrewsbury, England: Airlife, 1989), 26–29.
13. Francis Gary Powers and Curt Gentry, *Operation Overflight,* (New York: Holt, Rinehart and Winston, 1970), 43–56.
14. Research Publications Inc., Department of State 312, 1987.
15. *History of the 1110th Air Support Group, 1 July 56–31 December 56.*
16. Richelson, *American Espionage,* 117–120.
17. James E. Oberg, *Uncovering Soviet Disasters,* (New York: Random House, 1988), Chapter 13. It was a SAM site guarding the Kyshtym 40 complex that brought down Francis Gary Power's U-2. The complex was also the site of the "Urals nuclear disaster" in September of 1957, when some type of explosion scattered radioactive waste over a wide area. This was apparently only one of a number of spills which have contaminated the forests and lakes in the region.
18. History of the 1110th Air Support Group, 1 January 57–30 June 57, Microfilm Roll MO 109, Air Force Historical Research Center, Maxwell AFB, Alabama.
19. Meeting: High Altitude Balloon Committee, Washington Airspace panel, 1110th Balloon Activities Group Headquarters, Lowry Air Force Base, Colorado, 11 and 12 June 1958, briefing by Captain James W. Taylor.
20. History of the 1110th Air Support Group, 1 January 57–30 June 57, Microfilm Roll MO 109, Air Force Historical Research Center, Maxwell AFB, Alabama.
21. Foreign Nuclear Detonations—Through 31 December 1981, Department of Energy.
22. Research Publications Inc., CIA 1544, 1984.
23. Ivan Borisenko and Alexander Romanov, *Where All Roads into Space Begin,* (Moscow: Progress Publishers, 1982), 14, 60, 61.
24. Dino A. Brugioni, "The Tyuratam Enigma," *Air Force Magazine,* (March 1984): 108, 109.
25. NOVA, "Spy Machines," KPBS Channel 15, 13 October 1987.
26. Richelson, *American Espionage,* 145.
27. Brugioni, "The Tyuratam Enigma," 108, 109.
28. Personal correspondence with James E. Oberg, 27 March 1984. The name "Tyuratam" means in the Kazakh language "arrow burial ground." The Soviets use the name "Baikonur" (master with the light brown hair) for the launch complex.
29. NOVA, "Spy Machines," KPBS Channel 15, 13 October 1987.
30. Research Publications Inc., CIA 1544, 1984.
31. Memo: Air Research and Development Command, Cancellation of ARDC System, Directive SD No. 119L, 30 January 1957, and ARDC System Directive SN No. 461L, 30 January 1957.
32. Memo: Air Research and Development Command, Amendment No. 1 to SN No. 461L, 20 June 1957. Letter: James A. Winker to Curtis Peebles, 6 June 1988.
33. Research Publications Inc., Department of State 1901, 1984.
34. Memorandum for Record, 3 July 1957, Dwight D. Eisenhower Library.
35. History of the Air Force Cambridge Research Center, Volumes XXVIII—XXIX, Part 1, 1 January–31 December 1958, 65, 66.
36. *History of 1st Air Division, Historical Study No. 62,* Headquarters Strategic Air Command, November 1956, 37.
37. Research Publications Inc., Department of State 2724, 1984.
38. Memorandum for Record, 7 March 1958, Dwight D. Eisenhower Library.
39. David A. Anderton, *North American F-100 Super Sabre,* (London: Osprey Publishing Limited, 1987), 181. It is worth noting that "Keyhole" was later used as the code name for photoreconnaissance satellites. The traffic was not all one way; through-

out the 1950s, MiGs would make overflights of Western Europe on a weekly basis.

40. Richard M. Buesuhel, *Communist Chinese Air Power,* (New York: Praeger, 1968), 29, 31.
41. Research Publications Inc., 1278, 1986.
42. Powers and Gentry, *Operation Overflight,* 47.
43. Curtis Peebles, *Guardians,* (Novato, Calif.: Presidio Press, 1987), Chapters 2 and 3.
44. Memorandum for Record, 17 May 1958, Dwight D. Eisenhower Library.
45. Memorandum for Record, 19 May 1958, Dwight D. Eisenhower Library.
46. Letter: Jeffrey Richelson to Curtis Peebles, n.d.
47. Roger Chesneau, *Aircraft Carriers of the World, 1914 to the Present: An Illustrated Encyclopedia,* (London: Arms and Armour Press, 1984), 238. During World War II, after several escort carriers were lost owing to uncontrolled fires, the story sprang up that the ship's designation "CVE" (carrier, heavier-than-air, escort) actually stood for "combustible, venerable, expendable."
48. *Dictionary of American Naval Fighting Ships Vol. VIII,* James L. Mooney, ed., (Washington, D.C.: Naval Historical Center, 1981), 404, 405. The USS *Windham Bay* was named for a bay on the southeastern coast of Alaska. Its keel was laid on January 5, 1944; it was launched on March 29 and set sail for its first voyage to the Pacific war zone on June 12, 1944. Over the next year, it made several trips to transport aircraft between the West Coast and the combat area. On the night of June 4/5, 1945, it was caught in a typhoon near Okinawa. It was battered by 75-foot waves and 127-knot winds. Each time the ship went over a wave, its propellers would be clear of the water. The forward lookout platform and two 40mm gunmounts were torn off. The forward flight deck then collapsed. Once the storm cleared, the *Windham Bay* sailed to San Diego for repairs. It arrived on July 11 and spent the next six weeks undergoing repairs and so missed the end of the war. After the Japanese surrender, it made several trips to the western Pacific to return troops to the United States. It was finally placed in moth balls in August 1946. With the outbreak of the Korean War, the *Windham Bay* was recommissioned on October 28, 1950, to again serve as an aircraft transport. It made its first trip from the West Coast to Japan on January 2, 1951. From that time until its involvement with WS-461L, it made regular West Coast/Japan voyages in support of fleet carriers in the western Pacific. WS-461L was the ship's swan song; in January 1959, it was decommissioned and subsequently sold to the Hugo Neu Steel Products Corp. The USS *Windham Bay* was scrapped in Japan in February 1961.
49. Deck Log, U.S.S. Windham Bay, TCVU-92, 25 June 1958 thru 2 July 1958.
50. Memorandum for The Secretary of Defense, 31 July 1958, Dwight D. Eisenhower Library.
51. Deck Log, U.S.S. Windham Bay, TCVU-92, 2 July 1958 thru 4 July 1958. Merton E. Davies and William R. Harris, *RAND's Role in the Evolution of Balloon and Satellite Observation Systems and Related U.S. Space Technology,* (Santa Monica: RAND, 1988), 78–85.
52. Deck Log, U.S.S. Windham Bay, TCVU-92, 5 July 1958 thru 21 July 1958. Letter: James A. Winker to Curtis Peebles, 6 June 1988.
53. Dwight D. Eisenhower, *Waging Peace 1956–1961,* (Garden City, N.Y.: Doubleday & Co., 1965), 226, 265–285.
54. Research Publications Inc., Department of State 1717, 1985.
55. John Foster Dulles, Papers, Telephone Series, Box 8, June–July 1958, (1).
56. Message from Mr. Ayer, Office of Staff Secretary: Subject Series, Alpha Subseries, Box 14, File Intel Matters, (5).

57. Memorandum for the Secretary of Defense, 31 July 1958, Dwight D. Eisenhower Library.
58. Eisenhower, *Waging Peace,* 292–294.
59. *Khrushchev Remembers the Last Testament,* Strobe Talbott, ed., (New York: Little, Brown and Co., 1974), 261, 262.
60. Buesuhel, *Communist Chinese Air Power,* 54.
61. Eisenhower, *Waging Peace,* 292, 293.
62. "Mixing the Potion of War?" *Newsweek,* (8 September 1958): 34.
63. Eisenhower, *Waging Peace,* 297.
64. Allen Rankin, "One of Our Airplanes is Missing—Again," *Reader's Digest,* (June 1959): 39–42.
65. James Bamford, *The Puzzle Palace,* (New York: Penguin Books, 1983), 232, 233.
66. Research Publications Inc., 3006, 1986. The reference to a large quantity of gold is unexplained. The use of decoy beacons continues to this day.
67. The Current Digest of the Soviet Press, Vol. X, No. 36, 16 (1958).
68. Eisenhower, *Waging Peace,* 300.
69. *New York Times,* 7 September 1958, 17.
70. Eisenhower, *Waging Peace,* 302.
71. Donald S. Zagoria, *The Sino-Soviet Conflict 1956–1961,* (Princeton: Princeton University Press, 1962), 210–214.
72. The Current Digest of the Soviet Press, Vol. X, No. 37, 24 (1958).
73. Eisenhower, *Waging Peace,* 303.
74. Zagoria, *The Sino-Soviet Conflict,* 213, 214.
75. "Aerial Piracy," *Time,* (29 September 1958), 12. Assuming the eyewitness report is correct, the question arises as to why the Soviets did not return the other eleven bodies. The Soviets did not admit, and have never admitted, they shot down the C-130A-II. They have always said it "crashed," implying mechanical failure. One possible explanation is that autopsies of the other bodies would have shown shell fragments from the repeated attacks. This would have proved the Soviets were lying. Whatever the reason and their true fate, the eleven crewmen's families were left uncertain.
76. Buesuhel, *Communist Chinese Air Power,* 54, 55.
77. "Deadly Sidewinder," *Newsweek,* (13 October 1958): 41.
78. Eisenhower, *Waging Peace,* 303.
79. The Current Digest of the Soviet Press, Vol. X, No. 41, 20, 21 (1958).
80. *New York Times,* 12 October 1958, 1.
81. The Current Digest of the Soviet Press, Vol. X., No. 41, 21 (1958).
82. Eisenhower, *Waging Peace,* 304.
83. Banford, *The Puzzle Palace,* 236–238.
84. Peebles, *Guardians,* 33–39.
85. Letter: Leroy C. Stables to Curtis Peebles, 11 November 1987.
86. Ellie Abel, *The Missile Crisis,* (New York: Bantam Books, 1966), 14, 15.
87. Peebles, *Guardians,* 79.
88. Chuck Kubin, "Not Just Hot Air," *Aerospace History,* (Spring, March 1988): 55–60.
89. Phone conversation with Jim Taylor, 27 October 1986.
90. James R. Chiles, "NASA giant research balloons are out of sight," *Smithsonian,* (March 1987): 83–92.
91. "That Outfit in Texas," *Sky and Telescope,* (November 1983): 386.
92. Letter: R. W. Koch to Curtis Peebles, 18 September 1986. Unlike Gopher, Grandson, Grayback, and Genetrix, the material on WS-461L is very limited. From the start of my research into balloon reconnaissance in the spring of 1986, I found

the main problem was WS-461L. The AF Historical Research Center at Maxwell AFB was able to supply only one document. The AF Museum, Strategic Air Command, Systems Command, and the AF Geophysical Lab were all unable to find any material in their files (either classified or declassified). Most of the information came from the U.S.S. Windham Bay Log, provided by the Navy History Center, and documents from the Eisenhower Library. In contrast, there were four official histories of Grayback/Genetrix. This had made it necessary to reconstruct WS-461L's history to a greater degree than with the other projects. I have tried my best to be careful in this but the threads are often thin and the possibility of error ever present.

Chapter 8

1. Memorandum for Record, Conference of Joint Chiefs of Staff with the President, 10 February 1956. "If these balloons had been sent over us, we might be talking about mobilizing." [10 February 1956]
2. Research Publications Inc., Department of State 316, 1985. "[The President] thought [overflights] might lead to a Soviet reaction which superficially at least, would seem justified. Such reaction might take place, for example, in Berlin." [22 January 1958]
3. Research Publications Inc., Department of State 2724, 1984. "The President expressed the view that any such operations carried a danger of starting a nuclear war by miscalculation. He said that his military advisers had pressed upon him the necessity of retaliation if there seemed to be a movement of Soviet planes towards the United States. The President felt the Soviets might have the same attitude and might misinterpret an overflight as being designed to start a nuclear war." [7 March 1958]
4. Carrollton Press, White House 622A, 1981. "The President is reserved on the request to continue reconnaissance flights on the basis that it is undue provocation. Nothing, he says, would make him request authority to declare war more quickly than violation of our air space by Soviet aircraft." [12 February 1959]
5. W. W. Rostow, *Open Skies,* (Austin: University of Texas Press, 1982), 191.
6. Francis Gary Powers and Curt Gentry, *Operation Overflight,* (New York: Holt, Rinehart and Winston, 1970), 139–141.
7. Jeffrey Richelson, *American Espionage and the Soviet Target,* (New York: William Morrow and Co., 1987), 139.
8. Letter: Robert Burch to Curtis Peebles, 21 September 1986.
9. *1st Air Division (Meteorological Survey) Final Report Project 119L,* 25.
10. Memorandum for Record, Conference of Joint Chiefs of Staff with President, 10 February 1956.
11. Rostow, *Open Skies,* 192, 193.
12. Curtis Peebles, *Guardians,* (Novato, Calif.: Presidio Press, 1987), Chapters 3 and 4.
13. Rostow, *Open Skies,* 193.
14. Peebles, *Guardians,* Chapter 9.